from this GENERATION for ever

Volume 1: Inspiration

A Study of God's Promise to Preserve His Word

Bryan C. Ross

Copyright © 2022, Bryan C. Ross

From This Generation For Ever: A Study of God's Promise to Preserve His Word

All Scriptures are quoted from the King James Version.

ISBN:

Trust House Publishers

P.O. Box 3181

Taos, NM 87571

www.trusthousepublishers.com

Ordering Information: Special discounts are available on quantity purchases by churches, associations, and retailers. For details, contact the publisher at the address above or call toll-free 1-844-321-4202.

1 2 3 4 5 6 7 8 9

The notes found in the book are designed to be used in conjunction with a King James Bible.

The following notes were taught to the saints of Grace Life Bible Church in Grand Rapids, MI between September 13, 2015, and April 17, 2016. The purpose of this project has been to set forth our belief that the King James Bible is God's Word for English speaking people. Our goal has been to enunciate a position on the final authority of the King James Bible that is scriptural, reasonable, factual, and historically accurate. The notes presented herein are the edited course notes that were distributed to participants when the lessons were originally taught. As of the publiciaton of the present volume the class is still being taught. To access the video and MP3 audio for these Lessons please visit the online classroom at bit.do/preservationproject or by visiting the School of Theology page on the Grace Life Bible Church website.

I would like to thank Sylvia and Mike Erspamer for their assistance every week in proofreading the notes. Many thanks are also in order to the members of the Adult Sunday School class at Grace Life Bible Church. Without your interest and support this class would not have been possible.

TABLE OF CONTENTS

LESSON 1 Course Introduction | **1**

LESSON 2 The "Yea, Hath God Said" Society | **13**

LESSON 3 The "Yea, Hath God Said" Society, Part 2 | **23**

LESSON 4 Originals Onlyism: A Position of No Practical Consequence | **35**

LESSON 5 Overcoming the Problem of "Verbatim Identicality" | **51**

LESSON 6 Understanding Basic Terminology: Revelation | **59**

LESSON 7 Understanding Basic Terminology: Inspiration and Illumination | **67**

LESSON 8 Understanding Basic Terminology: Preservation | **79**

LESSON 9 Understanding Basic Terminology: Preservation, Part 2 | **91**

LESSON 10	Understanding Basic Terminology: Preservation, Part 3	**101**
LESSON 11	Understanding the Various Theories of Inspiration	**133**
LESSON 12	Potential Pitfalls of Plenary Inspiration	**145**
LESSON 13	Passages Proving the Plenary Position	**156**
LESSON 14	Divine Dictation: The Mechanism of Inspiration? Part 1	**166**
LESSON 15	Divine Dictation: The Mechanism of Inspiration? Part 2	**177**
LESSON 16	Divine Dictation: The Mechanism of Inspiration? Part 3	**191**
LESSON 17	Divine Dictation: The Mechanism of Inspiration? Part 4	**202**
LESSON 18	God's Design in Inspiration	**214**
LESSON 19	The Living Word's Attitude Toward the Written Word	**227**
LESSON 20	The New Testament Writer's Attitude Toward the Written Word	**237**
LESSON 21	Internal Evidence of Inspiration: Undesigned Coincidences	**245**

LESSON 22	Internal Evidence of Inspiration: Undesigned Coincidences, Part 2	**261**
LESSON 23	Internal Evidence of Inspiration: Fulfilled Prophecy	**272**
LESSON 24	External Evidence of Inspiration: The Historicity of the Old Testament	**286**
LESSON 25	External Evidence of Inspiration: The Historicity of the New Testament	**294**
LESSON 26	External Evidence of Inspiration: The Transmission of the Text	**307**
LESSON 27	Disclaimers Regarding the Limitations of Inspiration	**321**

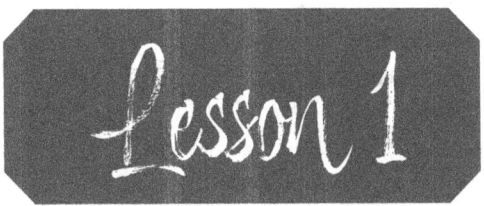

COURSE INTRODUCTION

INTRODUCTION

- Welcome to our new Grace Life School of Theology class From This Generation For Ever. As we begin our study this morning of all things related to the King James Bible, I would like to cover the following three points:

  - Why this class?
  - Personal history
  - List of topics to be covered

WHY THIS CLASS?

- Since the inception of Grace Life Bible Church (GLBC) in the fall of 2007, I have spoken numerous times on the subject of the King James Bible (KJB). In January and February of 2010, I taught a six part study titled *Final Authority: Locating God's Word in English* (Scroll down to access the audio recordings of these studies.). 2010 also saw the publication of my first booklet on the Bible issue *The Argument for Inerrancy and the King James Bible,* that effort was followed by *The Apocrypha and the King James Bible* in the spring of 2013. In 2011, as part of the festivities commemorating the 400th anniversary of the KJB, I spoke at both the Great Lakes Grace Bible Conference (Ohio) and the Grace School of the Bible Summer Family Bible Conference (Chicago) on issues related to the KJB. In the Grace History Project (GHP), I taught a two part study on the history of the doctrine of inerrancy (see Lessons 63 & 64). More recently, I spoke this past April (2015) at the GSB Pastor's Conference (also in Chicago) on the subject of *The Paulicians and the Preserved Text.* A month later, at the Great Lakes Grace Bible Conference I delivered a message titled *The Textual History of the English Bible.*

- So, having already taught on the KJB in a variety of formats and settings I would like to take some time and explain why I chose to do this class.

- First and foremost, the impetus for this class was questions that I have received over the years from you, the saints of Grace Life Bible Church (GLBC). In particular, Mike Erspamer has asked many important questions regarding a host of topics related to the KJB. Many of Mike's questions were involved, complex, and required further study in order to answer. In addition, there was never a good time to address them when we were going through the GHP material.

- Second, the board of GLBC has made the training of faithful men within the assembly a top priority. Our most recent 30-part study of Right Division 101 was done with the goal of creating a basic class for dispensational instruction for those interested in being trained to labor in word and doctrine within the assembly. In addition, properly understanding GLBC's stance on the Bible issue is also a must for those seeking to serve in a teaching capacity. This class will be geared to helping to meet that important need.

- o Article I. The Bible

    "We believe that the entire Bible is verbally inspired of God and is of plenary authority (2Timothy 3:16, 2Peter 1:20-21) and that God has providentially preserved His completed Word for us today (Psalms 12:6-7, Colossians 1:25, Isaiah 40:8). We believe that the Word of God exists in its preserved form in what is commonly called the *Textus Receptus* (Received Text) and that the King James Version (KJV) is the best English translation of the Received Text available today. We believe the KJV to be without error and disapprove of all attempts to "correct" the text of the KJV with manuscript evidence or supposed understanding of original languages.

    We are unashamedly literalist in our method of study and adhere to the principle God has set forth in the scriptures to rightly divide the Bible dispensationally (2Timothy 2:15). The literal, dispensational approach is the only way to understand the differences in God's various programs and dealings with mankind since the beginning of time and plays a vital role in establishing the believer and maintaining a distinct, clear gospel message (Romans 16:25-27). While we believe every word of the Bible is inspired and infallible, we recognize that Paul's writings alone (Romans – Philemon) contain the revelation of the mystery that is God's purpose during this dispensation of grace." (*GLBC Statement of Faith*)

- Third, I came to believe (especially since the 2011 Bible Conferences on the 400th anniversary of the KJB) that a new class on the KJB was in order. For the record, I am not seeking to replace or cast dispersion upon what Brother Richard Jordan taught in the Manuscript Evidence class in Grace School of the Bible (GSB). Brother Jordan's work has grounded many, including myself, with a clear understanding of the need for a final authority in our own language. That being said, the GSB is now nearly forty years old. During the intermittent four decades, the study of the historical and textual history of the KJB has progressed.

> o   When Pastor Jordan began teaching Manuscript Evidence in the fall of 1983 the following resources would have been available for the writing of the curriculum. *Note: This list does not claim to be an exhaustive listing of precisely the resources utilized by Brother Jordan. Rather this list seeks to identify the major works on the subject that would have been available for him to draw from prior to the fall of 1983 when the class began.*

- L. Gaussen
  - The Divine Inspiration of the Bible (1841)

- Alexander McClure
  - The Translators Revived (1858)

- John William Burgon
  - The Last Twelve Verses of Mark (1871)
  - The Revision Revised (1883)
  - The Traditional Text of the Holy Gospels (1896)
  - The Causes of Corruption of the Traditional Text of the Holy Gospels (1896)

- Philip Mauro
  - Which Version? Authorized or Revised (1924)

- Benjamin G. Wilkinson
  - Our Authorized Bible Vindicated (1930)

- Jasper James Ray
  - God Only Wrote One Bible (1955)

- Edward F. Hills
  - The King James Bible Defended (1956)
  - Believing Bible Study (1967)

- Peter S. Ruckman
  - The Bible "Babble" (1964)
  - Christian Handbook of Manuscript Evidence (1970)
  - The Monarch of the Books! (1973)
  - Problem Texts (1980)
  - The Differences in the King James Version Editions (1983)

- Ward S. Allen
  - Translating for King James (1969)

- David Otis Fuller
  - Which Bible? (1970)
  - True or False? (1973)
  - Counterfeit or Genuine? (1975)

- William Pickering
  - The Identify of the New Testament Text (1977)

- D.A. Carson
  - The King James Version Debate: A Plea for Realism (1979)

- Zane C. Hodges & Arthur L. Farstad
  - The Greek New Testament According to the Majority Text (1982)

    o Brother Jordan taught Manuscript Evidence before any of the significant works by the following King James advocates had been written: Samuel Gipp, D.A. Waite, William P. Grady, Gail Riplinger, Jack A Moorman, Lawrence M. Vance, David W. Cloud, Joey Faust, R.B. Ouellette, Thomas Holland, Jack McElrory, and many others. In addition, the first edition of James R. White's book *The King James Only Controversy: Can You Trust the Modern Translations* did not appear in print until 1995.

    o New discoveries were made in the 1950s and 1960s at libraries in Great Britain. Notable discoveries include MS 98, a manuscript of the Westminster Company that translated the New Testament epistles, the notes of John Bois, and Bod.1602 (a bound copy of a 1602 edition of the Bishops Bible with handwritten notes by the translators in the margin). These discoveries were studied throughout the 1970s with books explaining their significance first appearing in the 1969 (Bois Notes), 1977 (MS 98) and 1995 (Bod. 1602). Published works explaining the significance of these findings were not well known outside academic circles in the early 1980s.

- Ward S. Allen
  - Translating for King James: Notes Made by a Translator of King James's Bible (1969)
  - Translating the New Testament Epistles 1604-1611: A Manuscript of King James's Westminster Company (1977)
  - The Coming of the King James Gospels: A Collation of the Translators Work-in-Progress (1995)

    o The first half of the last decade (00 decade) saw the publication of two important works on the making of the KJB as well as its linguistic and cultural impact upon the English-speaking world. These titles include:

- Alister McGrath
  - In the Beginning: The Story of the King James Bible and How It Changed a Nation, a Language, and a Culture (2001)

- Adam Nicholson
  - God's Secretaries: The Making of the King James Bible (2003)

○ In 2005, Professor David Norton's ground-breaking book A Textual History of the King James Bible was published by Cambridge University Press. Moreover, Professor Norton's equally important *The King James Bible: A Short History from Tyndale to Today* was published in 2011 in commemoration of the 400th anniversary of the KJB. Both works by Norton are indispensable to a complete understanding of the history of the King James text. Moreover, Professor Norton has also written extensively on the subject of the Bible as literature in the following series of books:

- A History of the Bible as Literature 2Vol. (1993)
- A History of the English Bible as Literature (2000)

○ In addition, 2011 saw a flurry of scholarly works published in commemoration of the 400th anniversary of the King James Bible. There is much in these books that needs to be taken into account when considering this subject matter. A sampling of titles includes:

- Donald L Brake
  - A Visual History of the King James Bible (2011)

- David Crystal
  - Begat: The King James Bible & the English Language

- Leland Ryken
  - The Legacy of the King James Bible

- Jon M. Sweeney
  - Verily, Verily: The KJV — 400 Years of Influence and Beauty

- David Teems
  - Majestie: The King Behind the King James Bible

    o Earlier this year (2015), Lawrence M. Vance published the results of his collation comparing the text of the Bishops Bible New Testament with the King James New Testament in *The Making of the King James New Testament*.

    o In short, a class on the KJB that takes into account the latest research on the subject is long overdue.

- Fourth, I have concluded that historically (since the mid-1950s) the articulation of the King James position has been dominated by Acts 2 Baptists who not only disapprove of our dispensational position (mid-Acts) but in some cases believe things about the KJB that are detrimental to the position. Consequently, I have come to believe that it is incumbent upon Pauline Dispensationalists to forge and advance our own position on the KJB that is inline and consistent with both the historical and textual facts as well as our dispensational beliefs regarding God's working in time.

    o I am a King James Bible believer. I believe that the King James Bible is God's word for English speaking people. It has been translated from the preserved and proper text (*Textus Receptus* or *TR*) using the proper method (literal equivalency).

    o I am also a mid-Acts Pauline dispensationalist who believes some very specific things regarding God's working in time during the dispensation of grace. God is at work in the world today in the lives of His saints through His written word.

o I further maintain that what one believes about the Bible ought not conflict with what they believe about the other (God's working in time during the dispensation of grace). Doctrinal consistency is very important and should be sought after diligently.

o Herein lies a unique problem for all those who are King James Bible believers and mid-Acts Pauline dispensationalists. Historically, the King James position has been championed most visibly and vocally by Acts 2 Baptists who vehemently oppose our dispensational position (calling us hyperdispensationalists). Consequently, much has been said in pro-King James literature that is not only inconsistent with our dispensational position specifically; but is also detrimental to an accurate enunciation of the King James position in general.

o If asked, I would be hard pressed to think of even one book on the King James position that I could recommend to someone without reservation or equivocation. The available literature on the matter is full of doctrinal problems of a dispensational nature, documentation problems, plagiarism, ad hominem attacks, or tabloid style sensationalism.

- It is my prayer that the time we spend together studying these issues will be productive to these ends i.e., the forging of a position that is doctrinally, textually, and historically accurate but also dispensationally correct.

PERSONAL HISTORY

- I grew up reading and using the KJB. As child, all the verses I memorized in AWANA were from the KJB (at the time all AWANA books used the KJB.).
- Very early after his salvation, my father (Steve Ross) came to understand and appreciate that there were more differences between the KJB

and modern versions than just an updating of wording. For a time in the 1970s, my father contemplated attending Peter Ruckman's Pensacola Bible Institute in Pensacola, FL. After traveling to the school and meeting Dr. Ruckman he decided against attending there on account of the vicious/radical spirit he saw in Ruckman's followers.

- In the mid-1980s my father enrolled in GSB where he took Brother Jordan's Manuscript Evidence class. This class served to buttress his long-held preference and affinity for the KJB thereby turning it into a personal conviction.

- While I grew up using the KJB throughout my formative years in the 1990s, I had no real understanding of the reasons why my father advocated for its exclusive use. I knew that the NIV and other modern versions took out the "blood" in Colossians 1:14 (I know that I had been exposed to more teaching on the subject but either didn't pay attention, didn't understand, or didn't retain it). I also and saw Gail Riplinger's *New Age Bible Versions* on his bookshelf but beyond that I never questioned anything.

- It was not until I arrived at Grace Christian Universtiy (Grace Bible College at the time. GCU hereafter) in the fall of 1996 that I really began to have questions regarding the KJB versus modern versions debate. In the summer of 1997, I picked up a copy of Gail Riplinger's *New Age Bible Versions* at the GSB Summer Family Bible Conference and read it before going back to school for my sophomore year. In the summer of 1997, I also enrolled in GSB while at the same time being a student at GCU. During my second year of college I also picked up a few other titles, *The King James Bible Defended* by Dr. Edward F. Hills and *Which Bible?* by David Otis Fuller.

- That fall (1997), I began receiving videos from GSB and watching them in the basement of GCU's library. It was then that I began inhaling the Manuscript Evidence and Fundamentals of Dispensationalism classes. It the same time, in my second-year theology class we were learning about Westcott and Hort's theory of textual criticism and the alleged superiority of the Critical Text and its resultant modern versions over the Traditional Text of the *Textus Receptus* (TR) and the King James. At was a very exciting time for me to be able to study both theories at virtually the same time.

- By the end of my sophomore year (spring 1998), after a lengthy study of the issues I became convinced that the KJB was God's Word for English speaking people. My acceptance and advocacy of the King James position was not popular at school and caused many problems throughout the duration of my stay at GCU. While I was never threatened with expulsion over the issue I was called before the President of the college on more than one occasion to answer various false allegations that had been made against me by members of the student body.
- Since embracing the King James position I have taught and preached from it exclusively and promoted its superiority over all modern versions. Over the years, further study of the position has revealed that tweaking of my thinking on the matter was in order (most notably the inerrancy issue that I addressed in 2011 at the GSB Summer Family Conference in Chicago.).
- More recently, my commitment to the KJB has been called into question by some because I dared to consider the underlying Greek in addressing the joint-heir controversy of Romans 8:17. Some have accused me of having an indecent agenda of seeking to infect GSB with the Greek games and modern version leaven of GCU. Not only are *ad hominem* attacks such as these ignorant of the facts of my personal history, but they also highlight a growing trend in some quarters of calling into question one's commitment to the KJB in the face of doctrinal disagreement (many are labeled "Bible Greekers").

LIST OF TOPICS TO BE COVERED

- Given my experience with the GHP, I hesitate to even publish any type of course outline. I know that what I think the class will be now at the outset will change as we move through the material.
- Topics I plan on covering include:

    o   Inspiration

- Preservation
- Canonicity
- Transmission
- Formation of the *Textus Receptus*
- Pre-1611 English translations as rough drafts of the King James
- Political climate leading up to the decision to translate
- State of the English language at the time of the translation
- Translation process
- Textual history of the King James
- Reception and political implications of the translation
- Cultural and linguistic impact
- Westcott & Hort and the formation of the Critical Text
- The Critical Text and modern versions
- Dean Burgon's objection to the Critical Text
- The formation of the doctrine of inerrancy
- History and historiography of the King James only movement

- I have also created a website that will serve as an online extension of the class. As I did with the GHP, I plan on uploading all the video, audio, PDF notes, and PowerPoints files to the From This Generation For Ever website. The website can be found at:

fromthisgenerationforever.blogspot.com

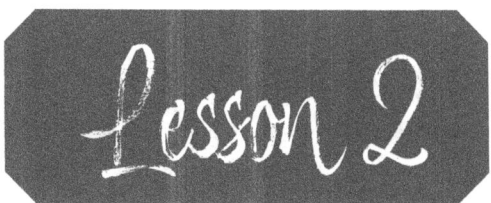

THE "YEA, HATH GOD SAID" SOCIETY

INTRODUCTION

- II Timothy 3:16 — at the outset it is important to note what the Bible claims for itself. The Bible claims to have a divine origin. This claim is not something that men have placed upon the Bible; rather it is the Bible's claim for itself.
- In the weeks and months leading up to the start of class I gave a lot of thought to how I should begin and the best order for covering the material. While I knew I was going to start with the issue of inspiration, originally, I thought I would cover the evidentiary proofs of inspiration first.
- As I pondered my options further I decided that beginning with an evidentialist approach might send the wrong message. I believe that

the Bible is the inspired word of God because that is the Bible's claim for itself. This does not mean that there are no evidentiary proofs that speak to the Bible's inspiration it just means that we need to base our study on the proper set of assumptions.

- o God exists. (Psalm 14:1)
- o God has magnified his word above his own name. (Psalm 138:2)
- o God's word is eternally settled in heaven. (Psalm 119:89)
- o God through the process of inspiration has communicated his word to mankind. (I Tim. 3:16 & II Peter 1:21)
- o God's words were written down so that they could be made eternally available to men. (I Peter 1:23)
- o God promised to preserve that which he inspired. (Psalm 12:6-7)

- So, for the purposes of this class we are going to initially adopt a Presuppositional approach that assumes the Bible to be the inspired word of God at the outset. This assumption is made on account of the fact that the Bible claims to be inspired by God. After we have learned what the Bible says about itself, we will consider the many evidential proofs that the Bible is in fact of divine origin.
- I am aware of the division that exists within Christian Apologetics between the Presuppositional by Evidential approaches. It is my view that both are valid and have a seat at the table. Consequently, throughout the course of this study we will be looking at both. There is ample internal and external evidence that the Bible was given by inspiration and God and is therefore of divine origin.
- Our studies together are going to be an in-depth study into the origin and the transmission of the written word of God. In other words, where did it come from? What is its origin? And, how did it get from the original autographs, when it was originally written, into our hands today?
- I want you to be able to identify and defend the word of God accurately and confidently. I want you to be able to know where it is and what it is.

SATAN: THE FIRST DESTRUCTIVE CRITIC

- Genesis 3:1-6 — the original standards of the original Textual Critic are preserved for you by God, and you can see the tactics, and the methods, and the approach, and the policy of evil that Satan has against God's word.

- Now, you need to get an understanding of this. How does Satan come at God's word? Before Eve ever took of that tree, there is a long discussion (5 verses) between her and Satan. In that whole discussion, the tactics and the policy of Satan's design against the word of God are laid out for you. And it is just as true today as it was then. In fact, today, we are in the advanced stages of that campaign.

- Genesis 3:1 — the very first thing that Satan does is question the word of God. He questions the scripture, Yea, hath God said . . .? Did God really say that? Are you sure God said that? He raises the question; Satan seeks to create doubt about what God actually said. This is his first tactic.

- Notice that he does it with a positive approach. You want to remember that. He says, "Yea, (yes), hath God said …." The root source of all questioning and doubt of the Bible comes from the Adversary.

- Genesis 3:2 — is that what God told them?

  o Genesis 2:16

- Do you see what Eve did in Gen. 3:2? She left a very important word out. She subtracted a word from the text. She subtracted the word "freely" from the text. The first mistake Eve made, outside of engaging the Adversary in a conversation, was subtracting from the text.

- Tactic 1 is to question the word whereas Tactic 2 is to subtract from the word.

- Genesis 3:3 — reveals the Adversary's 3rd and 4th tactics, ADD to the word of God and water it down.
- Genesis 2:16-17 — does the phrase "neither shall ye touch it" appear in these verses. Satan adds the phrase to the verse when he quotes it to Eve in Genesis 3:3?
- Genesis 3:3 — notice the ending of the verse "lest ye die."

  o Genesis 2:16-17 — the text states "thou shalt surely die."

- Notice how Genesis 3:3 waters the severity of the situation down, "thou shalt surely die" becomes "well, you might die."
- Genesis 3:4 — Satan's attack on the word of God culminates with his outright denial of what God said. The verse reads "Ye shall not surely die."

  o Genesis 2:17 — clearly states "thou shalt surely die"

- Notice what Satan denies. He did not deny the words *"you shall not possibly die"*. He denied the original version. He denied "Ye shall not surely die."
- Genesis 3:5 — The basis of Satan's denial of the word of God is a desire that he perceives in Eve for an independent viewpoint –for her own viewpoint, for her own knowledge. Here we see the origin of what Paul is talking about in I Cor. 1. Ultimately Satan wants to replace God's word and his wisdom with human viewpoint and the wisdom of men, i.e., the wisdom of this world.
- In summation, the Adversary's attack on the final authority of God's word is rooted in the following 5 tactics:

  o Tactic 1 — Question God's word (Gen. 3:1)
  o Tactic 2 — Subtract from God's word (Gen. 3:2)
  o Tactic 3 — Add to God's word (Gen. 3:3)

- - Tactic 4 — Water down God's word (Gen. 3:3)
  - Tactic 5 — Deny God's word (Gen. 3:4)

- Sin, on this planet earth, begins with an attack on God's word in Genesis 3. There is a satanic policy of evil against the word of God clearly laid out in the scripture, and the design is simply to destroy the final authority of your Bible. Satan wants to take that word of God and make it less than the final authority.

- Now, how is he going to do that? Well, if you have an authority and it speaks with authority, the tactic is to bring up another authority alongside of it and give that second authority equal weight with the first. Well, then how do you decide which is right? If you have two competing authorities, who decides what is right? A third authority decides – you do, or somebody does.

  - "For example: you have two baseball teams playing against each other. There is a close play at first base. Well, you know what they are all going to say, right? The guy in the field is going to say that he was out, and the guy running is going to say that he is safe. Now, what do you have in the game to take care of that? You have a final authority; you have an umpire. If that umpire says that someone is out, you can kick dirt on him all day long, but it does not change anything unless you can go convince the league commissioner that he was wrong. But, when that happens, nobody ever knows if they can be sure or not." (Jordan, MSS 101)

- So, Satan's goal is to get rid of that final authority by putting up a competing authority. And the policy, and the design, is to destroy that final authority in God's word.

  - Hegelian Dialectic—"usually presented in a threefold manner, was stated by Heinrich Moritz Chalybäus as comprising three dialectical stages of development: a thesis, giving rise to its reaction, an antithesis, which contradicts or negates the thesis, and the tension between the two being resolved by means of a synthesis. Although this model is often named after Hegel, he himself never used that specific formulation. Hegel ascribed that terminology to Kant. Carrying on Kant's work, Fichte greatly elaborated on the synthesis model, and popularized it." (Wikipedia Entry)

- Hegelian Dialectic certainly applies to the realm of human viewpoint or the wisdom of this world. It does not hold, however, when dealing with the word of God. God gave his word to be an anchor, no matter what your thesis is, if the old book stands up here and the old book is different from human viewpoint, that is the final authority. And it will look at your thesis and say that it is wrong. It may look at that guy's opinion and say that it is right. It stands. It is the authority.
- Satan wants to get rid of that authority. He does not want you to have the capacity, in your hands, to have what God Almighty says. You need to know where God's word is because Satan is interested, and he has a positive program in place to corrupt that book.

    o II Corinthians 2:17

- Amos 8:11-12 — now, notice that it says "words". That's the words on the page, not just the message but the words. There is going to be a famine, an inability to find God's word. Now, if you study the book of Amos, you will find that this passage is prophetic, not just of the captivity of Israel; but it is also prophetic of the tribulation period. In the tribulation period there will be two big issues.

    o Issue One—"Where is the promise of his coming?" (II Peter 3:4)
    o Issue Two — Where are the words of God? (Amos 8:11-12)

- Amos 8:13-14 — we see the results of not being able to find the words of God. They will be totally consumed by a religious system – no book, no light, no revelation. They will have their doctrinal statements – "Thy god, O Dan, liveth." They conform to the fundamentals of a creed. They are orthodox, but they do not have a book, and they do not have light; and God's judgment is on them. They are all swept off in judgment.

> o *"If you do not have an absolute final authority, don't you preach to anybody.* If you cannot find out what God's word is, and know what it is, and have it in your hand, and know you are preaching it, then you hang up your track shoes and you go fishing, but don't you preach. If you preach, all you are going to do is what that verse in Amos says. You are just going to build a bunch a people into a religious system that God Almighty is going to judge and condemn. . .
>
> Now, the world is hungry today for authority. They are hungry for leadership; they are hungry for purity; they are hungry for an honest message that has some power in it. And there is not any power, anywhere, except in that book. You know that, and that's the reason you are here. But I want you to understand that that's a fact. And that is why this issue is important.
>
> Folks, if you want power to get a drunkard saved, or you want power to get a proud boastful spirit in line, or you want power to overcome the sins of life in your life and the lives of those you will minister to, that power must come out of a book; and that book is God's book. You will need some authority. And that is what the world is after, and that is what the religious system does not have." (Jordan, MSS 101)

- Romans 10:17 — In the final analysis, the word of God, (your Bible), is the only ultimate proof that you have for your faith. The ultimate proof for your faith is in that book.

> o "Folks, if you use that book right, it is enough to overwhelmingly convince any honest and sincere listener. And that is the answer. Ultimately, you know you are right because of the Bible. Do you see why it is important to be able to know what that book is and where it is? If Satan can take that book away from you, he has destroyed the basis of your ministry." (Jordan, MSS 101)

CONCLUSION

- Given the adversary's tactics against the word of God we need to think about God's word accordingly. Three times the word of God warns against adding or subtracting from the scriptures.

    - Deuteronomy 4:1-2
    - Proverbs 30:5-6
    - Revelation 22:18-19

- II Corinthians 11:3 — the Adversary is willing to use whatever means necessary to undermine the final authority that God has placed in his word.
- In *Which Bible Would Jesus Use?* author Jack McElroy points out that "it's not politically correct to believe that one Bible is the final authority for Christians." (McElroy, 287) McElroy goes on to point out that no one who uses or promotes modern versions claims that any of them are "all the words of God without error."

    - "That's why you don't see any influential Christian leaders who profess to be NIV Onlyeist, ESV Onlyists, or NASB Onlyists or any other version Onlyist, and you never will. They all believe that their Bibles have errors in the text and translation and they're not ashamed to admit it. This is why they make the "Which Bible?" issue one of preference and not of conviction.

        Since they still aren't completely sure which words are original and which are imposters, the only thing that's really important to them is the message and not the words." (McElroy, 288)

- II Corinthians 13:14

    - Holman Christian Standard Bible (HCSB) does not contain it.
    - New American Standard Bible (NASB) and the English Standard Version (ESV) do contain it.

- Matthew 12:47

    - ESV does not contain it.
    - HSCB and the NASB do contain it.

- James 1:7

    - New Revised Standard Version (NRSV) does not contain it.
    - HSCB, NASB, and ESV do contain it.

- Matthew 21:44, Luke 24:12, and Luke 24:40

    - Revised Standard Version (RSV) does not contain these verses.
    - HSCB, NASB, ESV do contain them.

- "Almost all modern versions are nothing more than personal versions of "The Original Bible" the experts are still searching for. They are "personal versions" because they reflect the editor's choices as to which variant readings are authentic and which are not. Plus, they provide plenty of footnotes and encourage you to choose how "the Bible" should read." (McElroy, 290)
- According to Kurt and Barbara Aland's (the go-to folks in New Testament textual criticism) *The Text of the New Testament* there are at least 31 possibly as many as 39 complete verses that shouldn't be in

the Bible. (see pages 306-311) The fact that the editors and committees that produce and publish modern versions cannot agree with each other about what verses should and should not be in the Bible highlights an important point, according to Jack McElroy.

> o "The experts are all in competition with each other. They all claim that it's their mandate to update the "Word of God" or "The Bible" into a language you can understand, and yet they can't even agree on which verses they should translate, let alone how they should be translated." (McElroy, 291)

- The Adversary's attack and tactics have been successful. Scores of competing and contradictory Bibles have flooded the market place. Anything goes in Christian academia except the belief that there is one final absolute authority.

WORKS CITED

Aland, Kurt & Barbara. *The Text of the New Testament: An Introduction to the Critical Editions and to the Theory and Practice of Modern Textual Criticism.* 1987.

Jordan, Richard. *Manuscript Evidence 101.* Grace School of the Bible.

McElroy, Jack. *Which Bible Would Jesus Use? The Bible Version Controversy Explained and Resolved.* 2013.

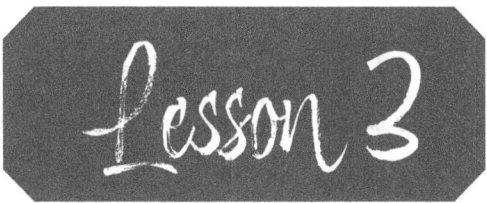

THE "YEA, HATH GOD SAID" SOCIETY, PART 2

INTRODUCTION/REVIEW

- In our last lesson we discussed the difference between Presuppositional and Evidential Apologetics and how every worldview operates on a set of assumptions.
- II Timothy 3:16 — at the outset it is important to note what the Bible claims for itself. The Bible claims to have a divine origin. This claim is not something that men have placed upon the Bible; rather it is the Bible's claim for itself.
- I believe that the Bible is the inspired word of God because that is the Bible's claim for itself. This does not mean that there are no evidentiary proofs that speak to the Bible's inspiration it just means that we need to base our study on the proper set of assumptions.

- God exists. (Psalm 14:1)
- God has magnified his word above his own name. (Psalm 138:2)
- God's word is eternally settled in heaven. (Psalm 119:89)
- God through the process of inspiration has communicated his word to mankind. (I Tim. 3:16 & II Peter 1:21)
- God's words were written down so that they could be made eternally available to men. (I Peter 1:23)
- God promised to preserve that which he inspired. (Psalm 12:6-7)

- Genesis 3:1-6 — the *modus operendia* of the original textual critic are preserved for you by God, and you can see the tactics, methods, approach, and the policy of evil that Satan has against God's word. In summation the Adversary's attack on the final authority of God's word is rooted in the following 5 tactics:

    - Tactic 1 — Question God's word (Gen. 3:1)
    - Tactic 2 — Subtract from God's word (Gen. 3:2)
    - Tactic 3 — Add to God's word (Gen. 3:3)
    - Tactic 4 — Water down God's word (Gen. 3:3)
    - Tactic 5 — Deny God's word (Gen. 3:4)

SATAN: THE FIRST DESTRUCTIVE CRITIC (CONTINUED)

- Amos 8:11-12 — now notice that it says "words". That's the words on the page, not just the message but the words. There is going to be a famine, an inability to find God's word. Now, if you study the book of Amos, you will find that this passage is prophetic, not just of the captivity of Israel; but it is also prophetic of the tribulation period. In the tribulation period there will be two big issues.

- Issue 1 — Where is the promise of His coming? (II Peter 3:4)
  - Issue 2 — Where are the words of God? (Amos 8:11-12)

- Amos 8:13-14 — we see the results of not being able to find the words of God. They will be totally consumed by a religious system – no book, no light, no revelation. They will have their doctrinal statements – "Thy god, O Dan, liveth." They conform to the fundamentals of a creed. They are orthodox, but they do not have a book, and they do not have light; and God's judgment is on them. They are all swept off in judgment.

  - *"If you do not have an absolute final authority, don't you preach to anybody.* If you cannot find out what God's word is and know what it is and have it in your hand and know you are preaching it, then you hang up your track shoes and you go fishing, but don't you preach. If you preach, all you are going to do is what that verse in Amos says. You are just going to build a bunch a people into a religious system that God Almighty is going to judge and condemn. . .
  - Now, the world is hungry today for authority. They are hungry for leadership; they are hungry for purity; they are hungry for an honest message that has some power in it. And there is not any power, anywhere, except in that book. You know that, and that is the reason you are here. But, I want you to understand, that that is a fact. And that is why this issue is important.
  - Folks, if you want power to get a drunkard saved, or you want power to get a proud boastful spirit in line, or you want power to overcome the sins of life in your life and the lives of those you will minister to–that power must come out of a book; and that book is God's book. You will need some authority. And that is what the world is after, and that is what the religious system does not have." (Jordan, MSS 101)

- Romans 10:17 — In the final analysis, the word of God (your Bible) is the only ultimate proof that you have for your faith. The ultimate proof for your faith is in that book.

- o "Folks, if you use that book right, it is enough to overwhelmingly convince any honest and sincere listener and that is the answer. Ultimately, you know you are right because of the Bible. Do you see why it is important to be able to know what that book is and where it is? If Satan can take that book away from you, he has destroyed the basis of your ministry." (Jordan, MSS 101)

THE SOCIETY'S MODERN CHAPTER

- Given the Adversary's tactics against the word of God we need to think about God's word accordingly. Three times the word of God warns against adding or subtracting from the scriptures.

    - o Deuteronomy 4:1-2
    - o Proverbs 30:5-6
    - o Revelation 22:18-19

- II Corinthians 11:3 — the Adversary is willing to use whatever means necessary to undermine the final authority that God has placed in His word.
- In *Which Bible Would Jesus Use?* author Jack McElroy points out that "it's not politically correct to believe that one Bible is the final authority for Christians." (McElroy, 287) McElroy goes on to point out that no one who uses or promotes modern versions claims that any of them has "all the words of God without error."

    - o "That's why you do not see any influential Christian leaders who profess to be NIV Onlyists, ESV Onlyists, or NASB Onlyists, or any other version Onlyists, and you never will. They all believe that their Bibles have errors in the text and translation and they are not ashamed to admit it. This is why they make the "Which Bible?" issue one of preference and not of conviction.

Since they still are not completely sure which words are original and which are imposters, the only thing that is really important to them is the message and not the words." (McElroy, 288)

- All the modern versions do not say the same thing. Take for example what the tabernacle (mentioned 297 times) was made out of.

  - KJB — And he made a covering for the tent of rams' skins dyed red, and a cover of badgers' skins above that.
  - NIV (1984)—Then they made for the tent a covering of ram skins dyed red, and over that a covering of hides of sea cow.
  - NASB (1995)—He made a covering for the tent of rams' skins dyed red, and a covering of porpoise skins above.
  - ESV (2001)—And he made for the tent a covering of tanned rams' skins and goatskins.
  - NIV (2011)—Then they made for the tent a cover of ram skins dyed red, and over that a covering of the other durable leather.

- All of these cannot be correct. This is a case where the same Hebrew word is translated 5 different ways.
- This is not just an issue of the KJB versus modern versions. The modern versions themselves can't even agree about how verses should read.

  - Ecclesiastes 8:10

    - NASB (1995)—Then I saw the wicked buried. They . . . were praised in the city. . .
    - ESV (2001)—So then, I have seen the wicked buried . . . they are soon forgotten in the city. . .

- Matthew 18:22

  - NIV (1984)—Jesus answered, "I tell you, not seven times, but seventy-seven (77) times."
  - ESV (2011)—Jesus said to him, I do not say to you seven times, but seventy times seven (490)."

- II Samuel 15:7

  - NASB (1995)—Now it came about at the end of forty years that Absalom said to the king, . . .
  - ESV (2011)—And at the end of four years Absalom said to the king, . . .
  - Dr. Albert Mohler Jr. president of Southern Baptist Theological Seminary said the following regarding the NASB and the ESV despite the clear contradiction in II Samuel 15:7:
    - NASB (40 Years)—"The New American Standard Bible has set the standard for faithful Bible translations for a generation. It is the favorite of so many who love the Bible and look for accuracy and clarity in translation. The New American Standard Bible should be close at hand for any serious student of the Bible. I thank God for this faithful translation." (Lockwood Foundation, "NASB Endorsements")
    - ESV (4 Years)—"The ESV represents a new level of excellence in Bible translations — combining unquestionable accuracy in translation with a beautiful style of expression. It is faithful to the text, easy to understand, and a pleasure to read. This is a translation you can trust." (Crossway, "MacArthur Study Bible: ESV")

- Luke 10:1

  - NASB (1995)—Now after this the Lord appointed seventy others...
  - ESV (2001)—After this the Lord appointed seventy-two others...

- Matthew 12:47

  - NASB (1995)—Someone said to Him, "Behold, Your mother and Your brothers are standing outside seeking to speak to you."
  - ESV (2011)—Omitted
  - Dr. Paige Patterson is the president of Southwestern Baptist Theological Seminary in Fort Worth, Texas. Dr. Patterson stated the following regarding the NASB and ESV.
    - NASB (Contains Matt. 12:47)—"The New American Standard Bible . . . is still the most accurate translation of the Greek and Hebrew Scriptures available. . ." (Lockwood Foundation, "NASB Endorsements")
    - ESV (Omits Matthew 12:47)—"For our churches and pulpits, as well as for our students, it is critically important to have a Bible translation that does not compromise orthodox theology or gender issues, and that is both faithful to the language of the text and eminently readable. The ESV unequally fulfills that prescription." (Crossway, ESV Endorsements)

- Acts 8:37

  - NASB (1995)—includes verse 37 in brackets with the following footnote attached. "Early mss do not contain this verse."
  - ESV (2011)—Omitted
  - NIV (2011)—Omitted

- o II Corinthians 13:14

  - Holman Christian Standard Bible (HCSB) does not contain it.
  - New American Standard Bible (NASB) and the English Standard Version (ESV) do contain it.

- o Matthew 12:47

  - ESV does not contain it.
  - HSCB and the NASB do contain it.

- o James 1:7

  - New Revised Standard Version (NRSV) does not contain it.
  - HSCB, NASB, and ESV do contain it.

- o Matthew 21:44, Luke 24:12, and Luke 24:40

  - Revised Standard Version (RSV) does not contain these verses.
  - HSCB, NASB, ESV do contain them.

- "Almost all modern versions are nothing more than personal versions of "The Original Bible" the experts are still searching for. They are "personal versions" because they reflect the editor's choices as to which variant readings are authentic and which are not. Plus, they provide plenty of footnotes and encourage you to choose how "the Bible" should read." (McElroy, 290)

- According to Kurt and Barbara Aland's (the go-to folks in New Testament textual criticism) *The Text of the New Testament,* there are at least 31, possibly as many as 39, complete verses that should not be in the Bible. (See pages 306-311)

- Matthew — 5:44, 6:13, 16:2b-3, 17:21, 18:11, 20:16, 20:22-23, 23:14, 25:13, 27:354
- Mark — 7:16, 9:44, 9:46, 11:26, 15:28
- Luke — 4:4, 9:54-56, 17:36, 23:17, 24:24
- John 5:3b-4
- Acts 8:37, 15:34, 24:6b-8, 28:16, 28:29

- The editors and committees responsible for the production of modern versions are in agreement about some of these but not all. The following is a list of verses that are placed in the text in brackets thereby showing their doubtful authenticity. So they are (by modern textual criticism standards) probably impure forgeries yet they are still placed within the text.

  - Mark — 10:7, 10:21, 10:24, 14:68
  - Luke –8:43, 22:43-44

- The fact that the editors and committees that produce and publish modern versions cannot agree with each other about what verses should and should not be in the Bible highlights an important point, according to Jack McElroy.

  - "The experts are all in competition with each other. They all claim that it's their mandate to update the "Word of God" or "The Bible" into a language you can understand, and yet they can't even agree on which verses they should translate, let alone how they should be translated." (McElroy, 291)

- The real question in who gets to pick which readings out of the pile are authentic. Even the editors of the Greek New Testament behind virtually all modern versions self-graded their choices regarding what the readings should be. According to the preface of the latest edition of the Greek text published by the United Bible Society (*USB4*) the grading system works as follows:

- A — Indicates the text is certain.
- B — Indicates the text is almost certain.
- C — Indicates the text is difficult to determine.
- D — Indicates the text is very difficult to determine. (Ballard)

- If you pay close attention you will run across instances of extreme candor on the part of the men doing the textual work to reconstruct the "original Bible." One such instance is provided by Eldon J. Epp, Professor of Biblical Literature at Case Western Reserve University in Cleveland, Ohio. In addition to serving as the president for the Society of Biblical Literature form 2003 to 2004, Professor Epp also coauthored *Studies in the Theory and Method of New Testament Textual Criticism* (1993) with Gordon D. Fee. As an expert and recognized authority in the field of New Testament textual criticism Professor Epp stats the following:

  - ". . . we no longer think so simplistically or so confidently about recovering "the New Testament in the Original Greek." . . . We remain largely in the dark as to how we might reconstruct the textual history that has left in its wake — in the form of MSS and fragments — numerous pieces that we seem incapable of fitting together. . . we seem to have no such theories and no plausible sketches of the early history of the text that are widely accepted. What progress, then, have we made? Are we more advanced than our predecessors where, after showing their theories to unacceptable, we offer no such theories at all to vindicate our accepted text?" (Epp and Fee, 114-115)

- In the end, the only thing textual critics/experts are certain of is that the King James Bible is not the word of God for English speaking people. There is not a book in existence today that can rightly be called the word of God, according to the prevailing thoughts of Christian academia.
- The Adversary's attack and tactics have been successful. Scores of competing and contradictory Bibles have flooded the marketplace. Anything goes in Christian academia except the belief that there is one final absolute authority.

WORKS CITED

Aland, Kurt & Barbara. *The Text of the New Testament: An Introduction to the Critical Editions and to the Theory and Practice of Modern Textual Criticism.* 1987.

Ballard, Peter. *Is the Bible Reliable Despite Textual Errors.* http://peterballard.org/catalog.html.

Epp, Eldon J. and Gordon D. Fee. *Studies in the Theory and Method of New Testament Textual Criticism.*

Jordan, Richard. *Manuscript Evidence 101.* Grace School of the Bible.

McElroy, Jack. *Which Bible Would Jesus Use? The Bible Version Controversy Explained and Resolved.* 2013.

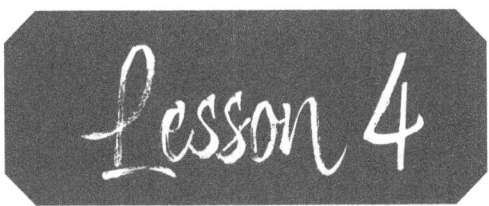

ORIGINALS ONLYISM: A POSITION OF NO PRACTICAL CONSEQUENCE

INTRODUCTION

- I would like to begin this morning by just making a general statement about our progression through the content contained in this class. I am trying to present the information in what I believe to be the most logical progression possible. With a topic this large it is not possible to say everything one might like at the outset. If I were to address certain topics prematurely before having given you the background or prerequisite information first, you would not understand my reasoning. In other words, I am going to ask your patience that as the course develops all your questions will be answered in due time.

- That said, this morning we are going to address an issue that I originally planned on tackling a bit later in the class. However, it has come up a couple different times already and is related to the topic of inspiration, so I decided to cover it, at least in part, in this lesson.
- The topic relates to what I am calling "Originals Onlyism" or the belief that only the original autographs of the Biblical writings are inspired and inerrant.
- Last week we learned that the "Bible Issue" is not just a King James versus modern version debate but that not all modern versions say the same thing. Neither is this just a question of translation philosophy and methodology, i.e., dynamic versus formal equivalence. There are substantive differences in meaning between modern versions. Textual scholars cannot even agree among themselves on what verses should be in the text much less how each verse should read.

ORIGINALS ONLYISM

- For the last 130 years or so, Fundamental and Evangelical leaders have taught that "the real Bible" is not a book anyone today can hold in their hands. Much ink has been spilt defending the inspiration and inerrancy of the Bible while "the Bible" they're defending never actually existed in one place at one time in world history.
- The Bible they are defending is one whose text is made up of an unavailable collection of original autographs that comprise a book they call "The Original Bible."
- Dr. Randall Price, Professor and Executive Director of the Center for Judaic Studies at Liberty University summarized the "Original Bible" concept in his book *Searching for the Original Bible*. Dr. Price states,

    o "*Autograph* is the accepted term for the original edition of a particular work, written or dictated by the author. It is the *earliest* copy, from which the *apographs* (all later copies) are ultimately descended... Although neither the Hebrew nor the Greek original manuscripts ever existed in a form resembling our present Bible, and in some cases they were edited by others before assuming the form we know today, their collective existence as original manuscripts constitutes the *autographa*, or the "Original Bible." (Price, 33-34)

- Despite Price's own admission that no such document ever existed, virtually all Fundamental and Evangelical leaders claim that this unavailable collection of writings ought to be the final authority for Christian belief and practice. Christian scholars boldly utter proclamations such as "I believe the Bible is the inspired and inerrant word of God!" and "The book is our only authority." Yet they are admittedly speaking about a Bible that they are still searching for. They teach that the only "scripture" that was inspired and without error is this "Original Bible." They say that the words we have today are inspired and inerrant only so far as they match the wording of the "Original Bible." Yet they remain unsure as to the exact wording of the "Original Bible." (McElroy, 4)
- Moreover, these scholars teach that no book in existence today contains all of God's words and only God's words. Worse yet, they believe all Bibles today contain errors and/or have readings that may not be "original." Yet as we saw last week, they can't even agree on what verses and or readings are authentic and representative of the "Original Bible."
- Who is making these claims? For starters the following Christian leaders and theologians recommend Dr. Randall Price's book *Searching for the Original Bible* (quoted from above):

    o   Kenneth L Barker, ThM, PhD — General Editor of the NIV Study Bible

    o   Dr. Wayne House — Distinguished Research Professor of Biblical and Theological Studies at Faith Evangelical Seminary in Tacoma, WA

    o   Walter C. Kaiser Jr.—President Emeritus of Gordon-Conwell Theological Seminary in Hamilton, MA

    o   Colman M. Mockler — Distinguished Professor of Old Testament at Gordon-Conwell Theological Seminary in Hamilton, MA

- - Dr. Charles C. Ryrie — former professor at Dallas Theological Seminary and author of the *Ryrie Study Bible*.
- Dr. Ryrie is also the author of the introductory Systematic Theology book *Basic Theology*. In the section on the Bible, Ryrie takes up a discussion of how the doctrines of inspiration and inerrancy apply to the original autographs alone. Notice how Ryrie struggles to defend these important doctrines when they are applied to the "originals" only.

  - - "The second excuse for diluting the importance of inerrancy is that since we do not possess any original manuscripts of the Bible, and since inerrancy is related to those originals only, the doctrine of inerrancy is only a theoretical one and therefore nonessential. We do not possess any of the original manuscripts of the Bible, and the doctrine of inerrancy, like inspiration is predicated only on the original manuscripts, not on any of the copies. The two premises in the statement above are correct, but those particular premises do not prove at all that inerrancy is a nonessential doctrine.

      Obviously, inerrancy can be asserted only in relation to the original manuscripts because only they came directly from God under inspiration. The very first copy of a letter of Paul, for instance, was in reality only a copy, and not the original that Paul himself wrote or dictated. Both inspiration and inerrancy are predicated only on the originals." (Ryrie, 80)

- In Volume One of his *Systematic Theology*, Dr. Norman Geisler follows suite by stating:

  - - "The inspiration of Scripture is the supernatural operation of the Holy Spirit who, through the different personalities and literary styles of the chosen human authors, invested the very words of the original books of Holy Scripture, alone and in their entirety, as the very Word of God without error in all that they teach (including history and science) and is thereby the infallible rule and final authority for the faith and practice of all believers." (Geisler, 498)

- In *The Moody Handbook of Theology*, Paul Enns offers the following definition of inerrancy:

    o "Inerrancy means that when all the facts are known, the Scripture in their original autographs and properly interpreted will be shown to be wholly true in everything they teach, whether that teaching has to do with doctrine, history, science, geography, geology, or other disciplines or knowledge." (Enns, 167)

- Lastly, the popular *Evangelical Dictionary of Theology* edited by Walter A. Elwell records the following definition for inerrancy (the entry is written by Paul D. Feinberg):

    o "Inerrancy is the view that when all the facts become known, they will demonstrate that the Bible in its original autographs and correctly interrupted is entirely true and never false in all it affirms, whether that relates to doctrine or ethics or to the social, physical, or life sciences.

    A number of points in this definition deserve discussion. Inerrancy is not presently demonstratable. Human knowledge is limited in two ways. First, because of our finitude and sinfulness human beings misinterpret the data that exists. For instance, wrong conclusions can be drawn from inscriptions or texts. Second, we do not possess all the data that comes to bear on the Bible. Some of that data may be lost forever, or they may be awaiting discovery by archeologists. By claiming inerrancy will be shown to be true after all the facts are known, one recognizes this. The defender of inerrancy argues only that there will be no conflict in the end.

    Further, inerrancy applies equally to all parts of the Bible as originally written. This means that no present manuscript or copy of scripture, no matter how accurate, can be called inerrant." (Elwell, 156-157)

- This entry by Paul D. Feinberg is truly puzzling. According to this definition it is totally pointless to affirmatively argue for inerrancy since all of the information is not known. This so-called definition proves nothing. All Mr. Feinberg has done is leave the doors open for modern textual critics such as Bart D. Ehrman, author of *Misquoting Jesus*, and his troop to attack the veracity of God's written word.

- In October 1978 a group of 300 scholars, pastors, and laymen came together in Chicago, IL for The International Conference on Biblical Inerrancy (ICBI). Here is a sampling of what their document said regarding the doctrines of inspiration and inerrancy.

    - Article VI — *WE AFFIRM* that the whole of Scripture and all its parts, down to the very words of the original, were given by divine inspiration.

    - Article X — *WE AFFIRM* that inspiration, strictly speaking, applies only to the autographic text of Scripture, which in the providence of God can be ascertained from available manuscripts with great accuracy. We further affirm that copies and translations of Scripture are the Word of God to the extent that they faithfully represent the original.

    - Article X — *WE DENY* that any essential element of the Christian faith is affected by the absence of the autographs. We further deny that this absence renders the assertion of Biblical inerrancy invalid or irrelevant. (Geisler, *Inerrancy*, 494-502)

- There you have it. According to leading Evangelical scholars including James Boice, Norman L. Geisler, John Gerstner, Carl F. H. Henry, Kenneth Kantzer, Harold Lindsell, John Warwick Montgomery, Roger Nicole, J. I. Packer, Robert Preus, Earl Radmacher, Francis Schaeffer, R. C. Sproul, and John Wenham:

    - 1) inspiration applies only to the autographic text of Scripture,
    - 2) copies and translations of Scripture are the Word of God to the extent they faithfully represent the original, and
    - 3) they admit that the autographs are "absent."

- So how do they really know what they claim to know when their standard for judging, by their own admission, is a document that doesn't exist? This is a doctrine of no practical consequence.

INSPIRATION WITHOUT PRESERVATION IS MEANINGLESS

- In 1980, Normal Geisler edited a book called *Inerrancy*. This book contained 14 scholarly essays that had been edited from the transcripts of lectures presented at the ICBI in 1978. One of the essays, written by Greg L. Bahnsen is titled "*The Inerrancy of the Autographa*." We will have more today about Bahnsen's articles at a future date when we discuss the doctrine of inerrancy in greater depth. For now, please note that all of these quotations come from the same essay.

    o   *No Originals No Scripture*—"We can believe our copies of Scripture and be saved without having the autographic codex, for the Bible itself indicates that copies can faithfully reflect the original text and therefore function authoritatively. Second, the paramount features and qualities of Scripture — such as inspiration, infallibility, and inerrancy — are uniformly identified with God's own original word as found in the autographic text, which alone can be identified and esteemed as God's own word to man." (Geisler, 169-170)

    o   *The Logical Implication*—"There is circulating at present a rather serious misunderstanding of the evangelical restriction of inerrancy (or inspiration, infallibility) to the autographic text and the implications of that restriction. DeKoster claims that there are only two options: either the Bible on our pulpits is the inspired Word of God, or it is the uninspired words of man. Because inspiration and inerrancy are restricted to the autographa (which are lost, and therefore not found in pulpits), then our Bibles, it is argued, must be the uninspired words of man and not the vitally needed word of God. Others have misconstrued an epistemological argument for biblical inerrancy and hold that, if the Bible contains even one mistake, it cannot be believed true at any point; we cannot then rely on any part of it, and God cannot use it to communicate authoritatively to us. From this mistaken point critics go on to say that the evangelical restriction of inerrancy to the autographs means that, because of errors in all present versions, our Bible today cannot be trusted at all, cannot communicate God's word to us, and cannot be the inspired word of God. If our present Bibles, with their errors, are not inspired, then we are left with nothing (since the autographa are lost)." (Geisler, 172)

o *Mistaken Bibles Are Still the Word of God*—"It needs to be reiterated quite unambiguously that evangelical restriction of inerrancy to the autographa 1) is a restriction to the autographic text, thereby guarding the uniqueness of God's verbal message and 2) does not imply that present Bibles because they are not fully inerrant, fail to be the Word of God. . . So also my American Standard Version of the Bible contains mistaken or disputed words with respect to the autographic text of Scripture (how would he actually know this), but it is still the very Word of God, inspired and inerrant — to the degree that it reflects the original work of God (because of the objective, universally accepted, and outstanding degree of correlation in the light of textual criticism) is a qualification that is very seldom in need of being stated." (Geisler, 173)

o *No Promise of Preservation*—"God has not promised in His Word that the Scriptures would receive perfect transmission, and thus we have no ground to claim it a priori. Moreover, the inspired Word of God in the Scriptures has a uniqueness that must be guarded from distortion. Consequently, we cannot be theologically blind to the significance of transmissional errors, nor can we theologically assume the absence of such errors. We are therefore theologically required to restrict inspiration, infallibility and inerrancy to the autographa. . . Scripture nowhere give us ground to maintain that its transmission and translation would be kept without effort by God. There is no scriptural warrant for holding that God will perform the perpetual miracle of preserving His written Word from all errors in its being transcribed from one copy to another. Since the Bible does not claim that every copier translator, typesetter, and printer will retain the infallibility of the original document, Christians should not make such a claim either. The doctrine is not supported by Scripture, and

Protestants are committed to the methodical principle of sola Scriptura." (Geisler, 175-176)

o *Theological Doubt-Talk: Providential Bible Copying*—"... the preservation of the text of Scripture is part of the transmission of the knowledge of God, it is reasonable to expect that God will provide for it lest the aims of His revealing Himself to man be frustrated. The providence of God superintended matters so that copies of Scripture do not become so corrupt as to become unintelligible for God's original purposes in giving it or so corrupt as to create a major falsification of His message's text... Faith in the consistency of God — His faithfulness to His own intention to make men wise unto salvation — guarantees the inference that He never permits Scripture to become so corrupted that it can no longer fulfill that end adequately. We can conclude theologically that, for all practical purposes, the text of Scripture is always sufficiently accurate not to lead us astray. If we presuppose a sovereign God, observes Van Til, it is no longer a matter of great worry that the transmission of Scripture is not all altogether accurate; God's providence provides for the essential accuracy of the Bible's copying...our copies virtually supply us with the autographic text. All the ridicule that is heaped on evangelicals about the "lost autographa" is simply vain, for we do not regard their text as lost at all! ... The doctrine of original inerrancy, then, does not deprive believers today of the Word of God in an adequate form for all the purpose of God's revelation to His people. Presupposing the providence of God in the preservation of the biblical text and noting the outstanding result of the textual criticism of Scriptures, we can have full assurance that we possess the Word of God necessary for our salvation and Christian walk. As a criticism of this evangelical doctrine, suggestions that the autographic text has been forever lost are groundless and futile. The Bibles in our hands are trustworthy rendition of God's original message, adequate for all intents and purposes as copies and conveyors of God's autoreactive word." (Geisler, 185-189)

- To say there is confusion in Bahnsen's essay quoted above would be an understatement to say the least.

- Perhaps sensing the inconsistency of Christian academia's position, Geisler hedges as to the reliability of the available copies. In Volume One of his *Systematic Theology*, Dr. Geisler seeks to debunk ten of the most common objections to the doctrine of Inerrancy. In the section, "The Objection That Inerrancy Is Based on Non-Existent Originals," Geisler offers the following counterpoint:

    o "Some object to inerrancy because it affirms that only the original text is inerrant (there being admitted errors in the copies), and the originals are not extant. Hence, all the doctrine of inerrancy provides is a non-existent authority; supposedly, this isn't any different than having no Bible at all.

    This allegation is unfounded. First of all, it is not true that we do not possess the original text. We do possess it in well preserved copies; it is the original manuscripts we do not have. We do have an accurate copy of the original text represented in these manuscripts; the nearly 5,700 New Testament manuscripts we possess contain all or nearly all of the original text, and we can reconstruct the original text with over 99 percent accuracy...

    In brief, the Bible in our hands is the infallible and inerrant Word of God insofar as it has been copied accurately. And it has been copied so accurately as to assure us that nothing in the essential message has been lost." (Geisler, 503)

- Geisler's double-speak in compounded is the next section where he tackles "The Objection That Inerrancy is Unnecessary:"

    o "The answers to the previous objections lead to another: If errant copies of the original text are sufficient, then why did God have to inspired errorless originals? If a scratched record can convey the music of its master, then an errant Bible can convey to us the truth of the Master.

    The response is simple. The reason the original text cannot err is that it was breathed out by God, and God cannot err. The copies, while demonstrated to have been providently preserved from substantial error, are not breathed out by God. Hence there can be errors in the copies." (Geisler, 503-504)

- Notice that Geisler mentions the issue of providential preservation, yet he does not define it or elaborate upon it in any way. Is Dr. Geisler really saying that God is incapable of accurately preserving that which he inspired?
- All the confusion we observed in our last lesson regarding the reconstruction of the Biblical text stems from an improper understanding of the twin doctrines of inspiration and preservation.
- Systematic Theology books are filled with information about inspiration and inerrancy but none of them contain any exposition of the doctrine of Preservation. In preparation for these studies, I searched the Systematic Theology books by the following Christian authors looking for information on the doctrine of preservation.

    o   Norman L. Geisler — *Systematic Theology, Volume I*
    o   Lewis Sherry Chaffer — *Systematic Theology*
    o   Charles C. Ryrie — *Basic Theology*
    o   Paul Enns — *Moody Handbook of Theology*
    o   Wayne Grudem — *Systematic Theology: An Introduction to Christian Doctrine*
    o   Millard J. Erickson — *Christian Theology*
    o   Alister McGrath — *Christian Theology: An Introduction*
    o   Charles F. Baker — *A Dispensational Theology*

- Why did former evangelical Bart D. Ehrman (graduate of Moody Bible Institute and Wheaton College) become an agnostic? It was largely due to his lingering doubts over the inspiration and inerrancy of Scripture. In *Misquoting Jesus: The Story Behind Who Changed the Bible and Why*, Ehrman gives his reasons for opposing the historicity of both the original text and the transmission of the text.

- o "... the reality is that we don't' have the originals — so saying they were inspired doesn't help much, unless I can reconstruct the originals. Moreover, the vast majority of Christians for the entire history of the church have not had access to the originals, making their inspiration a moot point... I came to realize that it would have been no more difficult for God to preserve the words of scripture than it would have been for him to inspire them in the first place. If he wanted this people to have his words, surely he would have given them to them (and possibly even given them the words in a language they would understand, rather than Greek and Hebrew). The fact that we don't have the words surely must show, I reasoned, that he did not preserve them for us. And if he didn't perform that miracle, there seems to be no reason to think that he performed the earlier miracle of inspiring those words." (Ehrman, 10-11)

- Ehrman's honesty regarding the implications of his evangelical training led him to agnosticism.
- By limiting inerrancy to the originals and failing to acknowledge the doctrine of preservation, Evangelical scholars neglect to protect the doctrine of inspiration. If God went to the trouble to perfectly inspire his word only to allow substantive errors and mistakes to creep into the text it would be inconsistent with His nature and character.
- In fact, just as the Bible internally claims to have been given by inspiration of God it also says that God intends to preserve the very words that God breathed. However, one does not learn about preservation in the evangelical systematic theology books because the topic has been totally overlooked
- Just as the Bible claims to be inspired it also records God's promise to preserve that which he inspired.

  - o Psalm 12:6-7 — "The words of the LORD are pure words: as silver tried in a furnace of earth purified seven times. 7) Thou shalt kept them, O LORD, thou shalt preserve them from this generation for ever."

- Psalm 33:11 — "The counsel of the Lord standeth for ever, the thoughts of his heart to all generations."
- Psalm 119:152 — "Concerning thy testimonies, I have know of old that thou hast founded them for ever."
- Psalm 119: 89 — "Forever, O LORD, thy word is settled in heaven."
- Isaiah 30:8 — "Now go, write it before them in a table, and note it in a book, that it may be for the time to come for ever and ever."
- Matthew 5:18 — "For verily I say unto you, Till heaven and earth pass, one jot or one tittle shall in no wise pass from the law, till all be fulfilled."

- Believers are thus forced into an interesting predicament. One can either believe these verses or not. As we have already established, none of the original autographs remain, yet God promises that his words will remain throughout all eternity. Therefore, God did not use the original manuscripts as the vehicle through which preservation would take place.
- So then, where does this eternal preservation take place if not in the original autographs? The believing Bible student will let the Word of God answer this question as well. Consider II Timothy 3:15:

  - "And that from a child thou hast known the holy scriptures which are able to make thee wise unto salvation through faith which is in Christ Jesus."

- Paul, writing under the influence of the Holy Spirit, tells Timothy that from the time of his childhood he knew the Holy Scriptures. Did Timothy's family possess the original manuscripts for every book of the Bible written at that time? No, they had copies. Notice that Paul calls the copies that Timothy's family possessed "Scripture". In other words, the copies in their possession were just as authoritative as the original manuscripts.
- It is God's design to preserve His word through a multiplicity of accurate, reliable copies that are just as authoritative as the original.

During his earthly ministry, Jesus Christ expressed the same attitude as Paul regarding the copies that were available to Him. Please consider Matthew 22:29-31:

- ○ "Jesus answered and said unto them, Ye do err not knowing the scriptures, nor the power of God.

    For in the resurrection they neither marry, nor are given in marriage, but are as the angles of God in heaven."

    But as touching the resurrection of the dead, have ye not read that which was spoken unto you by God, saying. . .

- Christ rebukes the Sadducees because they did not know the Scriptures. Does this mean they did not possess the original manuscripts? Certainly not, it means, as verse 31 states, they did not know the Scriptures because they had not read the copies they had in their possession.

CONCLUSION

- Eloquent arguments aside, the prevailing wisdom within Christendom regarding the inspiration and inerrancy of Scripture is meaningless because leading theologians only apply these doctrines to the originals which no longer exist. The Bible teaches that God has promised to preserve the inerrant words of his inspiration through a multiplicity of accurate copies that are just as authoritative as the originals.

- A side-by-side examination of modern versions with the King James text reveals startling differences that impact the major doctrines of the faith. These differences cannot be attributed to differences in how words are translated out of Greek and Hebrew into English. Rather the underlying texts used by the translators are different thereby resulting in different readings in English.

- As we saw in the previous lesson, the same problem exists for modern version proponents when dealing with what verses should and should not be included. Logic dictates that when two things are different, they cannot be the same thus making it impossible for divergent translations containing substantive differences in meaning to both be the Word of God.

- God did not go through all the trouble to perfectly inspire his word only to have it disappear with the originals.

WORKS CITED

Ehrman, Bart. *Misquoting Jesus: The Story Behind Who Changed the Bible and Why*. Harper One, 2005.

Elwell, Walter. *Evangelical Dictionary of Theology 2nd Edition*. Baker Book House, 2001.

Enns, Paul. *The Moody Handbook of Theology*. Moody Press, 1989.

Geisler, Norman L. *Inerrancy*. Zondervan, 1980.

Geisler, Norman L. *Systematic Theology Volume I*. Bethany House, 2002.

Price, Randall. *Searching for the Original Bible*. Harvest House Publishers, 2007.

Ryrie, Charles R. *Basic Theology*. Moody Press, 1999.

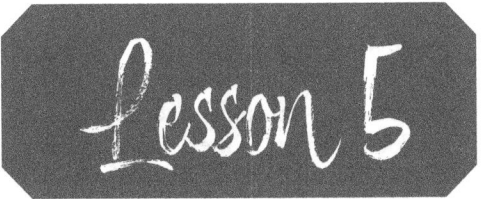

OVERCOMING THE PROBLEM OF "VERBATIM IDENTICALITY"

INTRODUCTION

- At this point it seems prudent to take stock of what we have studied so far. Thus far, the course introduction notwithstanding, we have had three lessons that have ranged over a host of introductory topics. In summation, these topics have included the following:

    o   Basic presuppositions regarding God and the Bible (Lesson 1).

    o   Satan's five-part strategy against the word of God: question it, subtract from it, add to it, water it down, and deny it (Lesson 1).

    o   Lack of textual agreement among modern Evangelical scholars regarding which readings are authentic and which ones are not. This is not just a KJB versus modern versions issue, but rather a problem that exists within the scholarship that is critical of the KJB and promotes the merits of modern versions (Lesson 2).

   o The prevailing position within Christian academia (for the last 130 years or so) is that only the original autographs are inspired and inerrant. This assertion is made despite admittance by these same scholars that the original autographs are "absent." This topic also included a discussion of the overlooked nature of the doctrine of perseveration by leading Fundamental and Evangelical scholars (Lesson 3).

- I am aware that these lessons have generated much discussion. As I said, in the introduction to last week's notes, I request your patience over the coming weeks/months as the class unfolds. I have been praying for myself and all of you students that we can have these hard discussions in a manner that is productive, honoring to the Lord as well as to one another. My prayer is that these lessons will produce light and not heat.

THE CONTINUUM OF POSITIONS

- For purposes of illustration, please consider the following continuum of views regarding the Bible issue. On one side, let's place the "Originals Only" position we discussed in the previous lesson. This side says little if anything meaningful about the doctrine of preservation and admittedly relies upon the discipline of textual criticism to reconstruct the "Original Text." This side generally maintains that the KJB is based upon old or outdated textual theories and therefore advocates for the use of modern versions and their underlying Greek text on account of the fact that they are more accurate.

- On the other side of the continuum, we find the King James extreme view that God supernaturally inspired the King James translators in the same manner that the original writers of Scripture were inspired. This group basically believes in the notion of "Double Inspiration" or the idea that God "re-inspired" His word in English in the early 17th century.

- In between these two views there are other less extreme options that have been articulated. Some examples include the following:

  o *I Prefer the KJB or I Like the KJB Best Position* — folks in this group view the KJB as the single best English translation available today. This belief is generally held for any of the following reasons: rhythmic beauty, historical importance, or its cultural and literary impact upon the English-speaking world.

  o *Majority Text Position* — is characterized by the common belief that the underlying Hebrew and Greek texts used by the King James translators are superior to those utilized by modern textual scholarship. Those holding this position point to the numerical superiority of the manuscripts found in the Byzantine Text type as a more faithful guide for reconstructing the text. Supporters of this position do not necessarily view the KJB as inerrant but that it more accurately reflects the original writings. Zane C. Hodges stands out as the leading proponent of this position.

  o *Textus Receptus or Received Text Only Position* — this position maintains that the *Textus Receptus* (*TR*) Greek text preserved the words of the originals in their inerrant condition. This position would not necessarily insist that the KJB is an inerrant translation of these texts, thereby leaving open the possibility for a better translation of the *TR*. The *TR* position acknowledges the importance of the *Majority Text* but takes into account the testimony of other witnesses such as early translations, patristic quotations, and early church lectionaries in seeking to establish the authenticity of a reading. Dean John William Burgon stands out as a leading proponent of this position. Burgon objected to the replacing of the Traditional Greek Text or *TR* with the new and improved Critical Text of Wescott and Hort.

- I believe that the "Originals Only" position was forged by Warfield and Hodge in the late 19th century in response to a growing chorus of voices that were critical and seeking to undermine the Bible. I further believe that the "Inspired King James" view was a reaction against the "Originals Only" position and its reliance upon textual criticism as well as its promotion of modern versions.

THE PROBLEM OF "VERBATIM IDENTICALITY"

- In reality, both of these views, the "Originals Only" and "King James Inspired" positions are seeking to address the problem of *Verbatim Identicality*. It is a known fact that there are textual variations in the Hebrew and Greek manuscripts supporting the English Bible. One side seeks to deal with the problem by appealing to the nonexistent "Original Autographs" while the other side sees the KJB as a divine act on par with the inspiration of the originals in the first place.

- The "Originals Only" position, as we saw last week, largely ignores the doctrine of preservation. Meanwhile, many King James defenders want to argue that preservation assures the *verbatim indenticality* of every word as originally written under inspiration. Unfortunately, this type of *verbatim* or *xeroxed identicality* of wording understanding of preservation cannot be sustained by a consideration of the historical and textual facts. Even among the manuscripts comprising the Byzantine Text Type and utilized by both the Majority Text and the *TR* positions, there is not *verbatim* wording across all the manuscript witnesses.

- The manuscripts in the Byzantine Text Type, while not possessing xeroxed or verbatim wording across the board, demonstrate an "agreeance" as to how passages should read in terms of their doctrinal substance.

- This is important because it recognizes the difference between 1) different ways of saying the same thing and 2) substantive differences in meaning. Even within the King James Bible one is forced to acknowledge the existence of different ways of saying the same thing. Consider the following example:

Isaiah 61:1-2	Luke 4:18-19
"The Spirit of the Lord GOD is upon me;	"The Spirit of the Lord is upon me,
because the <u>LORD</u> hath anointed me to preach <u>good tidings</u> unto the <u>meek</u>;	because <u>he</u> hath anointed me to preach <u>the gospel</u> to the <u>poor</u>;
he hath sent me <u>to bind up</u> the brokenhearted,	he hath sent me <u>to heal</u> the brokenhearted,
to <u>proclaim liberty</u> to the captives,	to <u>preach deliverance</u> to the captives,
	(and recovering of sight to the blind),
and the <u>opening of the prison</u> to them that are <u>bound</u>;	to <u>set at liberty</u> them that are <u>bruised</u>,
To <u>proclaim</u> the acceptable year of the LORD,	To <u>preach</u> the acceptable year of the Lord.

- These passages from within the KJB do not exhibit *verbatim identicality* yet the Lord Jesus Christ called the copy He was reading from in Nazareth "Scripture."
- Problems are compounded from the standpoint of modern scholarship when one considers there are two so-called oldest and best manuscripts: Codex Vaticanus (B) and Codex Sinaiticus (ℵ). After completing a complete collation of these manuscripts against the TR and each other, Dean Burgon concluded the following:

  o "... all four are discovered on careful scrutiny to differ essentially not only from ninety-nine out of a hundred of the whole body of extant MSS besides, even from one another... they stand asunder in every page; as well as differ widely from the commonly received Text, with which they have been carefully collated. On being referred to this standard, in the Gospels alone, B is found to omit at least 2,877 words; to add 536: to substitute 935: to transpose 2098: to modify 1132 (in all 7,578):--the corresponding figures for ☒ being 3455, 839, 1114, 2299, 1265 (in all 8,972). And be it remembered that the omissions, additions, substitutions, transpositions, and modifications, are by no means the same in both. It is in fact easier to find two consecutive verses in which these two MSS differ one from the other, than two consecutive verses in which they entirely agree." (Burgon, 11-12)

- In the previous lesson we considered an essay titled "The Inerrancy of the Autographa" by Greg L. Bahnsen found in Norman L. Geisler's book *Inerrancy*. As part of that consideration, we looked at the following quotes:

    o *No Promise of Preservation*—"God has not promised in His Word that the Scriptures would receive perfect transmission, and thus we have no ground to claim it a priori. Moreover, the inspired Word of God in the Scriptures has a uniqueness that must be guarded from distortion. Consequently, we cannot be theologically blind to the significance of transmissional errors, nor can we theologically assume the absence of such errors. We are therefore theologically required to restrict inspiration, infallibility and inerrancy to the autographa . . . Scripture nowhere gives us ground to maintain that its transmission and translation would be kept without effort by God. There is no scriptural warrant for holding that God will perform the perpetual miracle of preserving His written Word from all errors in its being transcribed from one copy to another. Since the Bible does not claim that every copier, translator, typesetter, and printer will share the infallibility of the original document, Christians should not make such a claim either. The doctrine is not supported by Scripture, and Protestants are committed to the methodical principle of sola Scriptura." (Geisler, 175-176)

    o *Theological Double-Talk: Providential Bible Copying*—". . . the preservation of the text of Scripture is part of the transmission of the knowledge of God, it is reasonable to expect that God will provide for it lest the aims of His revealing Himself to man be frustrated. The providence of God superintended matters so that copies of Scripture do not become so corrupt as to become unintelligible for God's original purposes in giving it or so corrupt as to create a major falsification of His message's text... Faith in the consistency of God — His faithfulness to His own intention to make men wise unto salvation — guarantees the inference that He never permits Scripture to become so corrupted that it can no longer fulfill that end adequately. We can conclude theologically that, for all practical purposes, the text of Scripture is always sufficiently accurate not to lead us astray. If we presuppose a sovereign God, observes Van Til, it is no longer a matter of great worry that the transmission of Scripture is not all altogether accurate; God's providence provides for the essential accuracy of the Bible's copying . . .our copies virtually supply us with the autographic text. All the ridicule that is heaped on evangelicals about the "lost autographa" is simply vain, for we do not regard their text as lost at all! . . . The doctrine of original inerrancy, then, does not deprive believers today of the Word of God in an adequate form for all the purposes of God's revelation to His people. Presupposing the providence of God in the preservation of the biblical text, and noting the outstanding result of the textual criticism of Scriptures, we can have full assurance that we possess the Word of God necessary for our salvation and Christian walk. As a criticism of this evangelical doctrine, suggestions that the autographic text has been forever lost are groundless and futile. The Bibles in our hands are a trustworthy rendition of God's original message, adequate for all intents and purposes as copies and conveyors of God's autoreactive word." (Geisler, 185-189)

- Bahnsen is partly right and partly wrong. He is right in the sense that God did not supernaturally overtake the pen of every scribe, translator, and typesetter to ensure the preservation of *verbatim* wording. To think otherwise is to stand in opposition to the plain historical and textual facts. Yet, the doctrine of preservation necessitates that we have more than just a shell of the "Original Bible." In other words, the truth lies in the middle between the two extreme positions identified above.

- One position leaves believers without a Bible they can hold in their hands today while the other outstrips the textual facts and creates the opposite problem.

- Overcoming the problem of *verbatim identicality* is the key to forging an accurate and meaningful position that does not over or understate the case and is in line with the historical and textual facts. After all, I stated the following in the Course Introduction:

    o "I have come to believe that it is incumbent upon Pauline Dispensationalists to forge and advance our own position on the KJB that is in line and consistent with both the historical and textual facts as well as our dispensational beliefs regarding God's working in time."

- The goal of this class is to attempt such an articulation. To this objective we will now turn our attention.

WORKS CITED

Burgon, John William. *The Revision Revised*. 1883.

Geisler, Norman L. *Inerrancy*. Zondervan, 1980.

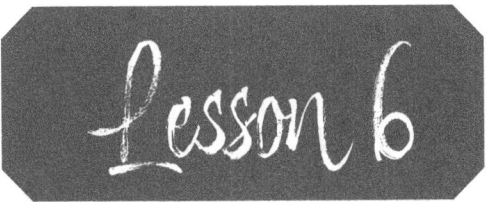

UNDERSTANDING BASIC TERMINOLOGY: REVELATION

REVIEW/CLARIFICATION

- In our last lesson we addressed the problem of verbatim identicaltiy by outlining a continuum of positions with respect to the Bible issue. On one side, we had the Originals Only Position (the view that only the Original Autographs are inspired and inerrant) and on the other side, the King James Inspired position (the view that the KJB was a second divine act of inspiration). In the middle we noted a variety of positions including the following: 1) I Prefer the KJB, 2) Majority Text Only, and 3) *Textus Receptus* or *TR* Only.
- In doing so, we observed that both positions on either side of the continuum are seeking to address the problem of *verbatim identicality* or the fact that there are variant readings in all manuscript

traditions. The Originals Only position was forged by Warfield and Hodge in the late 19th century in response to contemporary attacks on the word of God from Englightment Rationalism and German Higher Criticism. Meanwhile the King James Inspired position is a response against the Originals Only view and its advocacy for the Critical Greek Text and its support of modern versions.

- While I stopped short of articulating a position of my own, I did say that truth lies in the middle. The Originals Only crowd is correct in that God did not overtake the pen of every scribe who ever copied God's word to ensure *verbatim* wording across all the manuscript copies. Yet the doctrine of preservation ensures that we possess more than a shell of the "Original Bible" that the scholars are still searching for.

- One of the primary objectives of this class from here on out will be to accurately articulate a position that is both in line with the relevant Biblical doctrines as well as both the textual and historical facts. It is here that I beg your patience as we will begin our study of the Biblical doctrine in this lesson. In short, we cannot put the cart before the horse.

- Furthermore, during our last study, I was asked a question regarding the feasibility of a new translation of the *Textus Receptus* (*TR*) into English. I said that such a translation was "theoretically possible." I would like to take a few moments to clarify those statements.

- While I hypothetically acknowledge that a new translation of the TR into English is possible, I am not calling for one. Furthermore, I would be highly skeptical of any such call for the following reasons:

    o The KJB is a literary masterpiece. The extended verb ending "eth" enhances the rhyme and meter of the text.

    o The KJB has a proven track record of being considered the word of God in English for the better part of 400 plus years.

    o The KJB, while possessing some archaic language, facilitates study in a way that modern English versions do not.

    o The KJB's archaic wording is more precise in conveying the truths of Scripture. For example, the word "ye" is plural whereas the word "you" is singular.

- o The KJB clearly maintains the integrity of the dispensational approach to Bible study.
- o The KJB's translators were the most scholarly and linguistically gifted group of men ever assembled to complete the task of translating the Bible into English.
- o The KJB was produced using the best methodology i.e., the company approach where each company checked the work of the others and culminated in an audible reading of the text.
- o The questionable existence of such a company of scholastic men today who would faithfully follow the *TR* when doing the work of translating.

- These points being noted, we cannot ignore the fact that the KJB does contain some archaic words and/or common words whose meanings may have changed in the last 400 plus years. Therefore, I am not opposed to the use of reputable dictionaries such as the *Oxford English Dictionary* and/or Noah Webster's *American Dicitonary of the English Language* to assist the Bible student in discerning the meaning of English words.

INTRODUCTION: TEXTUAL CRITICISM AND CHRISTIAN FAITH

- Many encounter problems studying manuscript evidence because they approach the subject from the vantage point of human viewpoint. In other words, the subject is broached with a lack of thorough understanding of the fundamental underlying doctrines. Consider the following from the pen of Dr. Edward F. Hills:

  - o "The Christian Church has long confessed that the books of the New Testament, as well as those of the Old, are divine Scriptures, written under the inspiration of the Holy Spirit. . . Since the doctrine of divine inspiration of the New Testament has in all ages stimulated the copying of these sacred books, it is evident that this doctrine is important for the history of the New Testament text, no matter whether it be a true doctrine or only a belief of the Christian Church." But what if it be true? What if the original New Testament manuscripts actually were inspired of God? If the doctrine of divine inspiration of the New Testament is a true doctrine, then New Testament textual criticism is different from the textual criticism of ordinary books." (Hills, 1-2)

    o "Thus there are two methods of New Testament textual criticism, the *consistently Christian* method and the *naturalistic method*. These two methods deal with the same materials, the same Greek manuscripts, and the same translations and biblical quotations, but they interpret the materials very differently. The *consistently Christian* method interprets the materials of New Testament textual criticism in accordance with the doctrines of the divine inspiration and providential preservation of the Scriptures. The *naturalistic method* interprets these same materials in accordance with its own doctrine that the New Testament is nothing more than a human book." (Hills, 3)

- Consequently, before proceeding any further with this course, we need to thoroughly study the following basic terminology: revelation, inspiration, illumination, and preservation. In this lesson we will focus on revelation. In Lesson 7 we will focus on inspiration and illumination.

- Grounding ourselves in these basic concepts will help us wade through the manuscript and textual issues later on. Possessing the ability to judge the textual and historical information from the vantage point of what the Bible teaches about itself is the only source of clarity on these difficult issues. In short, if our doctrine is correct, it ought to commend itself to us in both history and our experience.

REVELATION

- Hebrews 1:1 — the term "revelation" is talking about God's disclosure of Himself. Without God taking the initiative and revealing things about Himself, you would never know anything about Him.

- Romans 16:25 — *apokalupsis* is the Greek word translated "revelation" and it literally means "to unveil a thing."

    - I Corinthians 2:7
    - Galatians 1:12
    - Ephesians 3:3

- According to Noah Webster's *American Dictionary of the English Language*, the English word "revelation" carries the following meanings:

    - "The act of disclosing or discovering to others what was before unknown to them; appropriately, the disclosure or communication of truth to men by God himself, or by His authorized agents, the prophets and apostles. How that by revelation he made known to me the mystery, as I wrote before in few words. Ephesians 3."
    - "That which is revealed; appropriately, the sacred truths which God has communicated to man for his instruction and direction. The revelations of God are contained in the Old and New Testament."
    - "The Apocalypse; the last book of the sacred canon, containing the prophecies of St. John."

- Essentially, revelation is *the content of God's communication to man*. Revelation is God's disclosure of Himself to mankind. Mankind cannot know anything about God apart from God choosing to reveal Himself to mankind.

- In order for revelation to occur, the following three prerequisites or preconditions must exist:

    - "A being capable of giving revelation — God is an eternal being (Genesis 1:1; John 1:1-4)
    - A being capable of receiving revelation — Man is a rational and moral being made in the image and likeness of God (Genesis 1:26-27)

- A medium through which revelation can be given — reason and language (Isaiah 1:18, Genesis 2:16-17, 3:8-10)" (Geisler, 49)

- Pastor Richard Jordan teaches in Grace School of the Bible that there are three types of revelation: natural, special, and written.
- Natural Revelation — is the revelation that God has provided of Himself in creation. All men have access to the revelation that God has placed in creation.

    - Romans 1:18-20
    - Psalm 19:1
    - Romans 1:19 — God has given natural revelation *in creation* and also *in man*.
    - Romans 2:14-15 — there is natural revelation. All men have it. They have it from creation; they have it within themselves from conscience.

- Special Revelation — this is what Hebrews 1:1 is referring to.

    - Genesis 18 — God appeared to Abraham and conversed with him in his tent.
    - Genesis 32 — God wrestled with Jacob.
    - Exodus 3 — God appeared to and spoke with Moses in the burning bush.
    - Matthew 16:17 — God the Father gave a special revelation to Peter as to the person of Christ.
    - Galatians 2:2 — Paul got some information from God that told him to go up to Jerusalem.

- Written Revelation — is not just something that God has placed innately in man, or in nature, as a testimony. It is not just a special time when God communicated with somebody, but it is what God caused to be written down.

- John 20:30-31 — God has those things written down for a purpose.

- The main point of revelation is the fact that God communicates, unveils, and reveals himself to mankind. Without revelation man would be incapable of knowing anything about God.
- Other Bible teachers break things down slightly differently. For example, in his *Systematic Theology* Norman Geisler distinguishes between God's General and Special Revelation.

General Revelation	Special Revelation
In Physical Nature	Bible Alone is Infallible and Inerrant
In Human Nature	Bible Alone Reveals God as Redeemer
In Human History	Bible Alone Has the Message of Salvation
In Human Arts	Bible Alone Contains the Written Norm for Believers
In Human Music	

- Geisler summarizes the relationship between General and Special Revelation as follows:

General Revelation	Special Revelation
God as Creator	God as Redeemer
Norm for Society	Norm for the Church
Means of Condemnation	Means of Salvation
In Nature	In Scripture

(Geisler, 53)

- Dr. Geisler sees the doctrine of revelation as a prerequisite or precondition to Christian Theology. Therefore, he includes a chapter on

Revelation in the Prolegomena or Introduction section of his *Systematic Theology*. Other Preconditions identified by Dr. Geisler include the: Metaphysical, Supernatural, Rational, Semantical, Epistemological, Oppositional (Exclusivism), Linguistic, Hermeneutical, Historical, and Methodological.

WORKS CITED

Geisler, Norman L. *Systematic Theology: In One Volume*. Bethany House, 2011.

Hills, Edward F. *The King James Version Defended*. Christian Research Press, 1956.

Jordan, Richard. *Manuscript Evidence 101*. Grace School of the Bible.

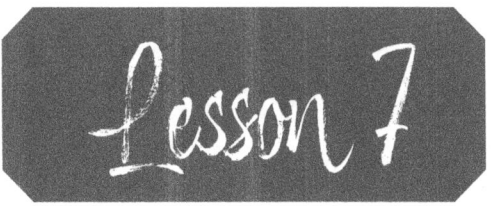

UNDERSTANDING BASIC TERMINOLOGY: INSPIRATION AND ILLUMINATION

INTRODUCTION

- In Lesson 6, we summarized two different approaches to New Testament textual criticism identified by Dr. Edward F. Hills; the *naturalistic* and *consistently Christian* methods. According to Dr. Hills, "These two methods deal with the same materials, the same Greek manuscripts, and the same translations and biblical quotations, but they interpret the materials very differently." (Hills, 3)

- Consistently Christian Method—"... interprets the materials of New Testament textual criticism in accordance with the doctrines of the divine inspiration and providential preservation of the Scriptures."

  - Naturalistic Method—"... interprets these same materials in accordance with its own doctrine that the New Testament is nothing more than a human book." (Hills, 3)

- Also, in Lesson 6, we began our study of some basic theological terminology as it related to God's Word. I stated in part:

  - "... before proceeding any further with this course, we need to thoroughly study the following basic terminology: revelation, inspiration, illumination, and preservation... Grounding ourselves in these basic concepts will help us wade through the manuscript and textual issues later on. Possessing the ability to judge the textual and historical information from the vantage point of what the Bible teaches about itself is the only source of clarity on these difficult issues. In short, if our doctrine is correct, it ought to commend itself to us in both history and our experience." (Lesson 6)

- Revelation was the only term of the four identified above that we had time to consider in Lesson 6. Essentially, we defined revelation as, "*the content of God's communication to man. Revelation is God's disclosure of Himself to mankind. Mankind cannot know anything about God apart from God choosing to reveal Himself to mankind.*" (Lesson 6)

- In addition to identifying the prerequisites or preconditions that make God's disclosure of himself possible, we also considered the following three types of revelation:

  - Natural Revelation — is the revelation that God has provided of Himself in creation as well as in man. All men have access to the revelation that God has placed in creation.

- o Special Revelation — this is what Hebrews 1:1 is referring to; God making Himself known to particular people in specific ways throughout Scripture (Genesis 18, Matthew 16:17, Galatians 2:2)
- o Written Revelation — is not something that God has placed innately in man, or in nature, as a testimony. It is not a special time when God communicated with somebody, but it is what God caused to be written down.

- In this lesson we will touch upon the mechanism that makes written revelation possible i.e., inspiration. If we have time, we will also discuss illumination.

INSPIRATION

- With revelation the information comes from God to man; in inspiration the information moves from man to paper. Man writes that which God wants written down.

- II Timothy 3:16 — All scripture is given by inspiration of God, and is profitable for doctrine, for reproof, for correction, for instruction in righteousness:

  - o The Greek word for scripture is *graphē*, and it means "that which is written down." Inspiration has to do with what is written down. Inspiration is not God just giving the information to man. That is revelation. But inspiration is man putting the thing on paper, and the issue is what is written down on that paper.

- The phrase "is given by inspiration of God" is a translation of the Greek word *theopneustos*. This is the only time the Greek word *theopneustos* occurs in the New Testament.

- Noah Webster's *American Dictionary of the English Langauge* offers the following relevant meanings for the English word inspiration:

- o "The act of drawing air into the lungs; the inhaling of air; a branch of respiration and opposed to expiration.
- o The act of breathing into anything.
- o The infusion of ideas into the mind by the Holy Spirit; the conveying into the minds of men, ideas, notices or monitions by extraordinary or supernatural influence; or the communication of the divine will to the understanding by suggestions or impressions on the mind, which leave no room to doubt the reality of their supernatural origin.

  All Scripture is given by inspiration of God. 2 Timothy 3:16."

- Please note that when Noah Webster published his famous dictionary in 1828, the definition of the English word inspiration had nothing to do with the original writings. Rather it was referring to the supernatural process whereby God the Holy Spirit infused into the minds of men the ideas of Almighty God.
- Then the dictionary gives II Timothy 3:16 as the verse to illustrate the concept. In other words, inspiration is the supernatural process whereby God the Holy Spirit moved upon human authors to have them record in writing those aspects of God's revelation (written revelation) that He wanted mankind to possess forever (Isaiah 30:8).
- II Peter 1:21 — "For the prophecy came not in old time by the will of man: but holy men of God spake as *they were* moved by the Holy Ghost."

  - o It was the supernatural force of God the Holy Spirit that caused the prophets of old to speak.

- Job 32:8 — "But there *is a* spirit in man: and the inspiration of the Almighty giveth them understanding."

  - o The giving of the Scripture is not the only thing God did by inspiration. *Nĕshamah* is the Hebrew word translated inspiration in Job 32:8 and it occurs 24 times in 24 verses in the

Hebrew text supporting the KJB. It is variously rendered as 'breath' seventeen times, 'blast' three times, 'spirit' two times, 'inspiration' one time and 'souls' one time.

- o Given the fact that Job was the first book of the Bible written, it is not possible that Elihu is using the word inspiration here in reference to the giving of the Scriptures as in II Timothy 3:16. Rather, Elihu is referring to the fact that there is something unique about man; via inspiration, God has given mankind the capacity for understanding.

- Job 33:4 — "The Spirit of God hath made me, and the breath of the Almighty hath given me life."

    - o Mankind was created by "the breath of the Almighty."

- Genesis 2:7 — "And the LORD God formed man of the dust of the ground, and breathed into his nostrils the breath of life; and man became a living soul."

    - o Adam and, by extension, all of humanity owes their very existence to the breath of God.
    - o Genesis 1:27-28 — So God created man in his own image, in the image of God created he him; male and female created he them. 28) And God blessed them, and God said unto them, Be fruitful, and multiply, and replenish the earth, and subdue it: and have dominion over the fish of the sea, and over the fowl of the air, and over every living thing that moveth upon the earth.
    - o This helps explain how God created man in his own image.

- Please recall the second definition of the English word inspiration presented above, "the act of breathing into anything." Life was brought to Adam through an act of inspiration on the part of God.

- Psalm 33:6 — "By the word of the LORD were the heavens made; and all the host of them by the breath of his mouth."

  - God used the same process to create the heavens and all the hosts thereof.
  - Genesis 1:3, 6, 9, 11, 14, 20, 24, 26, 28, 29

- The testimony of Scripture is that God inspired at least three things:

  - The creation of heaven and earth.
  - The creation of man.
  - The giving of the Scriptures.

- II Timothy 3:16 — "God exercised the same supernatural force to inspire His word that He utilized when He created heaven, earth, and mankind."
- Inspiration is the supernatural process whereby God recorded in writing (*graphē*) those aspects of His revelation that he wanted mankind to possess forever (Isaiah 30:8).
- Hebrews 4:12-13 — "For the word of God is quick, and powerful, and sharper than any twoedged sword, piercing even to the dividing asunder of soul and spirit, and of the joints and marrow, and is a discerner of the thoughts and intents of the heart. 13) Neither is there any creature that is not manifest in his sight: but all things are naked and opened unto the eyes of him with whom we have to do."

  - This understanding of inspiration helps one understand how the word of God can be "quick and powerful." God literally breathed His own life into His word just as He did into mankind and all of creation.

- Does anyone doubt that inspiration sets the Bible apart from any other book of antiquity? Therefore, taking a *neutral* or *naturalist approach* to textual criticism is out of step with God's word for a Bible believer.

ILLUMINATION

- Illumination is a theological word that does not appear in the Bible, much like the words "Trinity" or "Rapture". Illumination is a term used by theologians to describe the process whereby the truth of Scripture gets off the page and into the soul of the believer.
- I Corinthians 2:9-16 — "Paul is talking about the teaching ministry of the Holy Spirit (Illumination) whereby He takes the words on the page and communicates them to your understanding, and then stores them in your soul, i.e., your inner man."
- I Corinthians 2:14 — "But the natural man receiveth not the things of the Spirit of God: for they are foolishness unto him: neither can he know them, because they are spiritually discerned."

    o "Scripture is very plain that the natural mind of man does not receive and cannot know the things of the Spirit of God." (Baker, 45)

- I Corinthians 2:12 — "Now we have received, not the spirit of the world, but the spirit which is of God; that we might know the things that are freely given to us of God."

    o "This same passage teaches that God has given us His Spirit, so that we might know the things which are freely given us of God. This work of the Spirit of God in making known to the individual the things which God has prepared for them that love Him is called Illumination." (Baker, 45)

- "Revelation has been given to only a select few through whom God chose to give His Word. Illumination is available to every believer. Revelation has been completed . . . Illumination is a continuing process. Revelation has to do with the impartation of truth. Illumination has to do with the understanding of truth." (Baker, 45)

- Ephesians 1:17-18 — "That the God of our Lord Jesus Christ, the Father of glory, may give unto you the spirit of wisdom and revelation in the knowledge of him: 18) The eyes of your understanding being enlightened; that ye may know what is the hope of his calling, and what the riches of the glory of his inheritance in the saints,"

  - Indicates that Paul recognized the need of all saints for illumination.

- Luke 24:45-46 — "Then opened he their understanding, that they might understand the scriptures, 46) And said unto them, Thus it is written, and thus it behooved Christ to suffer, and to rise from the dead the third day:"

  - Christ opened their understanding, thereby causing them to understand the Scriptures.

- John 16:7-15 — "Nevertheless I tell you the truth; It is expedient for you that I go away: for if I go not away, the Comforter will not come unto you; but if I depart, I will send him unto you. And when he is come, he will reprove the world of sin, and of righteousness, and of judgment: Of sin, because they believe not on me; Of righteousness, because I go to my Father, and ye see me no more; Of judgment, because the prince of this world is judged. I have yet many things to say unto you, but ye cannot bear them now. Howbeit when he, the Spirit of truth, is come, he will guide you into all truth: for he shall not speak of himself; but whatsoever he shall hear, that shall he speak: and he will shew you things to come. He shall glorify me: for he shall receive of mine, and shall shew it unto you. All things that the Father hath are mine: therefore said I, that he shall take of mine, and shall shew it unto you."

- - Even in time past in Israel's program, one of the functions of God the Holy Spirit was to teach, instruct, and guide the kingdom saints.
  - I John 2:20, 27
- Lewis Sperry Chafer views these passages from John as the "seed-plot" for the doctrine of illumination that is later developed by Paul in I Corinthians 2:9-3:4. Regarding these verses Chafer states in part:

  - "It is not difficult to believe that the Third Person of the Godhead is in possession of all truth; the marvel is that this Third Person indwells the least Christian, and thus places that Christian in a position to receive and understand that transcendent truth which the Spirit knows. Within his own capacity, the child of God can know no more than "the things of a man," which are within the range of "the spirit of man which is in him." Amazing, indeed, is the disclosure that "the Spirit which is of God" has been received, and for the express purpose in view that the child of God "might know the things that are freely given to us of God." (Chafer, 111-112)

- Dr. R.B. Ouellette, pastor of First Baptist Church in Bridgeport, MI and author of *A More Sure Word: Which Bible Can You Trust?* summarizes illumination as follows:

  - "Illumination is when God "turns the light on" for us on a certain passage. This process is a work that is done by the Holy Spirit, the writer and interpreter of Scripture. This is a present-tense work accomplished by the Spirit. Whereas inspiration was completed in the past, preservation began in the past and carries through today; illumination is for us today in the present." (Ouellette, 34)

- II Peter 1:21 — "For the prophecy came not in old time by the will of man: but holy men of God spake as they were moved by the Holy Ghost."

- o   God the Holy Spirit was the active agent in the process of revelation and inspiration.

- I Thessalonians 5:23 — "And the very God of peace sanctify you wholly; and I pray God your whole spirit and soul and body be preserved blameless unto the coming of our Lord Jesus Christ."

    - o   As humans we possess a spirit.

- Romans 8:9-11 — "But ye are not in the flesh, but in the Spirit, if so be that the Spirit of God dwell in you. Now if any man have not the Spirit of Christ, he is none of his. 10) And if Christ be in you, the body is dead because of sin; but the Spirit is life because of righteousness. 11) But if the Spirit of him that raised up Jesus from the dead dwell in you, he that raised up Christ from the dead shall also quicken your mortal bodies by his Spirit that dwelleth in you."

    - o   The same Spirit of God that moved upon the Biblical writers thereby causing them to record God's words dwells within the believer.
    - o   I Corinthians 3:16
    - o   II Timothy 1:14

- Essence communicates with essence. Illumination is the spiritual process that occurs in the inner man of the believer as God the Holy Spirit takes the written word of God that the Spirit wrote and communicates it to the believer's inner man. This is how spiritual growth and learning take place and how sound doctrine is stored up in the believer's soul.

WORKS CITED

Baker, Charles F. *A Dispensational Theology*. Grace Bible College Publications, 1971.

Chafer, Lewis Sperry. *Systematic Theology Vol. I*. Dallas Theological Seminary, 1947.

Hills, Edward F. *The King James Version Defended*. Christian Research Press, 1956.

Jordan, Richard. *Manuscript Evidence 101*. Grace School of the Bible.

Ouellette, R.B. *A More Sure Word: Which Bible Can you Trust?* Striving Together Publications, 2008.

UNDERSTANDING BASIC TERMINOLOGY: PRESERVATION

INTRODUCTION/REVIEW

- In Lesson 7, we continued our consideration of Basic Terminology by looking at the terms inspiration and illumination.

- Essentially, we defined inspiration as "the supernatural process whereby God the Holy Spirit moved upon human authors to have them record in writing those aspects of God's revelation (written revelation) that He wanted mankind to possess forever (Isaiah 30:8)." (Lesson 7)

- Furthermore, we studied the occurrence of the word "inspiration" in Job 32:8 and learned that inspiration was the supernatural process whereby God: 1) created the heavens and the earth (Psalms 33:6), 2) brought life to the first man Adam (Genesis 2:7), and 3) recorded in writing (*graphē*) those aspects of His revelation that He wanted mankind to possess forever (II Timothy 3:16, Isaiah 30:8).

- This understanding of inspiration helps one understand how the word of God can be "quick and powerful" (Hebrews 4:12-13). God literally breathed His own life into His word just as He did into mankind and all of creation. Inspiration sets the Bible apart from any other book of antiquity.

- Second, we discussed illumination as a term used by theologians to describe the process whereby the truth of Scripture gets off the page and into the soul of the believer. Illumination is the spiritual process that occurs in the inner man of the believer as God the Holy Spirit takes the written word of God that the Spirit wrote and communicates it to the believer's inner man. This is how spiritual growth and learning take place and how sound doctrine is stored up in the believer's soul.

- I Corinthians 2:9-16 is the Pauline passage that sets forth the normative ministry of God the Holy Spirit in terms of illumination for the body of Christ during the dispensation of grace. Other passages such as John 16:7-15 and I John 2:20-27 describe illumination in terms of God's dealings with the nation of Israel in time past and in the ages to come.

- In this lesson we want to conclude our discussion of Basic Terminology by looking at some information regarding preservation as well as consider the terminological relationships of all four of our basic terms: revelation, inspiration, illumination, and preservation.

PRESERVATION

- Preservation deals with the process whereby the words of Scripture, given by inspiration, are passed on from generation to generation.

- Noah Webster's *American Dictionary of the English Language* defines the English word "preservation" as follows:

- o The act of preserving or keeping safe; the act of keeping from injury, destruction or decay; as the preservation of life or health; the preservation of buildings from fire or decay; the preservation of grain from insects; the preservation of fruit or plants. When a thing is kept entirely from decay, or nearly in its original state, we say it is in a high state of preservation.

- Last week we observed from Dr. R.B. Ouellette's book A *More Sure Word: Which Bible Can You Trust?* that "... inspiration was completed in the past, preservation began in the past and carries through today..." (Ouellette, 34)
- There are a host of verses that could be used to establish this doctrine.

  - o Psalms 33:11 — "The counsel of the Lord standeth for ever, the thoughts of his heart to all generations."
  - o Psalms 105:5 — "He hath remembered his covenant for ever, the word *which* he commanded to a thousand generations.»
  - o Psalms 119:89 — "For ever, O LORD, thy word is settled in heaven."
  - o Psalms 119:111 — "Thy testimonies have I taken as an heritage for ever: for they *are* the rejoicing of my heart."
  - o Psalms 119:152 — "Concerning thy testimonies, I have known of old that thou hast founded them for ever."
  - o Psalms 119:160 — "Thy word *is* true *from* the beginning: and every one of thy righteous judgments *endureth* for ever."
  - o Isaiah 30:8 — "Now go, write it before them in a table, and note it in a book, that it may be for the time to come for ever and ever."
  - o Isaiah 40:8 — "The grass withereth, the flower fadeth: but the word of our God shall stand for ever."
  - o Matthew 24:35 — "Heaven and earth shall pass away, but my words shall not pass away."
  - o I Peter 1:23-25 — "Being born again, not of corruptible seed, but of incorruptible, by the word of God, which liveth and abideth for ever. For all flesh *is* as grass, and all the glory of man as the flower of grass. The grass withereth, and the flower thereof falleth

away: But the word of the Lord endureth for ever. And this is the word which by the gospel is preached unto you."

- Regarding this passage Ouellete points that "this is a quotation of Isaiah 40," (see above) and thereby serves as "an indirect 'proof'" that this Scripture had already been preserved for over seven hundred years." (Ouellette, 33)

- One will notice that I did not include Psalms 12:6-7 in the preceding list. This was done on purpose to make a point. Psalms 12:6-7 is shrouded in some controversy as to whether or not God is preserving his "words" or his "people." For the sake of clarity, I am not abandoning this passage to the opposition. We will deal with it in detail and specificity when we study preservation. For now, what I am saying is that one does not need Psalms 12:6-7 to understand and establish the doctrine of preservation. The verses outlined above establish the doctrine quite clearly without needing to appeal to the passage in question.
- According to R.B. Ouellette, the verses quoted above are sufficient for establishing the doctrine of preservation irrespective of Psalms 12:6-7.

    o "There are seminaries that exist today that seem to 'explain away' every verse that teaches preservation. I have a problem with some who feel that verses or doctrine must be 'explained away.' I prefer to read the Bible and understand it literally. When God says His word will last forever, that it will last for a thousand generations, I believe that means God will preserve His word forever.

    In the Bible, the writers had no problem quoting Scripture that had been preserved up to that time. Peter quotes Isaiah 40 (I Peter 1:23-25); Paul quotes extensively from the Old Testament in Romans 9-11. Each time a New Testament writer quotes from the Old Testament, he is demonstrating that God has been able to preserve His word. Preservation is highly debated today because ultimately, the preservation issue will decide the translation issue — and preservation is completely a matter of faith in God's power." (Ouellette, 33)

- Elsewhere Ouellette states the following regarding Matthew 24:35, Psalms 119:60, and Psalms 119:89 (see list of verses above):

    o "It sounds to me as though God is teaching us a doctrine of preservation. The Scriptures clearly teach that even if Heaven and Earth were to pass away, the words would not. We are clearly taught that the righteous judgements of God endure forever, and that His Word has been forever settled in Heaven." (Ouellette, 47)

- We have already seen in Lesson 3 that any discussion of the doctrine of preservation is largely omitted from the Systematic Theology books authored by the following leading Evangelical authors.

    o Norman L. Geisler — *Systematic Theology, Volume I*
    o Lewis Sperry Chaffer — *Systematic Theology*
    o Charles C. Ryrie — *Basic Theology*
    o Paul Enns — *Moody Handbook of Theology*
    o Wayne Grudem — *Systematic Theology: An Introduction to Christian Doctrine*
    o Millard J. Erickson — *Christian Theology*
    o Alister McGrath — *Christian Theology: An Introduction*
    o Charles F. Baker — *A Dispensational Theology*

- When not outright silent on the doctrine of preservation, Ouellette points out that many within Evangelical academia seek to "explain away the clear teaching of Scripture" with respect to preservation. Ouellette cites the following statements issued by Detroit Baptist Theological Seminary (DBTS) and Gordon Fee in his book *The Textual Criticism of the New Testament* as a case in point.

    o "While the Bible teaches the ultimate indestructibility of the verbal revelation of God (Matthew 24:35; I Peter 1:25), it does not tell us how and where the written manuscript linage of that word is preserved. We believe that God has providentially preserved His Word in the many manuscripts, fragments, versions, translations, and copies of the Scripture that are available and that by diligent study, comparison, and correlation, the original text (words) can be ascertained. We therefore hold that the integrity of any text type, translation, version, or copy of the Scriptures is to be judged by the autographs (original manuscript) only . . ." (DBTS Statement from 1996 quoted in Ouellette, 47-48)

- o "The doctrine of preservation of Scripture . . . is not a doctrine that is explicitly taught in Scripture, nor is it the belief that God has perfectly and miraculously preserved every word of the original autographs in one manuscript or text-type. It is the belief that God has providently preserved His Word in and through all the extant manuscripts, versions, and other copies of Scripture. . . God has wonderfully and providently preserved His Word in a multiplicity of extant manuscripts. No passage of Scripture promises this, but the evidence of history leaves no doubt that such is the case." (Fee, 420 quoted in Ouellette, 50)

- In response to these two statements quoted above, Dr. Ouellette states:

  - o "Based on this view, how can the Christian be sure that he has the right words — which ones did God preserve and which ones did over-zealous scribes add? Apparently, he must diligently compare, correlate, and study the manuscripts, fragments, versions, translations, and copies of scripture that are available. The statement made above sounds academic, theological, and spiritual, but it has no practical value to a searching Christian. The end of the logic, if you hold to that statement, is that, due to our endless comparisons and discovery, we cannot ever believe that we have the authoritative Word of God in English. . .
  - o There are serious problems with the logic that is used to come to such conclusions and with the obvious denial of a basic Bible promise. For example, we read that "no passage of Scripture promises" preservation. This is simply a false statement. All would agree that the originals were given

by inspiration of God — there is no room for question or debate concerning inspiration. Again, we have no inspired originals today. Therefore, when someone states that we are to determine the accuracy of the copies we have based upon their correlation to the original autographs, we find ourselves in an indefinable position. The Bible can no longer be our final authority. Rather, we must look to God's working in history and to the expert opinions of scholars to validate our translations.

Those who would hold to the Critical Text position believe we can know by studying history that God has preserved His Word. Yet, how can one know by looking at history, when, to begin with, no one knows what it looked like? There is no way that historical observation can give documented proof that nothing has been changed. This is against the laws of scientific observation. Our position on preservation must be a "faith-based" approach. Certainly, this is a watershed issue, but we must let the Bible speak for itself.

... issues related to the biblical text are matters of faith — regardless of which side of the issue one takes. Textual scholarship should not operate solely upon scientific principles as though there was nothing divine about the origin of our Bible. The Bible does have something to say about its own preservation, thus necessitating a doctrine of preservation.

Bible-believing Christians, whether ministers or laymen, must go about the process of identifying the correct biblical text within the context of the biblical doctrine of preservation. The question that must be answered is: For what will you trust the scholars, and which scholars will you trust?

... While there is more to what the Bible says about its own preservation, enough has been given to demonstrate that those who take the Critical Text approach to the textual issue have to "explain away"—under the guise of scholarship — what the Bible clearly teaches.

For now, it is important to remember that not only is the doctrine of preservation diluted or deleted, but that there is also a subtle attack on doctrinal purity as well. (Ouellette, 48-52)

- In a later chapter Ouellette summarizes his thoughts regarding preservation with the following statement, "Those who advocate the Westcott and Hort position (i.e., the Critical Text) always have trouble with the preservation issue because it negates their practice. In the question of Bible translations, one either has a "preserved" Bible or a "restored, reconstructed" Bible." (Ouellette, 83)

    - The central question is: Do we have a preserved word or a restored, reconstructed word?

- Majority Text proponent Wilbur Pickering contributed an essay titled "John William Burgon and the New Testament" to David Otis Fuller's 1973 publication *True or False?* In addition to proving that Burgon believed in inspiration, preservation, and inerrancy, Pickering states the following about the need for preservation.

    - "... if the Scriptures have not been preserved then the doctrine of Inspiration is a purely academic matter with no relevance for us today. If we do not have the inspired words or do not know precisely which they be, then the doctrine of Inspiration is inapplicable." (Fuller, 269)

- While it is necessary to acknowledge the Bible's own teaching regarding preservation, it is equally important not to demand more from the doctrine than can be historically and/or textually proven. Regarding the doctrine of preservation Dr. Edward F. Hills states the following in *The King James Version Defended*:

    - "If the doctrine of divine inspiration of the Old and New Testament Scripture is a true doctrine, the doctrine of the providential preservation of the Scriptures must also be a true doctrine. It must be that down through the centuries God has exercised a special providential control over the copying of the Scriptures and the preservation and use of the copies, so that trustworthy representatives of the original text have been available to God's people in every age.

> God must have done this, for if He gave the Scriptures to His Church by inspiration as the perfect and final revelation of His will, then it is obvious that He would not allow this revelation to disappear or undergo any alteration of its fundamental character.
>
> Although this doctrine of the providential preservation of the Old and New Testament Scriptures has sometimes been misused, nevertheless, it also has been held, either implicitly or explicitly, by all branches of the Christian Church as a necessary consequent of the divine inspiration of these Scriptures. (Hills, 2)

- Please note that even Dr. Hills acknowledges what preservation does and does not assure. Preservation does not assure *verbatim identicality* of wording across every manuscript copy ever produced. Rather preservation secures that God will not allow his "revelation to disappear or undergo any alteration of its fundamental character." (Hills, 2)

- Elsewhere in *The King James Bible Defended*, when discussing the minor differences that exist in the various editions of the *TR*, Dr. Hills recognizes a difference between what he calls providential and miraculous preservation.

    o "The texts of the several editions of the *Textus Receptus* were God-guided. They were set up under the leading of God's special providence. Hence the differences between them were kept to a minimum. But these disagreements were not eliminated altogether, for this would require not merely providential guidance but a miracle. In short, God chose to preserve the New Testament text providentially rather than miraculously, and this is why even the several editions of the *Textus Receptus* vary from each other slightly." (Hills, 222-223)

- To accomplish preservation with *verbatim identicality* God would have had to supernaturally overtake the pen of every scribe, copyist, typesetter, and printer who ever handled the text to ensure that no differences of any kind ever entered the text. That God did not choose to accomplish preservation in this manor is apparent because there are slight differences even in the manuscripts comprising the Byzantine Text Type not to mention the various editions of the *TR*.

- This is where we must recognize the difference between: 1) different ways of saying the same thing and 2) substantive differences in meaning. The manuscripts of the Byzantine Text Type as well as the various editions of the *TR* contain *an agreement as to the doctrinal content of the readings*. Conversely, when the *TR* is compared with the Critical Text there *are substantive differences in meaning as to the doctrinal content of the readings*.

- Psalms 12:6-7 — what the doctrine of preservation assures is exactly what verse six states, namely the preservation of a Pure Text i.e., a text that does not report information about God, His nature or character, His doctrine, His dispensational dealings with mankind, history, archeology, or science that is false. In short, God's promise to preserve His word assures the existence of a text that has not been altered in its "fundamental character" or doctrinal content despite not being preserved in a state of *verbatim identicality*.

- If *verbatim identicality* of wording were the issue with God in preservation, then why did He not just preserve the originals and remove all doubt? The main reason is that God, at every turn, is testing the believer to see if he or she is going to walk by faith in what God said.

  - I Corinthians 1:27-29, 2:5
  - Hebrews 11:6

- I believe that God preserved his word for the same reason I believe that God inspired it. Preservation is the Bible's claim for itself. The doctrine of preservation impacts how one ought to look at the textual and translational issues and ensures that we have more than just a shell of the "original Bible" as the Originals Only position maintains.

WORKS CITED

Fee, Gordon D. *The Textual Criticism of the New Testament* in *Expositor's Bible Commentary* (Ed. Frank Gaebelein). Grand Rapids, MI: Zondervan, 1979.

Hills, Edward F. *The King James Version Defended*. Des Moines: IA, Christian Research Press, 1956.

Jordan, Richard. *Manuscript Evidence 101*. Grace School of the Bible.

Ouellette, R.B. *A More Sure Word: Which Bible Can you Trust?* Lancaster, CA: Striving Together Publications, 2008.

Pickering, Wilbur N. "John William Burgon and the New Testament" in *True or False?* (Ed. David Otis Fuller). Grand Rapids, MI: Grand Rapids International Publications, 1973.

UNDERSTANDING BASIC TERMINOLOGY: PRESERVATION, PART 2

INTRODUCTION

- In Lesson 8 we considered the doctrine of preservation as the fourth and final of our four basic terms: revelation, inspiration, illumination, and preservation.

- In doing so I gave the following definition of preservation, "the process whereby the words of Scripture, given by inspiration, are passed on from generation to generation." (Lesson 8) In addition, we noted from the pen of Dr. R.B. Ouellette that whereas "inspiration was completed in the past, preservation began in the past and carries through today." (Ouellette, 34)

- After looking at ten passages that clearly establish the doctrine of preservation, we noted that preservation in our day is either ignored outright or explained away by many leading voices within Christian academia.
- Last week's lesson proved Dr. Ouellette's point regarding the hotly debated nature of preservation in our day.

  o Preservation is highly debated today because ultimately, the preservation issue will decide the translation issue — and preservation is completely a matter of faith in God's power." (Ouellette, 33)

- After quoting Wilbur Pickering and Dr. Edward F. Hills regarding preservation, I stated the following in Lesson 8.

  o "Preservation does not assure the "exact sameness" or "verbatim wording" across every manuscript copy ever made. Rather preservation secures that God will not allow his "revelation to disappear or undergo any alteration of its fundamental character." (Hills, 2)

  ... In order to accomplish preservation of "exact sameness" God would have had to supernaturally overtake the pen of every scribe, copyist, typesetter, and printer who ever handled the text to ensure that no differences of any kind ever entered the text. That God did not choose to accomplish preservation in this manor is apparent because there are slight differences even in the manuscripts comprising the Byzantine Text Type not to mention the various editions of the *TR*.

  This is where we must recognize the difference between: 1) different ways of saying the same thing and 2) substantive differences in meaning. The manuscripts of the Byzantine Text Type as well as the various editions of the *TR* contain an agreement as to the doctrinal content of the readings. Conversely, when the *TR* is compared with the Critical Text there are substantive differences in meaning as to the doctrinal content of the readings.

Psalms 12:6-7— what the doctrine of preservation assures is exactly what verse six states, namely the preservation of a Pure Text i.e., a text that does not report information about God, His nature or character, His doctrine, His dispensational dealings with mankind, history, archeology, or science that is false. In short, God's promise to preserve His word assures the existence of a text that has not been altered in its "fundamental character" or doctrinal content despite not being preserved in a state of *verbatim identicality*.

If verbatim identicality of wording were the issue with God in preservation, then why did He not just preserve the originals and remove all doubt? The main reason is that God, at every turn, is testing the believer to see if he or she is going to walk by faith in what God said. (I Cor. 1:27-29, 2:5; Heb. 11:6).

I believe that God preserved his word for the same reason I believe that God inspired it. Preservation is the Bible's claim for itself. The doctrine of preservation impacts how one ought to look at the textual and translational issues and ensures that we have more than just a shell of the "original Bible" as the Originals Only position maintains. (Lesson 8)

- In this lesson, I would like to take some time to clarify my thinking on some of the issues raised in Lesson 8.

CLARIFICATIONS

- In Section I would like to clarify my thinking with respect to the following three points:

  o The importance of understanding the issue of *verbatim identicality*.

  o Use of the terminology "providential preservation."

  o The difference between the Dynamic View of inspiration and the Dynamic philosophy of translation.

Verbatim Identicality

- It is my personal private subjective opinion that the issue of what I am calling *verbatim identicality* or *xeroxed identicality* is the key to accurately unraveling the Bible version controversy. These are not ideas that you will encounter in other written works but are my own conclusions after studying the relevant issues.

- Until the summer of 2011, I would have and did demand *verbatim identicality* as the standard when discussing the preservation and translation of the Bible. On Sunday, February 7, 2010, as part of a six part series of studies titled *Final Authority: Locating God's Word in English*, I taught the following to the saints of Grace Life Bible Church in a sermon titled "The Place of Preservation, Part 2:"

  o "First principles are the foundation of knowledge. Without them nothing could be known. First principles undeniably apply to reality. The very denial that first principles apply to reality used first principles in the denial.

  The Principle of Noncontradiction: Being Is Not Nonbeing. Being cannot be nonbeing, for they are direct opposites. And opposites cannot be the same.

  The Principle of Excluded Middle: Either Being or Nonbeing. Since being and nonbeing are opposites (i.e. contradictory), and opposites cannot be the same, nothing can hide in the cracks between being and nonbeing.

  Illustration using the shirts. How many differences do these shirts need to have before they are not the same? One.

  How many differences do we need to demonstrate in English Bibles before we can conclude that they are not the same? One.

  How many mistakes do we need to demonstrate in a so-called Bible before we conclude that it is not inerrant? One. Can we rightly call a Bible with a mistake in it the word of God? No. (Ross, 4)

- At the time, my standard for judging what was or was not God's word was the standard of *verbatim identicality* of wording even though I did not explicitly use that terminology. Please note that I did not make a distinction between 1) different ways of saying the same thing and 2) substantive differences in meaning in February 2010. Rather, any difference, of any kind, constituted a situation where one would be forced to choose which Bible was or was not God's word.

- Up until May 2011, I believed that the only differences between a 1611 and 1769 edition of the King James Bible were updates in punctuation and spelling and I was perfectly content to function with that understanding. It was during a visit to my home in May 2011, that Brother Craig first began to challenge this understanding based upon the findings of David Norton in his 2005 book *A Textual History of the King James Bible*.

- At first, I was not very open or receptive to what Craig had to say, much to his frustration. I did; however, agree to read a PDF copy of Norton's book. It was not long after I began reading Norton's work that I started to see Craig's point. The facts presented by Norton were contrary to what I had been led to believe. There are more differences between the various editions of the King James than simply the updating of spelling and punctuation.

- In Appendix 8 of his book David Norton spends 155 pages chronicling 952 verses where differences in wording exist between 1611 and 1769 editions of the King James Bible. Does everyone see the problem I was faced with, based upon my teaching from February 2010? If preservation and inerrancy demand *verbatim identiclaity* then one is forced to determine which edition of the King James text is inerrant and which one is not.

- It was then in the summer of 2011 while preparing to teach a seminar for the Grace School of the Bible Summer Family Bible Conference in Chicago, that I came to understand that the nature of the differences is what matters in seeking to identify God's word. It was then that I came to realize that there is a difference between 1) different ways of saying the same thing and 2) substantive differences in meaning.

- Since 2011, I have come to believe that the breakthrough regarding *verbatim identicality* has many and far-reaching implications for the rest of the Bible version debate.

- The reason why Warfield and Hodge limited inspiration and inerrancy to the original autographs in the late 19th century was because they were responding to their critics who were pointing out variant readings in the manuscript witnesses supporting the New Testament. Warfield and Hodge dealt with this lack of *verbatim identicality* by confining inspiration and inerrancy to the original autographs only thereby alleviating the problem pointed out by their critics.

- If you pay close attention to the statements made by modern Evangelical scholars, one can see that it is precisely this lack of *verbatim identicality* in terms of textual transmission that forces them to limit inspiration and inerrancy to the original autographs only. Please consider the following case in point from Greg L. Bahnsen essay "The Inerrancy of the Autographa" found in Geisler's book *Inerrancy*:

    o   "God has not promised in His Word that the Scriptures would receive perfect transmission, and thus we have no ground to claim it a priori. Moreover, the inspired Word of God in the Scriptures has a uniqueness that must be guarded from distortion. Consequently, we cannot be theologically blind to the significance of transmissional errors, nor can we theologically assume the absence of such errors. We are therefore theologically required to restrict inspiration, infallibility and inerrancy to the autographa." (Bahnsen in Geisler, 175)

- Retreating to the originals only is one way of dealing with the differences that exist within the extant manuscripts. On the other end of the spectrum, the King James Inspired position believes that God reinspired his word between 1604 and 1611 in response to the originals only position on *verbatim identicality*. Even if they do not say it this way or would not admit it, the extreme King James position is seeking to address the same problem of i.e., the lack of *xeroxed identicality* in the manuscript witnesses. On this view the problem is overcome by arguing that God reinspired (double inspiration) His word in English between 1604 and 1611.

- The brilliance of limiting inspiration, infallibly, and inerrancy to the originals only is that it alleviated the need for scholars to explain the variant readings in the extant manuscripts. They could simply call everything good because what God originally did in inspiring His word was perfect and without error. No one disputes this.

- There are multiple problems with this view. First, it ignores what the Bible teaches about itself with respect to preservation. Second, it is unscientific and unfalsifiable because it judges all the surviving data based upon a standard that not only does not exist but that no one has ever seen. It proves nothing to argue that the truthfulness of the surviving manuscripts can only be determined by the original autographs which no one, by their own admission, possesses.

- The doctrine of preservation mandates that we have more than just a shell of the nebulous "original Bible." Preservation is the process whereby God secured the transference of His word from one generation to the next. My point in Lesson 8 was that God did not need to preserve His word in a state of *verbatim identicality* in order to fulfill His fundamental promise of preservation. This is obvious because there are slight differences even in the manuscripts comprising the Byzantine Text Type not to mention the various editions of the *TR*.

- This is where we must recognize the difference between: 1) different ways of saying the same thing and 2) substantive differences in meaning. The manuscripts of the Byzantine Text Type as well as the various editions of the *TR* contain an agreement as to the doctrinal content of the readings. Conversely, when the *TR* is compared with the Critical Text there are substantive differences in meaning as to the doctrinal content of the readings (more on this below).

- On this point I agree with Dr. R.B. Ouellete, "Preservation is highly debated today because ultimately, the preservation issue will decide the translation issue — and preservation is completely a matter of faith in God's power." (Ouellette, 33)

- I cannot agree with the originals only position for the following primary reasons:

    o First, from the standpoint of logic, it is both unscientific and unfalsifiable and thereby fails to meet its own standard.

    o Second, and more importantly, God promised to preserve the words that He inspired forever. Either God did this, or He did not. If God did not do what he promised, that would make God out to be a liar and we know that God cannot lie (Numbers 23:19, Titus 1:2).

- o Third, that God did not see fit to accomplish preservation by preserving the original autographs is evident or else we would have them today.

- Determining exactly how God accomplished the preservation of His word without preserving the original autographs will be part of the goal of the duration of this course of study.

Providential Preservation

- Second, with respect to the terminology "providential preservation" utilized by Dr. Hills and others, I am not necessarily ascribing the term "providential" to my view or understanding of preservation. "Providential" is a loaded term that means different things to different people. For many, there is no difference in their understanding between the terms miraculous and providential. Meanwhile, as Brother Craig pointed out last week, if, by providential, one means to refer to the process that God established to accomplish the preservation of His word via Bible believing members of the body of Christ, that would certainly be an entirely different meaning of the term. Consequently, until further notice, you will always hear me speak of just preservation when seeking to articulate my own position, not "providential preservation."

- That being said, I need to be able to honestly handle the source material that I am quoting or referencing in class. Therefore, any use of the terminology "providential preservation" by quoted sources should not automatically be equated with my endorsement of the term "providential" as an adequate descriptor for how preservation was accomplished.

Dynamic Inspiration & Translation

- Thirdly, since it has come up multiple times already, we need to clarify the difference between the Dynamic or Concept View of inspiration and the Dynamic Philosophy of translation.
- As we will see in our next lesson, the Dynamic or Concept View of inspiration maintains that God inspired the ideas or concepts and left the human authors to express those ideas in their own words. In other words, this is a Dynamic view of the Bible's origin that holds that God did not inspire the very words of Scriptures themselves but merely the concepts.
- In contrast, the Dynamic Philosophy of translation practices the belief that what matters most when translating the Bible out of the donor language (Hebrew and Greek) and into the receptor language (English) is the expression of the thoughts and not the words themselves. Meanwhile, the Literal or Formal Equivalence Philosophy of translation differs from the Dynamic in that it seeks to translate every word found in the donor language into the receptor language (to the best of their ability). The King James Bible is the product of a Literal Philosophy of translation whereas the New International Version (NIV), for example, stands out as a representative of the Dynamic Philosophy of translation.
- Lastly, it is important to note that one can reject the Dynamic View of inspiration in favor of a Verbal View (the words not the thoughts are inspired) yet at the same time accept and utilize a Dynamic Philosophy of translation. These are different things and ought not to be confused.

WORKS CITED

Geisler, Norman L. *Inerrancy*. Zondervan, 1980.

Ouellette, R.B. *A More Sure Word: Which Bible Can you Trust?* Lancaster, CA: Striving Together Publications, 2008.

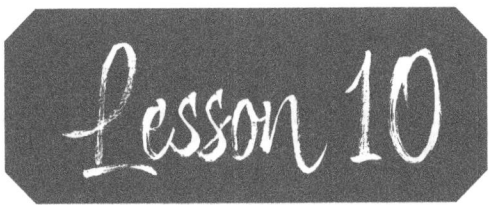

UNDERSTANDING BASIC TERMINOLOGY: PRESERVATION, PART 3

INTRODUCTION

- In Lesson 9, I sought to offer some clarifications on a few points raised in Lesson 8. Specifically, I clarified the following three points:

    o   The importance of understanding the issue of *verbatim identicality*.
    o   Use of the terminology "providential preservation."
    o   The difference between the Dynamic View of inspiration and the Dynamic philosophy of translation.

- In this lesson, I would like to respond further to some of the issues/questions raised in Lesson 8. After doing so, we will conclude the lesson by considering the terminological relationships between revelation, inspiration, illumination, and preservation.

COMMENTS ON ISSUES RAISED IN LESSON 8

- In this section I will comment on the following sub-points raised in Lesson 8.

    o The Doctrine of Repetition
    o Substantive Differences Affecting the Accuracy of the Text
    o Basic Factual Irregularities
    o Summary of Lessons 8-10

The Doctrine of Repetition

- In Lesson 8 (and twice referenced last week in Lesson 9) I stated, ". . . when the *TR* is compared with the Critical Text, there are substantive differences in meaning as to the doctrinal content of the readings." The notion that the differences between the *TR* and the Critical Text and their representative translations into English contain substantive differences in meaning that affect doctrine was openly questioned.
- This questioning was based in part on something called "the doctrine of repetition" or the idea that if one text seemed to undermine/weaken a particular doctrine in a given passage, the "doctrine of repetition" elsewhere protected that particular doctrine. When pressed for an example, I offered up the exclusion of the word "firstborn" from Matthew 1:25 in the Critical Text and its resultant English translations as an example of the weakening of the doctrine of the virgin birth.

- Since teaching Lesson 8, I have searched the internet and every theology book I own looking for more information on the "doctrine of repetition." While I could not locate the enunciation of a formal "doctrine of repetition" I was able to locate the concept in James R. White's book *The King James Only Controversy*. White touches upon the concept in a section of Chapter 3 subtitled "To Err is Human" beginning on page 36. Rather than using the phraseology "doctrine of repetition," White describes the notion by using the terms *harmonization* and *parallel influence*. (White, 37, 156-159) Essentially White reasons as follows:

  o "Let's say you were used to the way a particular phrase sounds in a particular passage of Scripture because your pastor uses that verse all the time in church. But let's say that a similar phrase occurs elsewhere in Scripture — similar, but not exactly the same. As you are copying the other passage of Scripture it would be very easy to inadvertently make that passage sound like the one you are accustomed to. You might not even know you had changed anything! But this kind of harmonization is found in many, many places.

  ... When Paul wrote to the Ephesians, he said, "Grace to you and peace from God our Father and the Lord Jesus Christ" (Eph.1:2, NASB). This phrase early on had a part in the liturgy of the church. It was a Christian greeting, a blessing of sorts. Many people continue to use it in that way to this very day. But, when writing to the Colossians, Paul was not so complete in his wording as when he wrote to the Ephesians. Instead he wrote, "Grace to you and peace from God our Father (Col. 1:2 NASB)." (White, 37)

Eph. 1:2 — KJB	Eph. 1:2 — NASB	Col. 1:2 — KJB	Col. 1:2 — NASB
Grace *be* to you, and peace, from God our Father, and *from* the Lord Jesus Christ.	Grace to you and peace from God our Father and the Lord Jesus Christ.	To the saints and faithful brethren in Christ which are at Colosse: Grace *be* unto you, and peace, from God our Father and the Lord Jesus Christ.	To the saints and faithful brethren in Christ *who are* at Colossae: Grace to you and peace from God our Father.

- Please note that the Colossian 1:2 passage in the NASB is missing the phrase "and the Lord Jesus Christ." The KJB contains the extended greeting in both Ephesians 1:2 and Colossians 1:2 because its underlying Greek text (*TR*) contains the phrase in both places whereas the Greek text supporting the NASB's reading only contains the phrase in Ephesians 1:2. White reasons that a scribe accustomed to hearing the longer greeting in Ephesians 1:2 inadvertently added the extra phrase to Colossians 1:2 to make it harmonize with Ephesians 1:2. Regarding this White states:

    o "This kind of harmonization is easy to understand, and it explains many of the most commonly cited examples of "corruption" on the part of the KJV Only advocates. . . The fact that all modern translations have "and the Lord Jesus Christ" at Ephesians 1:2 should certainly cause us to question anyone who would ask us to believe that there is some evil conspiracy at work behind the non-inclusion of the same phrase at Colossians 1:2. If someone were tampering with the texts, why not take out the phrase at Ephesians 1:2?" (White, 38)

- Later in the book White deals with Matthew 1:25.

KJB	NASB	ESV	NIV
And knew her not till she had brought forth her firstborn son: and he called his name JESUS.	but kept her a virgin until she gave birth to a Son; and he called His name Jesus.	but knew her not until she had given birth to a son. And he called his name Jesus.	But he did not consummate their marriage until she gave birth to a son. And he gave him the name Jesus.

- In this case the NASB and KJB readings constitute different ways of saying the same thing despite the NASB's reading not possessing the word "firstborn." The NASB still makes it clear that Mary was a virgin when she gave birth to Jesus which would have made Jesus her "firstborn" son. Meanwhile the ESV (Literal Translation) and

NIV (Dynamic Translation) readings leave open the possibility that Jesus was Mary's son sired by a different man other than Joseph. Moreover, the ESV and NIV renderings allow for the possibility that Mary could have had other children fathered by other men before the birth of Jesus. Two of these readings protect the doctrine of the virgin birth and two of them weaken it.

- Regarding the "firstborn" issue in Matthew 1:25, James White states,

    o "... Matthew 1:25 is often cited by critics of modern translations as an attempt to deny the virgin birth of Christ. Yet if a modern translation were to do this, why not remove the parallel occurrence of the term at Luke 2:7 where all modern translations contain the disputed term? In reality, we have here another example of parallel influence that caused a scribe, undoubtedly zealous for orthodox doctrine, to insert the term "firstborn" here so as to protect a sacred truth and bring this passage in line with Luke's account. Modern translations, far from seeking to denigrate such divine truths are simply seeking to give us what was written by the original authors." (White, 159)

- White's explanation only applies to the NIV's reading of Matthew 1:25 (ESV did not exist in 1995 when White wrote his book) and fails to address how the NASB secured the doctrine of the virgin birth in Matthew 1:25 without using the word "firstborn." In my opinion, this is yet another example of how the issue of *verbatim identicality* is lingering in unspoken fashion beneath the surface in all these discussions. White's entire explanation based upon *parallel influence* and *harmonization* is set up to explain why the NIV and KJB do not exhibit *verbatim* wording. When one breaks with the notion of "exact sameness" they are able to evaluate the doctrinal content of each reading as it stands before them.

- In my opinion, James White's analysis and explanation presented above exhibits the following problems:

    o First, as to the language "Let's say you were . . ." indicates, White is merely postulating this scenario. While it makes sense that someone could or would *harmonize* different passages he does

- not and cannot prove that is what occurred in any of the examples he cites of so-called *harmonization*.
- Second, without access to the original autographs how does White know what was written by the original authors? To make this statement White must presuppose that his textual position is correct. Moreover, he assumes that every variant of this type is the result of overzealous scribes seeking to *harmonize* texts based upon *parallel influence* when a scribe could have just as easily deleted a word or phrase either by accident or because they disagreed with it. Once again, this is an explanation of no practical consequence and an assumption on White's part because, in the absence of the original manuscripts, he cannot prove it.
- Third, how does White know which textual variants are explainable by his *harmonization* and *parallel influence* concepts and which are not?
- Fourth, as Pastor Lee pointed out during Lesson 8, if one says that it does not matter whether or not "firstborn" is found in Matthew 1:25 because the virgin birth is elsewhere affirmatively asserted, what does that do to one's stance for Plenary Verbal Inspiration or the idea that every word was inspired by God? It seems to me that this argument avoids the core question of whether or not the word "firstborn" belongs in the text of Matthew 1:25.
- Fifth, what does one do about doctrines that are taught in only one primary passage and are not repeated elsewhere? The whole idea of "rightly dividing the word of truth" in II Timothy 2:15 stands out as a possible prime example. The NASB's "accurately handling," the ESV's "rightly handling," or the NIV's "correctly handles" do not accurately convey the force of the Greek word *orthotomeō* which means to cut straight and divide. Even Dr. Dale DeWitt who has historically objected to the terminology "rightly dividing the word of truth" has recently acknowledged that the KJB's rendering accurately conveys the sense and the force of the word *orthotomeō*. In short, the principles of repetition, *harmonization*, and *parallel influence* could not secure the doctrinal content of truth conveyed via singular passages.
- Sixth, White's comments point out a phenomenon among most (not all) modern scholars. In the passages where the *TR* and the Critical Text disagree with one another the *TR* is always wrong.

Substantive Differences Affecting the Accuracy of the Text

- There is no doubt in my mind that there are substantive differences in meaning that affect the accuracy of the text between the *TR* and the Critical Text and their representative translations into English. Please consider the following examples. For the sake of clarity and consistency we will compare the King James with other literal translations namely, the New American Standard Bible (NASB) and the English Standard Version (ESV).

Mark 1:2-3

KJB	NASB	ESV
2) As it is written in the prophets, Behold, I send my messenger before thy face, which shall prepare thy way before thee. 3) The voice of one crying in the wilderness, Prepare ye the way of the Lord, make his paths straight.	2) As it is written in Isaiah the prophet: "BEHOLD, I SEND MY MESSENGER AHEAD OF YOU, WHO WILL PREPARE YOUR WAY; 3) THE VOICE OF ONE CRYING IN THE WILDERNESS, 'MAKE READY THE WAY OF THE LORD, MAKE HIS PATHS STRAIGHT.'"	2) As it is written in Isaiah the prophet, "Behold, I send my messenger before your face, who will prepare your way, 3) the voice of one crying in the wilderness: 'Prepare the way of the Lord, make his paths straight,'"

- Mark 1:2-3 contains quotations from Malachi 3:1 (Mark 1:2) and Isaiah 40:3 (Mark 1:3) as the KJB accurately reports with the use of "prophets" plural. Meanwhile the modern versions quoted above both read "As it is written in Isaiah the prophet" singular. This is a flat-out mistake in the NASB and ESV; one can read Isaiah from now till the rapture and not find the contents of Mark 1:2 in the book of Isaiah.

- This is not a "translation" issue. It is a "textual" issue. The issue here is not how to properly translate individual Greek words into English. The reason the English texts differ is because their underlying Greek texts differ. This is an example of a substantive difference in meaning. They both cannot be correct.

- This is a clear-cut case where modern versions and their underlying Greek text are wrong. They present information that is false. The Old Testament quotation found in Mark 1:2 cannot be found in the book of Isaiah.

Matthew 5:22

KJB	NASB	ESV
But I say unto you, That whosoever is angry with his brother without a cause shall be in danger of the judgment: and whosoever shall say to his brother, Raca, shall be in danger of the council: but whosoever shall say, Thou fool, shall be in danger of hell fire.	"But I say to you that everyone who is angry with his brother shall be guilty before the court; and whoever says to his brother, 'You good-for-nothing,' shall be guilty before the supreme court; and whoever says, 'You fool,' shall be guilty *enough to go* into the fiery hell.	But I say to you that everyone who is angry with his brother will be liable to judgment; whoever insults his brother will be liable to the council; and whoever says, 'You fool!' will be liable to the hell of fire.

- The phrase "without a cause" is missing from both the NASB and ESV. The reason the phrase is missing from both modern versions is because the underlying Greek text from which they are translated does not contain the phrase.

- The omission of the phrase "without a cause" seems to be a minor oversight in Matthew 5 but, when cross referenced with Mark 3:5, a theological problem is encountered. In Mark 3:5 Jesus gets angry due to the hardness of the heart exhibited by those in the synagogue. Does Jesus have cause to be angry? Yes. The omission of the phrase, "without a cause" in the Critical Text and its corresponding modern translations in Matthew 5 creates a doctrinal problem in Mark 3 when Jesus gets angry. Practically, the omission of the phrase "without a cause" results in Jesus condemning Himself out of His own mouth.

Luke 2:33

KJB	NASB	ESV
And Joseph and his mother marveled at those things which were spoken of him.	And His father and mother were amazed at the things which were being said about Him.	And his father and his mother marveled at what was said about him.

- Once again, why do these versions read differently in English? Because their underlying Greek texts are not the same. The *TR* and its subsequent translation into English via the KJB maintain the doctrinal integrity of the virgin birth. Joseph was not the father of Jesus as the modern translations of the Critical Text imply.

- What should one conclude when we find the same doctrine weakened in multiple places in the Critical Text and its corresponding modern versions? Consider Matthew 1:25 in the light of Luke 2:33:

    o KJB — And knew her not till she had brought forth her firstborn son: and he called his name JESUS.

    o ESV — but knew her not until she had given birth to a son. And he called his name Jesus.

Colossians 2:18

KJB	NASB	ESV
Let no man beguile you of your reward in a voluntary humility and worshipping of angels, intruding into those things which he hath not seen, vainly puffed up by his fleshly mind,	Let no one keep defrauding you of your prize by delighting in self-abasement and the worship of the angels, taking his stand on *visions* he has seen, inflated without cause by his fleshly mind,	Let no one disqualify you, insisting on asceticism and worship of angels, going on in detail about visions, puffed up without reason by his sensuous mind,

- Here we have a situation where the *TR* and the Critical Text are directly contradictory. This is not just a situation where one text leaves something out that the other one includes. One text, the Critical Text, says that you have seen the angels and visions while the other one (the *TR*) says that you have not. The reason they contradict in English is because they contradict in Greek.

- Here the principles of *Noncontradiction* and *Excluded Middle* absolutely apply because the two readings are directly contradictory and teach opposites. One reading says you have seen a thing while the other one says that you have not.

- Both readings cannot be correct because they possess substantive differences in meaning. One of them must be right and one of them has to be wrong or they are both wrong. We cannot even entertain the notion that they are both wrong on account of the doctrine of preservation.

- This passage is dealing with the doctrine of angels (*Angelology*) during the dispensation of grace. How many believers in our day claim to have guardian angels, seen angels, or heard messages from angels or received visions and revelations based upon their personal experience? Colossians 2:18 is the clearest verse in the Pauline epistles telling you that anyone making such claims does not know what they are talking about and is not to be trusted. More importantly, anyone dabbling in such doctrinal confusion is not holding Christ as the head as stated in the next verse (Colossians 2:19).

- Furthermore, the readings found in the NASB and ESV for Colossians 2:18, create an internal contradiction within the book of Colossians. Colossians 1:16 teaches that the principalities and powers in heavenly places and those beings occupying them are "invisible" i.e., you cannot see them. Now, one chapter later in chapter 2, modern versions have people seeing things that chapter 1 said were invisible.
- I fail to see how this difference does not affect doctrine as it relates to the body of Christ. I have dealt with many Pentecostals who have claimed to have had angelic visitations and have seen into the spirit world based upon the authority of Colossians 2:18 in their modern version.

John 1:18

KJB	NASB
No man hath seen God at any time; the only begotten Son, which is in the bosom of the Father, he hath declared *him*.	No one has seen God at any time; the only begotten God who is in the bosom of the Father, He has explained *Him*.

- Is Jesus Christ the "only begotten Son" or the "only begotten God" as the NASB states? The wording of the NASB asserts that Jesus Christ is a lesser God created by God Almighty and is not coequal with the Father. Theologically this is very close to what the Jehovah's Witnesses believe about Christ i.e., that he was not co-equal with God the Father but is a lesser created being. Once again it seems to me that this reading affects doctrine.

Basic Factual Irregularities

- The examples cited above do not even take into account the scores of omitted verses in the Critical Text or the fundamental lack of agreeance amongst Critical Text translations on even basic textual or historical details. As we studied in Lesson 3, this is not simply a King James versus modern versions problem. Even among modern versions, which subscribe to the same theories of textual criticism, there are substantive differences in meaning and lack of agreement about even basic facts. See the following examples:

II Samuel 15:7

KJB	NASB	ESV
And it came to pass after forty years, that Absalom said unto the king, I pray thee, let me go and pay my vow, which I have vowed unto the LORD, in Hebron.	Now it came about at the end of forty years that Absalom said to the king, "Please let me go and pay my vow which I have vowed to the LORD, in Hebron.	And at the end of four years Absalom said to the king, "Please let me go and pay my vow, which I have vowed to the LORD, in Hebron.

Ecclesiastes 8:10

KJB	NASB	ESV
And so I saw the wicked buried, who had come and gone from the place of the holy, and they were forgotten in the city where they had so done: this *is* also vanity.	So then, I have seen the wicked buried, those who used to go in and out from the holy place, and they are *soon* forgotten in the city where they did thus. This too is futility.	Then I saw the wicked buried. They used to go in and out of the holy place and were praised in the city where they had done such things. This also is vanity.

Luke 10:1

KJB	NASB	ESV
After these things the Lord appointed other seventy also, and sent them two and two before his face into every city and place, whither he himself would come.	Now after this the Lord appointed seventy others, and sent them in pairs ahead of Him to every city and place where He Himself was going to come.	After this the Lord appointed seventy-two others and sent them on ahead of him, two by two, into every town and place where he himself was about to go.

Matthew 12:47

KJB	NASB	ESV
Then one said unto him, Behold, thy mother and thy brethren stand without, desiring to speak with thee.	Someone said to Him, "Behold, Your mother and Your brothers are standing outside seeking to speak to You."	Omitted

- Once again, understanding how God accomplished His promise to preserve His word will be one of the main goals throughout the duration of this class. Before we can fully understand preservation though, we need to thoroughly ground ourselves in the doctrine of inspiration.

Summary of Lessons 8-10

- What was originally scheduled to be one basic introductory lesson on preservation in our mini-series on basic terminology has turned into three lessons. Over the course of the last three lessons, we have sought to establish the following points:

- o Preservation is the Bible's claim for itself (See the list of ten passages in Lesson 8). God promised to preserve that which he inspired.
- o God did not see fit to accomplish his fundamental promise of preservation by preserving the original autographs. This is evident because, had He chosen to accomplish preservation in this fashion, we would possess the originals today.
- o In order to accomplish the preservation of his word, God did not preserve it in a state of *verbatim identicality* but in a state of *substinative doctrinal pureness*.
- o There are substantive differences in meaning between the *TR* and the Critical Text that impact the accuracy of the text, some of which impact doctrine.

- The goal of Lessons 8 through 10 was not to set forth a fully developed doctrine of preservation. That task lies yet in the future after we have fully studied the doctrine of inspiration. One must first fully appreciate the doctrine of inspiration before being able to fully grasp the doctrine of preservation in its fullness. Put another way, if one does not accurately understand inspiration, they will struggle to understand what is being preserved and how to scripturally identify the process.

TERMINOLOGICAL RELATIONSHIPS: PUTTING IT ALL TOGETHER

- So, you have God revealing himself — communicating to man (*revelation*). Then He has a mechanism whereby man writes the communication down on a piece of paper (*inspiration*). Then He has a mechanism where the words on the piece of paper are stored up in the believer's soul (*illumination*). And then He has a mechanism where those words that are written down on a piece of paper are preserved from one generation to the next so that you and I can have them today (*preservation*).

- In Grace School of the Bible, Pastor Jordan summarized the relationships between these terms as follows (See the notes from Lessons 6 and 7 for Scripture references on revelation, inspiration, and illumination.):

    o "There is a sense in which *revelation* and *illumination* are associated, just as there is a sense in which *inspiration* and *preservation* are associated. It is important that you understand this issue.

    The first two (*revelation* and *inspiration*) are a unit, and the next two (*illumination* and *preservation*) are a unit. If *revelation* and *inspiration* go together then *illumination* and *preservation* go together. The reason that *inspiration* is possible is because of *revelation*, and the reason *preservation* is possible is because of *illumination*. You would not have a revelation if God did not give it. You would not have anything to write down unless God gave you some information – revelation, communication, unveiling of Himself. That is easy to see. There would not be preservation unless the word of God is stored in the soul of the believer. As the teaching ministry of the Holy Spirit, (illumination), identifies to the believer what God's word is, then consequently the true word of God is preserved through history.

    Let's say that there are five different Bible texts out there. How are you going to know which one is right one hundred years from now? Rather than writing down one manuscript and preserving that one manuscript through all of time, God has a mechanism whereby the church of the living God is the pillar and the ground of truth. And rather than preserving a single manuscript through time and saying, "That is it", and having everybody fall down and worship it, God has provided a mechanism whereby the Holy Spirit, that is in the believer, will be illuminated to the truth of the word of God and will be able to identify what is God's word and what is not, as He is instructed. Now we will see that as we go along.

    But, *revelation* and *inspiration* go together, and *illumination* and *preservation* go together.

    Revelation and *illumination* are similar things. They are a God-to-man kind of communication. *Inspiration* and *preservation* are associated because they have to do with the production and the preservation of the written word of God. *Revelation* and *illumination* are things that go on inside of the heart of a man, (or with revelation it could be an outward thing). But, they are subjective things. *Inspiration* and *preservation* are objective things.

Now, there is one other thing. *Revelation* and *inspiration* are complete. There is no more *revelation*, and there is no more *inspiration*. The second pair, *illumination* and *preservation*, are continuing. They involve a continuous process down through time. But, *revelation* and *inspiration* are finished. Why? The revelation is complete, and there is not any need for the inspiration that writes it down. There is not any need for any more revelation – God-to-man communication directly...

Illumination, (understanding, gaining knowledge of the scripture), is continuing. *Preservation* also continues right through time." (Jordan, Manuscript Evidence 101, Lesson 2)

WORKS CITED

Jordan, Richard. *Manuscript Evidence 101*. Grace School of the Bible.

White, James R. *The King James Only Controversy: Can You Trust Modern Translations?*. Bethany House Publishers: Minneapolis, MN: 1995.

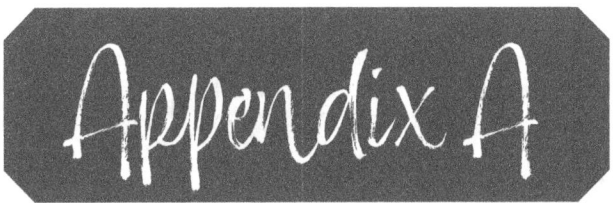

Response to Questions Raised During the Teaching of Lesson 10 Regarding Mark 1:2-3

INTRODUCTION

The following appendix was prepared in response to a question raised in Lesson 10 (originally taught on 11/29/15) regarding the manuscript support for the *TR*/King James reading found in Mark 1:2-3. It was argued based upon the findings of "textual criticism" that the reading found in the Critical Text and its resulting translations into English in Mark 1:2-3 is not a mistake. For the sake of clarity, we have reproduced the passage in question below.

Mark 1:2-3

KJB	NASB	ESV
2) As it is written in the prophets, Behold, I send my messenger before thy face, which shall prepare thy way before thee.	2) As it is written in Isaiah the prophet: "BEHOLD, I SEND MY MESSENGER AHEAD OF YOU WHO WILL PREPARE YOUR WAY;	2) As it is written in Isaiah the prophet, "Behold, I send my messenger before your face, who will prepare your way,
3) The voice of one crying in the wilderness, Prepare ye the way of the Lord, make his paths straight.	3) THE VOICE OF ONE CRYING IN THE WILDERNESS, 'MAKE READY THE WAY OF THE LORD, MAKE HIS PATHS STRAIGHT.'"	3) the voice of one crying in the wilderness: 'Prepare the way of the Lord, make his paths straight,'"

In Lesson 10, I offered the following commentary on the differences exhibited above.

- Mark 1:2-3 contains quotations from Malachi 3:1 (Mark 1:2) and Isaiah 40:3 (Mark 1:3) as the KJB accurately reports with the use of "prophets" plural. Meanwhile the modern versions quoted above both read "As it is written in Isaiah the prophet" singular. This is a flat-out mistake in the NASB and ESV; one can read Isaiah from now till the rapture and not find the contents of Mark 1:2 in the book of Isaiah.

- This is not a "translation" issue. It is a "textual" issue. The issue here is not how to properly translate individual Greek words into English. The reason the English texts differ is because their underlying Greek texts differ. This is an example of a substantive difference in meaning. They both cannot be correct.

- This is a clear-cut case where modern versions and their underlying Greek text are wrong. They present information that is false. The Old Testament quotation found in Mark 1:2 cannot be found in the book of Isaiah. (Lesson 10)

During the teaching of Lesson 10, two primary objections were raised in response to the information quoted above. First, the manuscript support for the reading "Isaiah the prophet" as contained in the Critical Text was cited as evidence that the *TR* reading is incorrect. Second, an objection to the *TR*'s reading was raised based upon 1st century Jewish forms of source citation which gave precedence to the major or more prominent author over a minor or less prominent author when dealing with "conflated" or compound quotations as found in Mark 1:2-3. According to this line of thought, there is nothing wrong with the Critical Text's reading, even though the content of Mark 1:2 cannot be found in Isaiah, because Isaiah is the major prophet and is therefore given precedence over Malachi in terms of source citation.

The goal of this appendix is to offer a written response to both objections. To that end, we will consider the writings of James R. White, a supporter of the Critical Text and Thomas Holland, a supporter of the *TR* or what he calls Traditional Text as representative of the two positions in question. Throughout and in summation, I will offer my own commentary and thoughts on the issues at hand.

JAMES R. WHITE & THE CRITICAL TEXT POSITION ON MARK 1:2-3

For purposes of comparison, we will use the comments found in James R. White's book *The King James Only Controversy: Can You Trust the Modern Versions* on Mark 1:2-3 as emblematic of the Critical Text position on this matter. White's comments are essentially identical to the objections raised during the public teaching of Lesson 10.

Manuscript Support for the Critical Text Reading

Regarding the manuscript support for the reading "Isaiah the prophet" as found in the Critical Text and modern versions, White offers the following comments in Part Two of his book on page 254.

- "The USB 4th assigns to the reading "Isaiah the prophet" a rating of {A}, and that for good reason. The reading has the support of both the external and internal evidence. Externally the word "Isaiah" is found in various forms in ℵ B D L Δ Θ f^1 33 205 565 700 892 1071 1241 1243 2427 l 253 arm geo Irenaeus^{gr} Origen Serapion Epiphanius Severian Hesychius and numerous Latin manuscripts, which alone would be sufficient." (White, 254)

For purposes of clarification, what White is trying to identify using scholarly language, symbols, numbers, and names are all the manuscript witnesses that contain the reading "Isaiah the prophet" as found in the Critical Text. For example, the symbols "ℵ B D L Δ Θ" designate Greek uncial manuscripts (Greek mss written in all capital letters) containing the reading whereas the numbers "33 205 565 700 892" are references to specific Greek minuscule manuscripts (Greek mss written in all lower-case letters) supporting the reading. Meanwhile, the names "Irenaeus^{gr} Origen Serapion Epiphanius Severian Hesychius" are references to the writings of the church fathers that support the reading "Isaiah the prophet" in Mark 1:2. Lastly, the statement regarding USB 4th assigning the reading "Isaiah the prophet" a rating of {A} is a reference to what I was talking about in Lesson 3. According to the preface of the latest edition of the Greek text published by the United Bible Society (USB5) the grading system works as follows:

- A — Indicates the text is certain;
- B — Indicates the text is almost certain;
- C — Indicates the text is difficult to determine;
- D — Indicates the text is very difficult to determine. (Ballard)

So, White's point in mentioning the {A} rating attached to Mark 1:2 in the 4th Edition of the Greek text published by the United Bible Society is that textual scholars are universally agreed that "Isaiah the Prophet" is the correct reading.

1st Century Jewish Forms of Source Citation

In the same paragraph quoted above, after presenting the external manuscript evidence for the reading "Isaiah the prophet," White turns his attention to the internal support for the reading which he views as "even stronger." By internal support, White is speaking about the 1st century Jewish method of source citation spoken about in the introduction to this appendix. Specifically, White states,

- "But the internal considerations are even stronger. The desire to rescue Mark from an (misapprehended) error in citing Isaiah when the quotation is from Malachi and Isaiah together (see our discussion in the text above regarding this) is a strong argument in favor of the reading found in the modern texts." (White, 254)

White's parenthetical note to "see our discussion in the text above regarding this" is a reference to his discussion of Mark 1:2-3 found in the main body of his book on pages 166-168. It is on these pages that one finds White's full explanation of why the Critical Text reading is acceptable based upon 1st century Jewish forms of source citation.

- "Why are KJV Only advocates so confident that "the prophets" is the only possible reading? The argument is that since part of the quotation given by Mark is from Malachi, Mark couldn't have written "in Isaiah the prophet," for this would be a "mistake" on the part of the inspired writer. Even though Mark 1:3 is from Isaiah, the preceding section is from Malachi, hence, it *must* be "in the prophets."

It is quite certain that some scribes early on in the transmission of the text of the New Testament had the very same thought. In fact, the reason why modern scholars are so confident that the proper reading is "in Isaiah the prophet" stems partly from this very fact: it is much easier to understand why a scribe would try to "help Mark out," so to speak, and correct what seems to be an errant citation than to figure out why someone would change it to "Isaiah the prophet." But as in so many instances where a scribe thought he had encountered an error in the text, the error was, in fact, the scribe's, not the text's.

The problem with the KJV Only argument at this point is simply one of ignorance of the common form of citation at the time of the writing of the New Testament. We have at least two instances recorded for us by the apostles where a conflated citation of two different Old Testament prophets is placed under the name of the more important or major of the two prophets. One of these instances is found in Matthew 27:9, where Matthew attributes to Jeremiah a quotation that is primarily drawn from Zechariah. We note in passing that the KJV has "Jeremiah" at Matthew 27:9, and hence must make reference to this phenomenon of citing a conflated Old Testament passage by the name of the more major of the two authors to explain this. Also we find the very same attempt on the part of some later scribes to change "Jeremiah" to "Zechariah" at Matthew 27:9, though in this case their attempts did not become the majority reading of the manuscripts. The other instance is here at Mark 1:2-3, where a conflated reading, combining Malachi 3:1 with Isaiah 40:3, is cited under the single name of the more major of the two prophets, Isaiah. This was, as we said, common practice in that day, and we cannot fault the apostolic writers for using the conventional means of expressing themselves. The "error" exists when modern readers try to force the ancient writers into modern standards of citation and footnoting.

We see, then, that Mark was quite accurate in his original wording and did not need the editorial assistance of later scribes, nor of KJV Only advocates, at all." (White, 167-168)

Once again, I would like to point out that White is very confident as to the "original wording" of Mark 1:2 despite never having seen an original manuscript a day in his life. His certainty that the Critical Text reading is correct, despite his admittance that the *TR* reading also dates from "early on in the transmission of the text of the New Testament," rests upon his knowledge of 1st century Jewish citation practices utilized by the apostles. White offers Matthew 27:9 as the lone supporting example for the apostles' "conventional means of expressing themselves" when dealing with "conflated" or compound quotations of the Old Testament. No other support for this notion is mentioned by White.

Having duly established White's reasoning for why the Critical Text reading is correct, we will now turn our attention to Dr. Thomas Holland's argument for the accuracy of the *TR*'s reading in Mark 1:2-3.

DR. THOMAS HOLLAND & THE *TR* POSITION ON MARK 1:2-3

Just as we used James R. White's book *The King James Only Controversy* as emblematic of the Critical Text position in the previous section of this appendix, in this section we will use Dr. Thomas Holland's book *Crowned with Glory: The Bible from Ancient Text to Authorized Version* as representative of the *TR* position on Mark 1:2-3. A portion of Holland's book was read during the public teaching of Lesson 10 (See Lesson 10 video).

For purposes of consistency, we will follow the format established in the previous section. First, we will address the manuscript support for the *TR* reading. Second, we will look at Holland's reply to the 1st century Jewish forms of citation argument summarized above by White.

Manuscript Support for the TR Reading

Holland chronicles the following manuscript support for the reading "written in the prophets" as found in the *TR* and the King James Bible for Mark 1:2.

- "The Traditional Text reads, "*As it is written in the prophets,*" and then cites from Malachi 3:1 and Isaiah 40:3. Other texts read, "As it is written in the Prophet Isaiah," before quoting Malachi and Isaiah. The reading of the Traditional Text has considerable support. It is found in many of the Greek uncials (A, K, P, W, Π), the majority Greek minuscules (28, 1009, 1010, 1079, 1195, 1216, 1230, 1242, 1252, 1344, 1365, 1546, 1646, 2148) and the majority of Greek lectionaries. Thus, the Greek support dates from the fourth century onward. Additionally, we find the same reading in the Syriac Harclean version (616 AD), the Armenian version (fourth/fifth century) and the Ethiopic versions of the sixth century. It also received patristic citations from many of the church fathers such as the Latin version of Irenaeus (202 AD), Photius (895 AD), and Theophlact (1077 AD)." (Holland, 146-147)

Textually, there is just as much if not more manuscript support for the *TR* reading of "written in the prophets" than there is for the reading "Isaiah the prophet" in the Critical Text. In addition, to the manuscript evidence catalogued above, King James Bible researcher Will Kinney adds that the *TR* reading is quoted by "Tertullian in 220, long before anything we have in the Greek copies." (Kinney, *Gospel of Mark: A Modern Version Mix-up*) In 202 AD Irenaeus stated the following in his *Against Heresies:*

- "Wherefore also Mark, the interpreter and follower of Peter, does thus commence his Gospel narrative: "The beginning of the Gospel of Jesus Christ, the Son of God; as it is written in THE PROPHETS, Behold, I send My messenger before Thy face, which shall prepare Thy way". . . Plainly does the commencement of the Gospel quote the words of THE HOLY PROPHETS and point out Him at once, whom they confessed as God and Lord;" (Book III, Chapter 10)

This Latin quotation from Irenaeus in 202 (White cites a Greek copy above that agrees with the Critical Text) coupled with the quotation by Tertullian in 220 highlights the fact that the manuscript evidence supporting the *TR* reading in Mark 1:2 is of equal antiquity with any of the witnesses supporting Critical Text reading. Therefore, secondary arguments regarding 1st century Jewish source citation are necessary on the part of textual scholars to justify their self-ascribed {A} rating for Mark 1:2 in the critical apparatus.

Response to 1st Century Jewish Forms of Source Citation Argument

Thomas Holland maintains that the notion posited by White and others that a copyist made the change from "Isaiah the prophet" to "the prophets" in Mark 1:2 in order to correct a perceived error is complete conjecture and cannot be proven. Furthermore, Holland argues that there are significant problems with the 1st century Jewish source citation argument. Holland writes:

- "Contextually there arises a problem with the reading as found in the Critical Text. The passage cites both the Prophet Malachi (3:1) and the Prophet Isaiah (40:3). The reading, "As it is written in Isaiah the Prophet," seems inconsistent. Nevertheless, it has been noted that Isaiah was the major prophet and therefore he takes preeminence over Malachi. To illustrate this point, scholars often refer to Matthew 27:9. They claim this passage is not really a citation of Jeremiah but instead a quotation of Zechariah 11:12. Jeremiah received the preeminence as the major prophet.

    However, this point can be argued. The text in Matthew does not say it was *written* as the passage in Mark does. Instead the text in Matthew states, "Then was fulfilled that which was *spoken* by Jeremy." God, the Author of Scripture, is aware of who writes what and who speaks what. Simply because Zechariah writes the passage does not mean Jeremiah did not speak it. Also, Zechariah warned Israel to pay attention to what the former prophets had spoken (Zech. 7:7). The ancient Jews had a saying that, "the spirit of Jeremiah was in Zechariah." Much of what

Zechariah received, he did so from both the Lord and the former prophet, Jeremiah.

The position presented by many that some copyist made the change from "Isaiah the Prophet" to "the prophets" in Mark 1:2 in order to correct what was perceived as a possible error is conjecture. One can just as easily speculate that an Egyptian copyist not overly familiar with Jewish Old Testament prophets recognized the Isaiah quote and made the change for what he considered to be better clarity. The point still remains that both sides have textual support for their respective positions. It also is understood, as Dr. George Kilpatrick has noted, that most of these types of textual variants were introduced into the manuscripts by the second century. Therefore, one reading is as likely (textually speaking) as the other. The difference is contextually. It is more truthful to say "the prophets" when citing two prophets. Accordingly, the reading in the Traditional Text is both textually substantial and contextually correct." (Holland, 147-148)

Dr. Holland argues for the validity of the *TR*'s reading in Mark 1:2 based upon the "substantial" nature of the manuscript evidence and the fact that the reading is "contextually correct." It is more accurate to say "the prophets" when citing two prophets than it is to say "Isaiah the prophet." Holland is not the only commentator to have reached this conclusion.

- o John Gill — "As it is written in the prophets ... Malachi and Isaiah; for passages out of both follow; though the Vulgate Latin, Syriac, and Persic versions read, "as it is written in the prophet Isaias"; and so it is in some Greek copies: but the former seems to be the better reading, since two prophets are cited, and Isaiah is the last; to which agree the Arabic and Ethiopic versions, and the greater number of Greek copies." (*John Gill's Exposition of the Bible*)

John Lightfoot in his *A Commentary on the New Testament from the Talmud and Hebraica* uses the exact same textual facts regarding the manuscript evidence from Mark 1:2-3 to make the exact opposite argument from James R. White. Rather than scribes changing the alleged original reading of "Isaiah the prophet" to "written in the prophets" to fix a perceived "error" as White contends, Lightfoot argues the converse. Lightfoot reasons that "written in the prophets" was the original reading based upon both the manuscript evidence and the "congruous" nature of the statement and that Christian Jews altered the text by inserting "in Isaiah the prophet" for "in the prophets" to make the passage conform to their custom.

- "[*As it is written in the prophets.*] Here a doubt is made of the true meaning: namely, whether it be *in the prophets*, or *in Esaias the prophet*. These particulars make for the former:

  When two places are cited out of two prophets, it is far more congruously said, *as it is written in the prophets*; than, *as it is written in Esaias*: but especially when the place first alleged is not in *Esaias*, but in another *prophet*.

  It was very customary among the Jews (to whose custom in this matter it is very probable the apostles conformed themselves in their sermons) to hear many testimonies cited out of many prophets under this form of speech, *as it is written in the prophets*. If one only were cited, if two, if more, this was the most common manner of citing them, *as it is written in the prophets*. But it is without all example, when two testimonies are taken out of two prophets, to name only the last, which is done here, if it were to be read, *as it is written in Esaias the prophet*...

  But what shall we answer to antiquity, and to so many and so great men reading, *as it is written in Esaias the prophet*? "I wonder (saith the very learned Grotius), that any doubt is made of the truth of this writing, when, beside the authority of copies, and Irenaeus so citing it, there is a manifest agreement of the ancient interpreters, the Syriac, the Latin, the Arabic." True, indeed; nor can it be denied that very many of the ancients so read: but the ancients read also, *as it is written in the prophets*. One Arabic copy hath, *in Isaiah the prophet*: but another hath, *in the prophets*. Irenaeus once reads *in Isaiah*: but reads twice, *in the prophets*. And "so we find it written," saith the famous Beza (who yet follows the other reading), "in all our ancient copies except

> two, and that my very ancient one, in which we read, *in Esaias the prophet*."
>
> The whole knot of the question lies in the cause of changing the reading; why, *as it is written in Esaias the prophet*, should be changed into, *as it is written in the prophets*. The cause is manifest, saith that very learned man, namely, because a double testimony is taken out of two prophets. "But there could be no cause (saith he) of changing of them." For if Mark, in his own manuscript, wrote, *as it is written in the prophets*, by what way could this reading at last creep in, *as it is written in Esaias*, when two prophets are manifestly cited?
>
> Reader, will you give leave to an innocent and modest guess? I am apt to suspect that in the copies of the Jewish Christians it was read, *in Isaiah the prophet*; but in those of the Gentile Christians, *in the prophets*: and that the change among the Jews arose from hence, that St. Mark seems to go contrary to a most received canon and custom of the Jews: "He that reads the prophets in the synagogues *let him not skip from one prophet to another*. But in the lesser prophets he may skip; with this provision only, that he skip not backward: that is, not from the latter to the former."
>
> But you see how Mark *skips* here from a prophet of one rank, namely, from a prophet who was one of the twelve, to a prophet of another rank: and you see also how he *skips* backward from Malachi to Isaiah. This, perhaps, was not so pleasing to the Christian Jews, too much Judaizing yet: nor could they well bear that this allegation should be read in their churches so differently from the common use. Hence, *in Isaiah the prophet*, was inserted for *in the prophets*." (Lightfoot)

So once again, we see the so-called experts contradicting each other in the realm of textual criticism. One thing is apparent; the situation with respect to Mark 1:2-3 is not as clear cut as James White leads his readers to believe in *The King James Only Controversy*. What does one do when two "scholars" interpret the exact same data in directly contradictory ways? Remember what we studied in Lesson 2 about Hegelian Dialectic and the tactics of the Adversary. Satan's objective from the beginning was to question and deny what God said with the goal of establishing a competing authority. Placed in this conundrum man would become his own authority as he gets to choose for himself what he believes God said. Who is right, White or Lightfoot?

As we saw in section 1, James R. White buttresses his belief that "Isaiah the prophet" is the correct reading based upon 1st century Jewish citation practices. To support this argument, Professor White appeals to Matthew 27:9-10 as another example of how Jewish scribes handled "conflated" or compound quotations from more than one prophet. The problem here is that White is making an apples to oranges comparison to try and prove his point. Mark 1:2-3 and Matthew 27:9 are not both examples of "conflated" or compound quotations from more than one prophet.

Mark 1:2-3	Matthew 27:9-10
2) As it is written in the prophets, Behold, I send my messenger before thy face, which shall prepare thy way before thee [Comes from Mal. 3:1].	9) Then was fulfilled that which was spoken by Jeremy the prophet, saying, And they took the thirty pieces of silver, the price of him that was valued, whom they of the children of Israel did value;
3) The voice of one crying in the wilderness, Prepare ye the way of the Lord, make his paths straight [Comes from Is. 40:3].	10) And gave them for the potter's field, as the Lord appointed me [The entire quote is from Zech. 11:12-13].

Mark 1:2-3 is a compound quotation to be sure in that its contents can be found in more than one prophet. Meanwhile, Matthew 27:9-10 is certainly not a "conflated" quotation seeing that its contents are only found in Zechariah 11:12-13. The passage that White directs his readers to (Matt. 27:9-10) in order to prove that 1st century Jewish citation practices explain why the Critical Text reading in Mark 1:2-3 is correct does not even exhibit the phenomenon that White is attempting to prove. White cannot even offer one apples to apples comparison within the Biblical text to prove his assertion regarding 1st century Jewish citation practices. Even from an extra Biblical standpoint, White offers no proof that 1st century Jews cited sources in the manner he is asserting. One is just supposed to take his word for it.

Dr. Holland compounds matters further for White when he points out that Mark 1:2-3 is discussing what was "written" by the prophets whereas Matthew 27:9-10 reports what was "spoken" by Jeremiah. Holland rightly points out that "God, the Author of Scripture, is aware of who writes what and who speaks what. Simply because Zechariah writes the passage does not mean Jeremiah did not speak it." In other words, Matthew 27:9 does not assert that Jeremiah *wrote* the words contained in Zechariah 11:12-13 but merely that Jeremiah said or *spoke* something similar. Dr. Holland then directs his readers attention to Zechariah 7:7 where the prophet tells his readers to pay attention to the things spoken by the former prophets (i.e. Jeremiah), "*Should ye* not *hear* the words which the LORD hath cried by the former prophets, when Jerusalem was inhabited and in prosperity, and the cities thereof round about her, when *men* inhabited the south and the plain?"

Textually, the Greek words translated "written" in Mark 1:2-3 and "spoken" in Matthew 27:9 are not the same and carry different meanings. This is true in both the *TR* and the Critical Text. The Greek word translated "written" in Mark 1:2 is *graphō* which means to write and is variously rendered as some form of "write" or "writing" in English. In contrast, the Greek word rendered "spoken" in Matthew 27:9 is the word *rheō* which means to utter audibly and is variously translated: "speak" twelve times, "speak of" three times, and "command" one time. Is James White really saying that there is not a difference between what was "written" down and what was "spoken?" It appears that he is.

In seeking to rescue the Critical Text from a clear mistake in Mark 1:2-3, White engages in a line of unfounded Biblical reasoning and sloppy reading of Biblical texts that he would never accept from anyone else he was debating on any other topic. Yet, explanations such as these are passed off as "scholarly" when they are used to defend the Critical Text and modern versions against the King James Bible and its underlying Greek text. If this does not constitute a double standard, I am not sure what does.

CONCLUSION

I maintain that the reading for Mark 1:2-3 as found in the King James Bible is the correct reading. First, there is ample early and abundant manuscript support for the reading across a host of various types of witnesses i.e., Greek manuscripts, early translations, lectionaries, and patristic citations. Second, the reading "written in the prophets" is contextually consistent with the fact that Mark is quoting from two different prophets, Malachi and Isaiah. Third, I find any arguments based upon unproven 1st century Jewish citations practices to be unconvincing, shabbily argued, and guilty of perpetrating greater damage to the text than what they are supposed to be fixing.

Remember the King James and its underlying text is presumed to be wrong by most modern textual scholars before any discussion of the facts commences. This is done in much the same way that many so-called scientists exclude the possibility of intelligent primary causes before they even begin investigating the question of origins. White conveniently leaves out of his book any discussion of manuscript evidence and/or scholarly opinion that contradicts the position he is advancing. Meanwhile, the Christian public is supposed to view this type of textual criticism as not only helpful but necessary for establishing the correct text.

Here again, as with parallel influence and harmonization, White and his troop are found to be grasping at straws in their attempt to disprove the validity of the *TR* and the KJB. Once again, in the absence of the "originals", how does White know that what the "original wording" of Mark 1:2-3 actually was? On the surface, White's arguments about parallel influence, harmonization, and 1st century Jewish citation practices sound reasonable and scholarly. But under closer inspection, White's reasoning falls apart because the verses he uses to build his argument do not even assert what he is trying to force them to say.

Must one read White, Holland, Gill, and Lightfoot in order to have confidence in the Bible they have before them? Does one need to know about 1st century Jewish citation practices to determine which reading of Mark 1:2 is correct? Are Protestant scholars who claim to believe in *sola scriptura* actually saying that one must consult extra Biblical data to identify scripture?

In the end, my main point from Lesson 10 stands. There are substantive differences in meaning that affect the accuracy of the text between *TR* and the Critical Text and their representative English translations. Determining which text or reading is correct cannot be determined by textual criticism alone without the aid of insight gained from the doctrine of preservation. It is the doctrine of preservation that will assist the Bible student in being able to determine which text/reading is correct, not so-called neutral or natural textual criticism which treats the Bible as though it were any other book. Textual criticism must be guided and reined in by the doctrine of preservation. Once again, this is why a proper grounding in what the Bible says about itself is a mandatory prerequisite to sorting out the textual and translational issues. It is to this task that we will now turn our attention to in Lesson 11 as we begin a detailed study of the doctrine of inspiration.

Lesson 11

UNDERSTANDING THE VARIOUS THEORIES OF INSPIRATION

INTRODUCTION

- In Lessons 6 through 10 we sought to establish an understanding of the following basic terminology: revelation, inspiration, illumination, and preservation. With that accomplished we can now turn our attention to a detailed study of God's written revelation and the process whereby that was accomplished, namely inspiration.

- We saw in Lesson 7 that inspiration is the Bible's claim for itself (II Timothy 3:16, II Peter 1:21). Moreover, we observed that God exercised the same supernatural force to inspire His word that He utilized when He created heaven, earth, and mankind. This understanding of inspiration helps one to understand how the word of God can be "quick and powerful" (Hebrews 4:12-13). God literally breathed His own life into His word just as He did into mankind and all of creation.

- In short, we defined inspiration as the supernatural process whereby God recorded in writing (*graphē*) those aspects of His revelation that He wanted mankind to possess forever (Isaiah 30:8).

- In this lesson we want to begin an exploration of the ideas that various people and theological systems have developed to try to explain what inspiration is and is not. These theories are varied and sundry and they come from theology, which unfortunately is often nothing more than merely human viewpoint.

- Today our objective is to survey the views of inspiration covered by Pastor Richard Jordan in Grace School of the Bible and use the writings of other theologians for elaboration or clarification where needed. These views include the following five:

    o Natural View
    o Dynamic View
    o Partial View or Spiritual-Rule-Only View
    o Existential View
    o Plenary Verbal View

NATURAL VIEW

- The *Natural View* says that the Bible is inspired in the same manner as William Shakespeare's *Romeo and Juliet*, or Homer's *Odyssey*, or Dante's *Inferno*. In other words, the Bible is just a high level of human achievement written by gifted men, but it was not written by God.

- This would be equivalent to the inspiration you felt when writing love notes, poems, and sonnets for your husband or wife when they first struck your fancy.

- Revelation 1:10 — "I was in the Spirit on the Lord's day, and heard behind me a great voice, as of a trumpet,"

    o People that believe the *Natural View* are talking about the Bible being written in the spirit. You are inspired; you are in the spirit. It is just a poetic sort of elevated human spirit.

- II Peter 1:2 1— "For the prophecy came not in old time by the will of man: but holy men of God spake as they were moved by the Holy Ghost."

    o Natural inspiration comes via the will of men and finds its origin in the heart of man. A man's soul may be stirred to write wonderful and sweeping prose, but this is a very different thing from a human being speaking because he is thusly moved by God the Holy Spirit.

- The following are a samplings of what leading Evangelical theologians have said regarding the *Natural View*:

    o Lewis Sperry Chafer — "As there have been exceptional artists, musicians, and poets who have produced masterpieces which have not been excelled, it is contended by the proponent of this theory that there have been exceptional men of spiritual insight who, because of their native gifts, were able to write the Scriptures. This is the lowest notion of inspiration and emphasizes the human authorship over the divine." (Chafer, 70)

    o Charles C. Ryrie — "This view understands the writers of the Bible to be men of great genius who did not need any supernatural help in writing the Bible." (Ryrie, 73)

    o Paul Enns — "This view teaches that there is nothing supernatural about biblical inspiration; the writers of Scripture were simply men of unusual ability who wrote the books of the Bible in the same way that an individual would write any other book today. The writers were men of unusual religious insight, writing on religious subjects in the same way like Shakespeare or Schiller wrote literature." (Enns, 160)

- Charles F. Baker — "This is the lowest concept of inspiration. It places the inspiration of Scripture on the same plane with so-called inspiring writings of the great authors and poets of history. But, as already noted, Biblical inspiration refers to the fact the Scriptures are God-breathed, not that they are inspiring to the reader." (Baker, 38)

DYNAMIC VIEW

- The *Dynamic Viewpoint* says that the content and the concept are important. You hear the word "dynamic" a lot when discussing Bible translations. The dynamic theory says that only the main thought of a particular writing is inspired. In other words, inspiration consists of ideas and thoughts; and it's the central message that is important. The dynamic viewpoint indicates that it is not just words, but what are important are the thoughts, the ideas, the flow, and the meaning behind the words.

- Matthew 24:35 — "Heaven and earth shall pass away, but my words shall not pass away."

    - The problem with the *Dynamic View* is that Christ said, "Heaven and earth shall pass away, but my words shall not pass away." So, it is not just the thoughts and the flow that are important, but it is the words themselves.

- In the coming weeks, as we study the issue of inspiration, you will see that there are times when single letters in words make all the difference in how one understands a passage of Scripture. An entire argument will hang on one letter and one word. This highlights the importance of words themselves in inspiration. With the dynamic viewpoint, it's the idea and the content that are important i.e., just the thoughts and the flow and not the words.

- In Grace School of the Bible, Brother Jordan equates the Dynamic View of inspiration with Neo-Orthodoxy's approach to Scripture.
    - "Neo-orthodoxy tells you that whether Adam was a real historical person or not is not what counts. It is the teaching of the passage that counts. Whether Cain and Abel were real individuals is not important, but it is the supra history – the thing that's above the actual details. It is the thought, the meaning, and the concept that is trying to be conveyed that is important." (Jordan, *MSS 101*-Lesson 2)

- Regarding the *Dynamic View* theologians have written the following:

    - Lewis Sperry Chafer—"This hypothesis attempts to conceive of thoughts apart from words, the theory being that God imparted ideas but left the human author free to express them in his own language. Quite apart from the fact that ideas are not transferable by any other medium than words, this scheme ignores the immeasurable importance of *words* in any message. Even a legal document which men execute over trivial matters may depend wholly upon the words therein." (Chafer, 69)
    - Charles C. Ryrie—"Some are willing to acknowledge that the concepts of the Bible are inspired but not the words. Supposedly this allows for an authoritative conceptual message to have been given but using words that can in some instances be erroneous. The obvious fallacy in this view is this: how are concepts expressed? Through words. Change the words and you have changed the concepts. You cannot separate the two. In order for concepts to be inspired, it is imperative that the words that express them be also." (Ryrie, 74-75)
    - Paul Enns—"This view suggests that only the concepts or ideas of the writers are inspired but not the words. In this view God gave an idea or concept to the writer who then penned the idea in his own words. According to this view there can be errors in Scripture because the choice of words is left to the writer and is not superintended by God."
    - Charles F. Baker—"Proponents of this theory (Concept Inspiration) state that God placed concepts of truth in the minds of the Bible writers but left it to them to give expression to these con-

cepts. If this view were true it would be inconsistent to call the Bible the Word of God, for it would be only the word of man. . . Further, it is questionable whether it is possible to convey a concept apart from words. Concepts become meaningful only as they are framed in words." (Baker, 39)

PARTIAL VIEW OR SPIRITUAL-RULE-ONLY VIEW

- In Grace School of the Bible Pastor Jordan separated the *Partial View* and *Spiritual-Rule-Only View*. Due to their close connection, I have elected to combine the two views and cover them together in one section.

- Partial Inspiration says that only certain parts of the Bible are inspired. This is the Modernist's view, and the Liberal's view. They only accept parts of the Bible. They talk about love and brotherhood, and they reject the part that deals with sin, and righteousness, and judgment.

    o   II Timothy 3:16 — "All scripture *is* given by inspiration of God, . . ."

- This view maintains that the Bible is an infallible rule in terms of faith and practice, matters of religion, ethics, and in matters of spiritual value, but not in its historical and scientific statements.

- In other words, if you want to know about creation, forget about going to the Bible. But if you want to know about ethics or morality it's fine to go to the Bible. As long as it's a spiritual, religious, or ethical question, the Bible has good information. But, if you want anything above that (if you are looking for historical accuracy), forget it! If you are looking for scientific statements, forget it! The Bible said that the sun stood still, but do not worry about that, because that is a way of looking at something back before man had better sense. The *Spiritual-Rule-Only View* maintains that just the ethical and spiritual content of the Bible is important.

- The problem here is that this is not what the Bible claims for itself.

- - John 17:17 — "Sanctify them through thy truth: thy word is truth."
    - The Lord Jesus Christ did not place a limit upon the truthfulness of his word.

  - John 3:12 — "If I have told you earthly things, and ye believe not, how shall ye believe, if I tell you of heavenly things?"
    - If the Bible cannot be trusted in terms of the earthly things it reports then how can it be trusted in terms of the spiritual things that it reports?

- Leading Evangelical theologians have stated the following regarding the *Partial View*.

  - Lewis Sperry Chafer—"According to this conception, inspiration reaches only to doctrinal teachings and precepts, to truths unknowable by the human authors. Thus the objective in all inspiration — to secure inerrant writings — is denied to certain parts of the Bible." (Chafer, 69)
  - Charles C. Ryrie—"Partial inspiration teaches that some portions are, in fact, not inspired at all. Usually the parts that are inspired are those which convey information otherwise unknowable (like the account of Creation or prophecies). Historical portions, on the other hand, which could be known from contemporary documents, do not need to be inspired. The contemporary expression of this view of inspiration teaches that the Bible is inspired in its purpose. That means we can trust the Bible when it tells us about salvation, but we may expect that errors have crept into other parts." (Ryrie, 74)
  - Paul Enns—"The partial inspiration theory teaches that the parts of the Bible related to matters of faith and practice are inspired whereas matters related to history, science, chronology, or other non-faith matters may be in error. In this view God preserves the message of salvation amid other material that may be in error. The partial theory rejects both verbal inspiration (that inspiration extends to the words of Scripture) and plenary inspiration (that inspiration extends to the entirety of Scripture)." (Enns, 161)

- Charles F. Baker — "A certain bishop is purported to have said that he believed the Bible to have been inspired in spots. When asked for the authority for such a statement, he quoted Hebrews 1:1, stating that this meant that God spoke at various times in varying degrees. Thus some spots were fully inspired, others were only partially inspired, and still other not inspired at all. The bishop was embarrassed when a layman asked: "How do you know that Hebrews 1:1, the one Scripture upon which you based your argument, is one of those fully inspired spots? . . . Who is to judge which parts of the Bible are to be accepted as truth? . . . Why should God guide a man to state the truth in one sentence and allow him to state error in the next? If He was able to guide him in the first case, why should He not also guide him at other times?" (Baker, 38-39)

- Charles F. Baker— "Some claim that the spiritual or doctrinal truth in the Bible is inspired but that the historical, geographical and scientific references are not, and are therefore liable to error. . . while inspiration pervades all parts of the Bible, it guarantees only the accurate communication of spiritual truth, and that in matters of historical, geographical, and scientific detail the writers employed only such information which they had at their natural disposal. Which may or may not have been in error." (Baker, 39-41)

EXISTENTIAL VIEW

- The *Existential View* says that the only parts of the Bible that are inspired are the parts that speak to you. A lot of Modernists and Liberals believe this kind of thing.
- Soren Kierkegaard developed what is called Existential Philosophy. He said that only the truth that edifies is truth for thee. In other words, the only time something is really truth is when it speaks to you and builds you up. So, the only parts of the Bible that are really true, and really God's word, and really inspired are the parts that really speak to you on a personal subjective level.
- This view says that when it speaks to you, it is the Bible; and when it does not speak to you, it is not the Bible.

- o Romans 3:4 — "God forbid: yea, let God be true, but every man a liar; as it is written, That thou mightest be justified in thy sayings, and mightest overcome when thou art judged."
    - God is true and that's all there is to it.
- o John 17:17 — "Sanctify them through thy truth: thy word is truth."

PLENARY VERBAL VIEW

- The fifth view of inspiration is the *Plenary Verbal View*, and this is the one that you aright to subscribe to. The word *Plenary* means "all" and the word *Verbal* means "words". The *Plenary Verbal View* of inspiration says that all the words are inspired by God.
- Matthew 24:35 — "Heaven and earth shall pass away, but my words shall not pass away."

    - o What's important is not just the ideas, the content, what it says about spiritual things, or when it speaks to you, but the words themselves are the issue in inspiration – "my words." It is not just the concepts, the message, or the thought, but the fact that the words that I speak to you shall not pass away.
    - o I Corinthians 14:37 — If any man think himself to be a prophet, or spiritual, let him acknowledge that the things that I write unto you are the commandments of the Lord.

- According to Brother Jordan, The *Plenary Verbal View* used to just be referred to as "Verbal Inspiration," but Plenary Verbal is the full title. You will never hear anybody refer to it as Plenary Inspiration, but you will occasionally hear somebody say that they believe in Verbal Inspiration. In time, other views came along, like the *Partial View*, and sought to modify people's understanding of inspiration. As we saw above, The *Partial View* maintains that only some of the words are inspired. So, in order to counteract the *Partial View*, theologians added the word "Verbal" to inspiration. Likewise, the *Existential View*, which maintains that the words are inspired when they speak to you, caused theologians to add the term "Plenary" to their definition of inspiration. Consequently, you will now see inspiration discussed in Systematic Theology books under the full descriptor of "Plenary Verbal Inspiration." So occasionally, especially in older books on the subject, you will encounter someone who just calls it Verbal Inspiration.

- II Timothy 3:16 — the doctrine of inspiration is primarily concerned with the words that were written down, not what happened to the writers themselves. You must remember that the Bible never says that the men were inspired. The Bible always says that what they wrote was inspired. All scripture, (*graphē*, that which is written down), was inspired. It is not the men that were inspired. Now, something happened to the men, "Holy men of God spake as they were moved by the Holy Spirit" (II Peter 1:21 — we will study what happened to them as well), but the issue in inspiration is what is written down on the page, not just what happened to the men.

- All the theological writings we have been surveying in this lesson, along with the addition Norman L. Geisler, adopt the *Plenary Verbal View* as the correct view of inspiration.

    o Lewis Sperry Chafer—"By *verbal* inspiration is meant that, in the original writings, the Spirit guided in the choice of the words used. However, the human authorship was respected to the extent that the writers' characteristics are preserved and their style and vocabulary are employed, but without the intrusion of error.

    By *plenary* inspiration is meant that the accuracy which verbal inspiration secures, is extended to every portion of the Bible so that it is in all its parts infallible as to the truth and final as to divine authority." (Chafer, 71)

    o Paul Enns—"The strongest defense of verbal plenary inspiration of the Scriptures is the testimony of Jesus Christ. He testified to the inspiration of the entire Scriptures, the various books of the Old Testament and the actual words of Scriptures as they had been originally recorded. The fact that He based His arguments on the precise wording of Scriptures testifies to His exalted view of Scripture. In addition, Paul acknowledged that all Scripture is

God-breathed; man was the passive instrument, being guided by God in the writing of Scripture. Peter's statement was similar in emphasizing that, in their passivity, men were carried along by the Holy Spirit in the writing of Scripture. The testimony of each of these witnesses draws attention to the verbal plenary inspiration of Scripture." (Enns, 166)

- o Charles F. Baker—"Verbal means that inspiration extends to the very words which the writers used in the original writings. This does not mean that God dictated the words, but that He so guided men to write in their own language, with their own words, and in their own style that when they had written they had said exactly what God wanted said... Plenary is usually taken to mean that inspiration is full, extending to all parts of the Bible. Paul did not say, "Some Scripture is inspired of God," but ALL Scripture. Since there are no degrees of inspiration, a writing is either inspired of God or it is not inspired." (Baker, 42)

- o Norman L. Geisler—"Numerous passages make it evident that the focus of revelation and inspiration is the written word, the Scriptures (*graphē*), not simply the idea or even the writer... So it wasn't simply God's message that men were free to state in their words; the very choice of the words was from God... Biblical inspiration is not only verbal (located in the words), but it is also plenary, meaning that it *extends to every part of the words and all they teach or imply*. Inspiration does guarantee the truth of all that the Bible teaches, implies, or entails... The inspiration of God, then extends to every part of Scripture, including everything God affirmed (or denied) about any topic. It is inclusive of not only what the Bible teaches explicitly but also with it teaches implicitly, covering not only spiritual matters but factual ones as well." (Geisler, 174-175)

WORKS CITED

Baker, Charles F. *A Dispensational Theology*. Grace Bible College Publications, 1971.

Chafer, Lewis Sperry. *Systematic Theology Vol. I*. Dallas Theological Seminary, 1947.

Enns, Paul. *The Moody Handbook of Theology*. Moody Press, 1989.

Geisler, Norman L. *Systematic Theology: In One Volume*. Bethany House, 2011.

Jordan, Richard. *Manuscript Evidence 101*. Grace School of the Bible.

Ryrie, Charles R. *Basic Theology*. Moody Press, 1999.

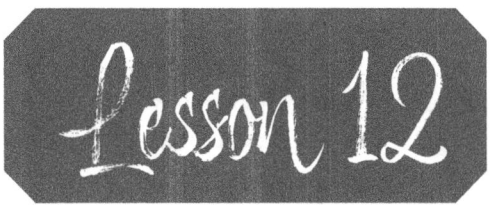

POTENTIAL PITFALLS OF PLENARY INSPIRATION

INTRODUCTION

- In Lesson 11 we began our study of inspiration by looking at the various views posited by theologians over the years to explain the doctrine. In summation these views included:

    o   Natural View
    o   Dynamic View
    o   Partial View or Spiritual-Rule-Only View
    o   Existential View
    o   Plenary Verbal View

- After surveying these views, we determined that the *Plenary Verbal View* is the correct position. The word *Plenary* means "all" and the word *Verbal* means "words". The *Plenary Verbal View* of inspiration says that all of the words are inspired by God.

- Matthew 24:35 — what is important is not just the ideas, the content, what it says about spiritual things, or when it speaks to you, but the words themselves are the issue in inspiration – "my words." It is not just the concepts, the message, or the thought, but the fact that the words that I speak to you shall not pass away.

- We concluded Lesson 11 with the following quotation from Norman L. Geisler's *Systematic Theology in One Volume* regarding *Plenary Verbal* Inspiration.

    o "Numerous passages make it evident that the focus of revelation and inspiration is the written word, the Scriptures (*graphē*), not simply the idea or even the writer. . . So it wasn't simply God's message that men were free to state in their words; the very choice of the words was from God. . . Biblical inspiration is not only verbal (located in the words), but it is also plenary, meaning that it *extends to every part of the words and all they teach or imply*. Inspiration does guarantee the truth of all that the Bible teaches, implies, or entails. . . The inspiration of God, then extends to every part of Scripture, including everything God affirmed (or denied) about any topic. It is inclusive of not only what the Bible teaches explicitly but also what it teaches implicitly, covering not only spiritual matters but factual ones as well." (Geisler, 174-175)

- As the title suggests in the lesson, we want to briefly consider some of the potential pitfalls or practical inconsistencies/misconceptions associated with the *Plenary Verbal* position.

POTENTIAL PITFALLS OF THE PLENARY POSITION

- I believe that the *Plenary Verbal View* is the correct Biblical view of inspiration. That being said there are a few potential pitfalls regarding Plenary Inspiration that we need to be aware of so that we can avoid them.
- We will discuss three potential pitfalls with the following subpoints.

    - The main issue with inspiration is the words on the page not what happened to the human authors.
    - *Plenary Verbal* inspiration is meaningless without Preservation.
    - *Plenary Verbal* on Inspiration but Dynamic on translation.

Words Not the Men

- In Grace School of the Bible, Brother Jordan highlights the first potential pitfall with the *Plenary Verbal View* of inspiration as being an over emphasis on what happened to the writers and not on their writings i.e., what they wrote down. He does this by comparing two different definitions of inspiration from the pens of Kenneth Wuest and W.E. Vine.

    - Wuest—"Inspiration is the act of God the Holy Spirit enabling the Bible writers to write down God-chosen words infallibly." (*Untranslatable Riches from the Greek New Testament*)
        - Regarding Wuest's definition, Brother Jordan stated, "Now, that is a good definition. God chose the words; and they write them down infallibly, which means they are all right, not just some of them but all of them. And it is the words!" (Jordan, MSS 101-Lesson 2)

    - Vine—"Inspiration attaches not only to the thought but to the words by which the thought is expressed. Words are signs with a definite value. Defect in the signs involves defect in the meaning conveyed. Inspiration of the scripture is inspiration of words, and the words themselves must be taken to express its real intention" (*The Divine Inspiration of the Bible*)

- In response to Vine's definition, Brother Jordan said, "Now that is good thinking. Dynamic Inspiration says that words are just signs that represent concepts and thoughts, so what is important is the concept and the thought. But, if you have a sign that does not convey the proper thought, then you will have a defect in communication. So, inspiration has to attach itself, not just to the thought but to the words that are conveyed; because the words are signs by which the thought is expressed, and words have a definite value. A defect in the sign of the word, involves defect in the meaning that is conveyed by the word. So, that is good thinking." (Jordan, MSS 101-Lesson 2)

- After commenting thusly, Brother Jordan prompts his students to note the subtle difference between the two definitions of inspiration presented above. Wuest placed the emphasis on "the act of God the Holy Spirit enabling the Bible writers to write" whereas Vine placed the emphasis on the "words" themselves and not on what happened to the human writers.

- II Timothy 3:16 — once again, the doctrine of inspiration is primarily concerned with the words that were written down, not what happened to the writers themselves. You must remember that the Bible never says that the men were inspired. The Bible always says that what they wrote is inspired. All scripture, (*graphē*, that which is written down), is inspired. It is not the men that are inspired. Now, something happens to the men, "Holy men of God spake as they were moved by the Holy Spirit" (II Peter 1:21 — we will study what happened to them as well), but the issue in inspiration is what is written down on the page, not just what happened to the men.

- In 1840, Swiss Protestant Louis Gaussen wrote *Theopneustia; or, the Plenary Inspiration of the Holy Scriptures* in French (*Théopneustie, Ou, Inspiration Plénière Des Saintes Écritures*). The following year, in 1841, an English version was published in Edinburgh, Scotland. Today, Gaussen's work was reprinted and made available by Kregel Publications in 1971 under the title *The Divine Inspiration of the Bible*.

- Originating in 1840, Gaussen's work sits at theological crossroads within the 19th century. Gaussen was aware of the textual work of Johann Jakob Griesbach from 1774-1775 but predated the discovery of Codex Sinaiticus, by Constantin von Tischendorf in 1844. Consequently, Gaussen's work represents a popular Protestant view of inspiration before the eruption of the following controversies in the latter half of 19th century: 1) Darwinian evolution, 2) German higher criticism, 3) textual theories of Westcott & Hort, and 4) the resulting debates between fundamentalists and modernists.

- Throughout his work Gaussen is clear that the main issue of inspiration is not what happened to the writers but what they wrote down. While examples abound, please consider the following few in summation of Gaussen's view of inspiration:

    o   "Theopneustia (inspiration) is not a system, it is a fact; and this fact, like everything else that has taken place in the history of redemption, is one of the doctrines of our faith. . .

        Meanwhile it is of consequence for us to say, and it is of consequence that it be understood, that this miraculous operation of the Holy Ghost had not the sacred writers themselves for its object — for these were only his instruments, and were soon to pass away; but that its objects were the holy books themselves, where were destined to reveal from age to age, to the Church, the counsels of God, and which were never to pass away." (Gaussen, 24)

    o   "Whether they recite the mysteries of a past more ancient than creation, or those of a future more remote than the coming of the Son of man, or the eternal counsels of the Most High, or the secrets of man's heart, or the deep things of God — whether they describe their emotions, or related what they remember, or repeat contemporary narratives, or copy over genealogy, or mark extract from uninspired documents — their writing is inspired, their narratives are directed from above; it is always God who speaks, who relates, who ordains or reveals by their mouth, and who, in order to do this, employs their personality in different measures: for "the Spirit of God has been upon them," it is written, "and his word has been upon their tongue." And though it be always the word of man, since they are always men who utter it, it is always, too, the word of God, seeing that it is God who superintends, employs, and guides them. They give their narratives, their doctrines, or their commandments, "not with the words of man's wisdom, but with the word taught by the Holy Ghost;" and thus it is that God himself had not only put his seal to all these facts, and constituted himself the author of these commands, and the revealer of all these truths, but that, further, has caused them to be given to his Church in the order, and in the measure, and in the terms which he has deemed most suitable to his heavenly purpose." (Gaussen, 25)

- o "And were we further, called to say at least what the men of God experienced in their bodily organs, in their will, or in their understandings, while engaged in tracing the pages of the sacred book, we should reply, that the powers of inspiration were not felt by all the same degree, and that their experiences were not at all uniform; but we might add, that the knowledge of such a fact bears very little on the interests of our faith, seeing that, as respects that faith, we have to do with the book, and not with the man. It is the book that is inspired, and altogether inspired: to be assured of this ought to satisfy us." (Gaussen, 26)

- o "These assertions (II Peter 1:21 and Psalm 12:6-7), which are themselves testimonies of the Word of God, have already comprised our last definition of Divine Inspiration, and lead us to characterize it, finally, as the inexplicable power which the Divine Spirit put forth of old on the authors of holy Scripture, in order to their guidance even in the employment of words they used, and to preserve them alike from all error and from all omission." (Gaussen, 34)

- Gaussen strongly asserts that the main issue of inspiration was the production of a book and the words contained within it. As we will see in a future lesson, Gaussen also had no problem maintaining a belief that God dictated the words of Scripture to the human authors while at the same time using each man's personality and style in the writing process. It was not until some years later, during their controversy with the Modernists that the notion of Divine Dictation fell out of favor with Fundamentalists and Evangelicals.

- Pastor Jordan offers the following theological definition of inspiration offered by Charles F. Baker in his *A Dispensational Theology* as an example of an inadequate definition of inspiration.

  - o "Theologically it means the supernatural divine superintendency exerted over the writers of the Scripture which guaranteed the accuracy of their writings." (Baker, 37)

- While Pastor Baker believed in the *Plenary Verbal View* (See *A Dispensational Theology* pages 42-45) his definition focuses more on what happened to the writers than on the words they actually wrote down.
- Potential pitfall number one of the *Plenary Verbal View* is to overemphasize what happened to the writers in inspiration instead of focusing on what was written down i.e., the words.

Preservation Secures the Plenary Position

- In Grace School of the Bible, Pastor Jordan explains that while *Plenary Verbal* is the correct view of inspiration, its acceptance is meaningless without also accepting the doctrine of preservation. It is the doctrine of preservation that will help the Bible student identify where the words originally given by inspiration can be found today.
- As we have already seen in this class, Brother Jordan is not alone regarding this conclusion. Many other pastors and theologians have come to similar conclusions. Agreement on every point with the writers quoted below should not be assumed.

  - o Edward F. Hills—"If the doctrine of divine inspiration of the Old and New Testament Scripture is a true doctrine, the doctrine of the providential preservation of the Scriptures must also be a true doctrine. It must be that down through the centuries God has exercised a special providential control over the copying of the Scriptures and the preservation and use of the copies, so that trustworthy representatives of the original text have been available to God's people in every age. God must have done this, for if He gave the Scriptures to His Church by inspiration as the perfect and final revelation of His will, then it is obvious that He would not allow this revelation to disappear or undergo any alteration of its fundamental character.

Although this doctrine of the providential preservation of the Old and New Testament Scriptures has sometimes been misused, nevertheless, it also has been held, either implicitly or explicitly, by all branches of the Christian Church as a necessary consequence of the divine inspiration of these Scriptures. (Hills, 2)

- Hills' point about the implicit belief in preservation is evident in Gaussen's book quoted above even though it is not explicitly stated.
  o Wilbur N. Pickering—". . . if the Scriptures have not been preserved, then the doctrine of Inspiration is a purely academic matter with no relevance for us today. If we do not have the inspired words or do not know precisely which they be, then the doctrine of Inspiration is inapplicable." (Fuller, 269)
  o R.B. Ouellette—"In the Bible, the writers had no problem quoting Scripture that had been preserved up to that time. Peter quotes Isaiah 40 (I Peter 1:23-25); Paul quotes extensively from the Old Testament in Romans 9-11. Each time a New Testament writer quotes from the Old Testament, he is demonstrating that God has been able to preserve His word. Preservation is highly debated today because ultimately, the preservation issue will decide the translation issue — and preservation is completely a matter of faith in God's power." (Ouellette, 33)

- In short, why go through all the trouble arguing for the inspiration of every word (*Verbal*) in all parts of Scripture (*Plenary*) and then fail to protect that doctrine by either ignoring or rejecting preservation? I agree with Pickering, if the Scriptures were not preserved "then the doctrine of Inspiration is a purely academic matter with no relevance for us today." (Fuller, 269)
- Potential pitfall number two is to accept the *Plenary Verbal View* of inspiration but fail to protect it with the doctrine of preservation.

Plenary Verbal on Inspiration but Dynamic on Translation

- A third caution is also offered by Brother Jordan regarding those who would identify themselves as believing in *Plenary Verbal* inspiration, yet at the same time adopt a *Dynamic* approach when it comes to translating God's word.

  o "Plenary Verbal is the right one, but we recognize a basic inadequacy in it, and that is that it does not equip us to also identify where those inspired words are. We will have to do that on our own, and I will show you how to do that.

  Let me explain the danger of the inadequacy. A man believes in Plenary Verbal Inspiration (every word is verbally inspired). There used to be a method of translating used down through the centuries called a Literal Equivalency. Because you believed in Plenary Verbal Inspiration, if you began to translate, what would you translate? You would translate every word. You would try to put the words in the other language, because the words are the issue. But, now we have something that is called Dynamic Equivalent, and that is the basis of the translating methods of the New International Version. That is the first version that has been put out in English in the last few years (it came out in 1976) that has gone over and taken Dynamic Inspiration and applies that method of inspiration to the practice of translating.

  Now, the men that did that believe in Plenary Verbal Inspiration, but when they began to handle the word of God, and when they got into the practice of translating the word of God, they adopted and were affected by Dynamic Inspiration in their translating methods. So, as far as their translating methods are concerned, they abandon the Plenary Verbal viewpoint, professing to hold it, and use Dynamic Inspiration." (Jordan, *MSS 101*- Lesson 2)

- Pitfall number three regarding *Plenary Verbal Inspiration* centers around one who accepts it as the correct view on the Bible's origin, yet functionally denies it when it comes to their philosophy of translation. In short it seems inconsistent to hold to the inspiration of every word only to turn around and advocate for a Dynamic Philosophy of translation.

- Brother Jordan also acknowledges that even the most literal of translations, such as the KJB, must from time to time utilize a *Dynamic* method when doing the work of translating. It is when translators adopt Dynamic Equivalency as their "total method" that the *Plenary Verbal View* of inspiration is undermined.

    o "Consequently, there is a method developed whereby every translator uses Dynamic Equivalency at times. When you read in your King James Bible where it says, "God Forbid", that is a dynamic equivalent. There is no word for "God" in the Greek text. In Greek it would just be, "Oh no!" Well, in our language, "God Forbid" is the same type of strong expletive. It is a dynamic equivalent.

    All translators use Dynamic Equivalency at some time or another in every situation. It especially helps you to get through idiomatic expressions, which is a legitimate thing. But, adopted as a total method, you abandon Plenary Verbal Inspiration. And you teach the next and the next and the next generation not to believe in Plenary Verbal." (Jordan, *MSS 101*-Lesson 2)

WORKS CITED

Baker, Charles F. *A Dispensational Theology*. Grand Rapids, MI: Grace Bible College Publications, 1971.

Fuller, David Otis. *True or False?*. Grand Rapids, MI: Grand Rapids International Publications, 1973.

Gaussen, Louis. *The Divine Inspiration of the Bible.* Grand Rapids, MI: Kregel Publications, 1971.

Geisler, Norman L. *Systematic Theology: In One Volume.* Minneapolis, MN: Bethany House, 2011.

Hills, Edward F. *The King James Version Defended.* Des Moines: IA, Christian Research Press, 1956.

Jordan, Richard. *Manuscript Evidence 101.* Grace School of the Bible.

Ouellette, R.B. *A More Sure Word: Which Bible Can you Trust?* Lancaster, CA: Striving Together Publications, 2008.

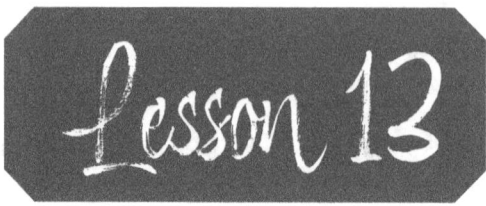

PASSAGES PROVING THE PLENARY POSITION

INTRODUCTION

- In Lesson 12 we sought to identify some of the potential pitfalls of the *Plenary Verbal View* of inspiration. Specifically, we discussed the following potential pitfalls:

    - *Words not the Men*— the main issue with inspiration is the words on the page not what happened to the human authors.
    - *Preservation Secures the Plenary Position*— the correct view of inspiration is meaningless without Preservation.
    - *Plenary Verbal on Inspiration but Dynamic on Translation* — it is inconsistent to hold to the inspiration of every word (*Plenary*

Verbal) only to turn around and advocate for a Dynamic Philosophy of translation.

- In this Lesson we want to consider some Biblical texts that prove the veracity of the *Plenary Verbal View* of inspiration.

PASSAGES PROVING THE PLENARY POSITION

- For this section we will consider the following subpoints.

    o The Bible self-authenticates its own claim of inspiration.
    o Practical examples that the words are the issue in inspiration.

Self-authenticating Nature of Inspiration

- II Timothy 3:16—"All scripture is given by inspiration of God. . ."

    o That is the Bible's claim for itself. That is what the Bible says about itself, and that is the boast that it makes for itself. "*Pas graphē theopneustos*" are the Greek words, and they simply mean "all scripture is inspired of God". "*Pas*" is the word for "all, every."

- Luke 24:44-46 — "And he said unto them, These *are* the words which I spake unto you, while I was yet with you, that all things must be fulfilled, which were written in the law of Moses, and *in* the prophets, and *in* the psalms, concerning me. Then opened he their understanding, that they might understand the scriptures [*graphē*], And said unto them, Thus it is written, and thus it behooved Christ to suffer, and to rise from the dead the third day:"

- o The word translated "scriptures" in verse 45 is the same word translated "scripture" in II Timothy 3:16; *graphē*. The Lord Jesus Christ called all three parts of the Hebrew Bible the Law, the Prophets, and the Psalms (our Old Testament), "Scripture".

The Law (*Torah*)	The Prophets (*Neviim*)	The Psalms (*K'thuvim*)
Genesis	Joshua	Psalms
Exodus	Judges	Proverbs
Leviticus	Samuel	Job
Numbers	Kings	Song of Songs
Deuteronomy	Isaiah	Ruth
	Jeremiah	Lamentations
	Ezekiel	Ecclesiastes
	12 Minor Prophets (1 Book)	Esther
		Daniel
		Ezra-Nehemiah
		Chronicles

- Therefore, our Lord's attitude toward the entire Old Testament was that all of it was scripture and inspired by God.
- I Timothy 5:18—"For the scripture [*graphē*] saith, Thou shalt not muzzle the ox that treadeth out the corn. And, The labourer *is* worthy of his reward."

  - o This verse is comprised of quotations from both the Old and New Testaments.
    - Deuteronomy 25:4—"Thou shalt not muzzle the ox that treadeth out the corn."
    - Matthew 10:10 and Luke 10:7—"The labourer *is* worthy of his reward."

- Now, do you see what Paul did? He quoted a passage out of Deuteronomy, (the words of Moses), and then he quoted a passage out of the Gospels (the words of Christ), and he called them both "scripture." Paul did not make any distinction between them. So, they are both scripture – the Old Testament and the New Testament. When he says "all scripture" he is literally talking about "all" or every part of it.
- II Corinthians 14:37 — "If any man think himself to be a prophet, or spiritual, let him acknowledge that the things that I write unto you are the commandments of the Lord."

    o The things Paul wrote are also the commands of the Lord.

- II Peter 3:15-16— "And account that the longsuffering of our Lord is salvation; even as our beloved brother Paul also according to the wisdom given unto him hath written unto you; 16) As also in all his epistles, speaking in them of these things; in which are some things hard to be understood, which they that are unlearned and unstable wrest, as they do also the other scriptures [*graphē*], unto their own destruction."

    o Peter calls everything Paul wrote in "all his epistles" scripture or *graphē*.

- Notice how in all these verses the Bible self-authenticates its own inspiration. In II Timothy 3 Paul teaches you that all scripture is given by inspiration of God. Then, in Luke 24, the Lord Jesus Christ names the threefold division of the Hebrew Old Testament and calls it scripture. Later, Paul in I Timothy 5 quotes both the Old Testament and Gospels and calls them scripture. Finally, in Corinthians 14, Paul claims that the things he is writing are also the "commandments of the Lord." Finally, in II Peter 3, Peter informs his readers that everything Paul had written was scripture as well. All parts of your Bible, both Old and New Testaments, are *graphē* or that which was written down by God Almighty.
- II Timothy 3:16 — "once again, the Greek word for "scripture" is "*graphē*". Our word "graph" comes from that word. "*Graphē*" means

"to write down, something that is written down". Now it is very important that you get this point. What does the verse say is inspired? Scripture is inspired; the writings are inspired. The thing that is written down on the page is the thing that is inspired. You want to be careful to notice that the verse says that the "writings" are inspired, not the "writers"."

Words not the Men: Practical Examples

- I Kings 13 is a passage that highlights the importance of the words and not what happened to the writers. In I Kings 13, there is a man who prophesies in the name of the Lord, without even foreseeing that he was going to do it. The following passages of scripture contain paraphrases).

    o I Kings 13:1-7 — God tells this young man of God to go down to the king and prophesy against him. He goes down and he does it, and the king reaches out to get him; but when he does, his hand withers up. The man of God prays for the king, and his hand is restored. Then, the king says, you come on down to my house, and I will give you a reward (verse 7).

    o I Kings 13:8-10 — God essentially tells the young man of God, "You go down there and tell them what I have to told you, and then get out of there. Do not eat anything and do not tarry. Do not even come back the same way. Do not get familiar enough with the territory to return the same way that you went." So, the man of God, following the Lord's instructions, goes back a different way and finds himself in Bethel at the end of verse 10.

    o I Kings 13:11-17 — on the way back, there is an old prophet living in Bethel. You know this old prophet had to be a 'compromiser' or God would have used him to start with to go down and rebuke the king. Anyway, this old prophet seeks out the man of God and tells him that he wants to meet and dine with him back at his house (He was an experienced man in the ministry, and he wanted to talk with the young man.). The man of God tells him in verses 16-17; no, I cannot come home with you. God told me not to stay, and not to eat, and not to drink and so forth.

- o I Kings 13:18 — the old prophet just flat out lies to the man of God. He tells the young man that God sent him a further revelation and you are supposed to come home with me.
- o I Kings 13:19 — so the man of God harkens unto the words of the old prophets and goes back with him to his house to eat and drink.
- o I Kings 13:20-22 — the word of the Lord came unto the old prophet to pronounce judgement upon the man of God for not harkening unto the words that God had previously given him.
- o I Kings 13:23-24 — before the man of God got home a lion slew him just as the old prophet had predicted by the word of Lord.

- There are many points of practical application that could be made from this passage. My main reasoning for bringing it up in this Lesson is to point out the following. That old lying prophet in Bethel has the man of God in trouble to start with. Then, suddenly, something happened to him that he was not used to have happening – the Lord came and put a word in his mouth and pronounced judgment on the man of God. That old prophet did not foresee that happening. This is an example of a man that spoke the word of the Lord without foreseeing that he was going to do it. He did not plan it, it just happened.
- This story from I Kings 13 helps to illustrate our main point regarding inspiration; the issue is the words not the instrument.
- John 11 provides a New Testament example of a similar phenomenon.

- o John 11:49-52 — Here Caiaphas prophesied something without even knowing what he was doing when he did it.

- According to the Holy Spirit's commentary in verses 51 and 52, Caiaphas said something that the Holy Spirit says is a prophecy about Christ dying for Israel and for the children of God that were scattered abroad. The rest of the nation is scattered to the four winds of the earth out there. And old Caiaphas never knew what he did. In fact, he probably died never knowing about it. The only way you know what he did is because the Holy Spirit wrote it down in the passage.

- So, there is a man who prophesied something (the passage said he did) but he did not know anything about it. My point to you is that the important issue is the words on the page, not the man.
- I Peter 1:10 — "Of which salvation the prophets have inquired and searched diligently, who prophesied of the grace that should come unto you:"

    o Many of the prophets spoke/wrote things that they did not fully understand.

- Our final example comes from the story of Balaam and Balak recorded in Numbers 22 -25[1].

    o Numbers 22:1-7 — the children of Israel have pitched camp near Moab, and Balak the King sees them, and he knows what they have done to everybody else that got in their way. So, Balak says, "I am going to get me a prophet to come down here and curse these people." So, he sends men to Balaam.

    o Numbers 22:8-12 — Balaam says, "Okay, but I have to pray about it before I go." So he went and prayed and asked the Lord about it, and the Lord said, "Number one, you cannot go. Number two, you cannot curse them because I have already blessed them. The Lord tells him *you cannot go with these guys anyway.*

    o Numbers 22:13— So, Balaam went back the next day and told the men of Moab that he could not go with them. Notice though that Balaam only tells them part of the story. He does not tell them that God forbade him from cursing Israel.

    o Numbers 22:14-19— So, Balak sent the men back to Balaam to offer him more money – "the reward of divination". The men did just that, and Balaam said, "Well, let me go pray about it again."

---

[1] Quotations in the following verses are paraphrased.

FROM THIS GENERATION FOR EVER

- o Numbers 22:20 — the Lord said, "Look Balaam, if the guys come to you in the morning and ask you to go, you can go." That being said, Balaam would still have to speak the word that God gave him.
- o Numbers 22:21 — so, in the morning Balaam woke up and told them that he is ready to go with them. But, that was not what the Lord had said. Balaam just decided to go and so he went.
- o Numbers 22:22-35 — Balaam and his donkey were withstood by the angels of Lord. In verse 35, Balaam is told again that he is allowed to speak only the words that he is given to speak.
- o Numbers 22:36-38 — in verse 38 Balaam tells Balak that he can only speak, "the word that God putteth in my mouth."
- o Numbers 23:1-10 — the next day Balaam double crosses Balak and blesses Israel according to the "word" the Lord put in Balaam's mouth.
- o Numbers 23:11 — Balak gets upset with Balaam for double crossing him. Balak said, "I am paying you wages and I put you up in the Holiday Inn. I am treating you real nice and buying you steaks for supper. But what are you doing? I hired, you to curse them and you are blessing them."
- o Numbers 23:12 — Balaam replies by saying I cannot speak anything other than what "the Lord hath put in my mouth."
- o Numbers 23:13-15 — Balak takes Balaam to a different place and goes through the whole religious charade again. In verse 15, Balaam tells Balak that he is once again going to go consult the Lord.
- o Numbers 23:16-24 — Balaam goes out and blesses Israel according to the "word" that the LORD put in Balaam's mouth. Balaam did not want to bless Israel, he wanted to curse them but every time he opened his mouth out came blessing.
- o Numbers 23:25-30 — now they go to a third spot.
- o Numbers 24:1-9 — Balaam blesses Israel for a third time.
- o Numbers 24:10-13 — after listening to Balaam tell him what will befall his people, Balak has a fit.

- My point in studying these passages with you is two-fold. First, I want you to understand whenever you see the issue of prophecy and this type of inspiration going on, the issue is not the people or the man, but the issue is the words that they are speaking and/or writing down, i.e., the *graphē*.

- II Timothy 3:16 — "All scripture is given by inspiration of God, and is profitable for doctrine, for reproof, for correction, for instruction in righteousness:"

    - o   The English word "inspiration" is a different word. The Greek word is *"theopneustos"* "*Theos*" means "God" and "*pneo*" means "to breathe". When you put those two words together, you have "God-breathed". All scripture is given by inspiration, "*theopneustos*" – God breathed it out. In other words, when it says that all scripture is given by inspiration, it means that God breathed it. What does that mean? It means that the scripture came out of the mouth of God. What do you do when you breathe? It goes in and comes out of your mouth. The scriptures came out of the mouth of God and that means that whatever the scripture says, who said it? Goddid. It came out of God's mouth.

- Psalms 33:6 — "By the word of the LORD were the heavens made; and all the host of them by the breath of his mouth."

    - o   Notice *Natural Revelation* in Psalms 33. Do you remember what Natural Revelation is? Natural Revelation is God's revelation in creation. We went over this in Lesson 6. Natural Revelation was authored in exactly the same way as the Written Revelation is authored.

- Second, in these accounts the various men speak the words that God put/placed in their mouths. In other words, God gave them the exact words He wanted said/written. Consider the following examples from the exchange between Balaam and Balak in Numbers 22-24.

- Numbers 22:38 — "And Balaam said unto Balak, Lo, I am come unto thee: have I now any power at all to say any thing? the word that God putteth in my mouth, that shall I speak."
  - Numbers 23:5— "And the LORD put a word in Balaam's mouth, and said, Return unto Balak, and thus thou shalt speak."
  - Numbers 23:12 — "And he answered and said, Must I not take heed to speak that which the LORD hath put in my mouth?"
  - Numbers 23:16 — "And the LORD met Balaam, and put a word in his mouth, and said, Go again unto Balak, and say thus."

- Verses such as these bring up the question of how inspiration occurred because they seem to imply the notion of dictation. God placed His word into the mouth of Balaam thereby causing Balaam to utter forth only those words that God gave him to speak.
- The notion of Mechanical or Divine Dictation as a descriptor for how *Plenary Verbal Inspiration* was accomplished has fallen on hard times in the past 150 years or so but this was not always the case. In the next Lesson we will begin looking at whether or not dictation was the mechanism by which inspiration was accomplished.

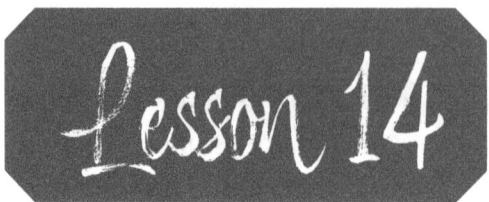

DIVINE DICTATION: THE MECHANISM OF INSPIRATION? PART 1

INTRODUCTION

- In Lesson 13 we looked at passages proving the *Plenary Verbal View* of inspiration. First, we looked at how the Bible self-authenticates its own inspiration. Second, we looked at some passages that demonstrated practically that the issue in inspiration is the words that are written down and not the men.

- - I Kings 13 — is an example of a man that spoke the word of the Lord without foreseeing that he was going to do it. He did not plan it, it just happened.
  - John 11 — Caiaphas said something that the Holy Spirit says is a prophecy and he never knew he did it.
  - Numbers 22-24 — Balaam did not want to bless Israel, he wanted to curse them, but he could only speak the words that God placed in his mouth.

- My goal in considering these passages was two-fold. First, I wanted you to grasp in a practical way that the main issue in inspiration is not the people or the man, but the words that are being spoken and/or written down, i.e., the *graphē*.

- Second, I wanted you to see that various men spoke the words that God put/placed in their mouths. In other words, God gave them the exact words He wanted said/written. Consider the following examples from the exchange between Balaam and Balak in Numbers 22-24:

  - Numbers 22:38 — "And Balaam said unto Balak, Lo, I am come unto thee: have I now any power at all to say any thing? the word that God putteth in my mouth, that shall I speak."
  - Numbers 23:5 — "And the LORD put a word in Balaam's mouth, and said, Return unto Balak, and thus thou shalt speak."
  - Numbers 23:12 — "And he answered and said, Must I not take heed to speak that which the LORD hath put in my mouth?"
  - Numbers 23:16 — "And the LORD met Balaam, and put a word in his mouth, and said, Go again unto Balak, and say thus."

- These verses in Numbers bring up an important question regarding the mechanism by which the inspiration of the words was accomplished. They seem to imply the notion of dictation; God placed His word into the mouth of Balaam thereby causing Balaam to utter forth only those words that God gave him to speak.

- The notion of Mechanical or Divine Dictation as a descriptor for how *Plenary Verbal Inspiration* was accomplished has fallen on hard times in the past 150 years or so but this was not always the case. In this lesson we want to begin a consideration of whether dictation is an appropriate Scriptural descriptor to explain how inspiration was accomplished.

- To accomplish this task, we will first survey what modern theologians have said regarding the notion of dictation. Second, we will consider historic articulations of inspiration before the publication of Darwin's *On the Origin of the Species* in 1859. Last, and most importantly, we will consider the Bible's testimony concerning itself.

DIVINE DICTATION AND MODERN THEOLOGIANS

- Virtually all modern Systematic Theology books discuss the notion of dictation under the heading of false or spurious views of inspiration along with the following: *Natural, Dynamic, Partial,* and *Existential Views* surveyed in Lesson 11. Consequently, the notion of dictation is almost universally rejected as false by modern Evangelical scholarship.

- It is also important to note that discussions of dictation in modern Systematic Theology books ascribe either of the following words to the notion: 1) Mechanical, or 2) Divine. Consequently, the terms Mechanical Dictation or Divine Dictation are synonyms for they are used interchangeably by modern authors.

- For the sake of consistency, we will sample the writings of the same authors cited in Lesson 11 when presenting the various theories of inspiration. We will include each author's terminology in parenthesis after his name.

    o Lewis Sperry Chafer (*Mechanical or Dictation Theory*)—"Had God dictated the Scriptures to men, the style and writing would be uniform. It would be the diction and vocabulary of the divine Author, and free from the idiosyncrasies of men (cf. 2 Pet. 3:15-16). All evidence of interest on the part of the human authors would be wanting (cf. Rom. 9:1-3). It is true that the human authors did not always realize the purpose of their writings. Moses could hardly have known the typical significance latent in the history of Adam, Enoch, Abraham, Isaac, and Joseph, or of the typology of Christ hidden in his description of the tabernacle which he wrote according to the pattern that was showed him in the Mount. . . A message which is dictated is obviously the product of the one who dictates; but if one is left free to write in behalf of another and then it is discovered that, while writing according to his own feelings, style, and vocabulary, he has recorded the precise message of the one in whose behalf he wrote and as perfectly as though it had been dictated by that one, the conviction is engendered that a supernatural accomplishment has been wrought. Under this arrangement, the human author is given full scope for his authorship, yet the exalted message is itself secured. The result is as complete as dictation could make it; but the method, though not lacking in mystery which always accompanies the supernatural, is more in harmony with God's ways of dealing with men in which He uses, rather than annuls, their wills. There is no intimation that God ever dictated any message to a man other than that which Moses transcribed when in Jehovah's presence in the holy Mount. This theory is easily classified as one in which the divine authorship is emphasized almost to the point of exclusion of the human authorship." (Chafer, 68)

- o Paul Enns (*Divine Dictation*)—the dictation view states that God dictated the words of Scripture and the men wrote them down in a passive manner, being mere amanuenses (secretaries) who wrote only the words they were told to write. This claim would render the Bible similar to the Koran which supposedly was dictated in Arabic from heaven. Although some parts of the Bible were given by dictation (cf. Ex. 20:1, "And God spake all these words"), the books of the Bible reveal a distinct contrast in style and vocabulary, suggesting the authors were not mere automatons. The beginning student in Greek will quickly discover the difference in styles between the gospel of John and the gospel of Luke. John wrote in simple style with a limited vocabulary, whereas Luke wrote with an expanded vocabulary and a more sophisticated style. If the dictation theory were true, the style of the books of the Bible should be uniform." (Enns, 161-162)

- o Charles F. Baker (*Mechanical Inspiration*)—"This is the view that the writers of the Bible were merely secretaries to whom God dictated the Bible. Thus it is sometimes referred to as the Dictation Theory of Inspiration. It is true that there are some parts of the Bible that might be classified as dictation, such as those passages which read, "Thus saith the Lord." It would also seem that it was a case of dictation when God spoke the law to Moses in the mount and said to him: "Write thou these words: for after the tenor of these words I have made a covenant with thee and with Israel." (Ex. 34:27)

The major portion of Scripture, however, cannot be classified a dictation. It is evident that the style and vocabulary differ from one writer to the next. Surely when the Apostles wrote letters expressing their feelings in the first person singular, this could not be classified as dictation from God. Hodge says:

> "The church has never held what has been stigmatized as the mechanical theory of inspiration. The sacred writers were not machines. Their self-consciousness was not suspended; nor were their intellectual powers superseded. Holy men spake as they were moved by the Holy Ghost. It was men, not machines; not unconscious instruments, but living, thinking, willing minds, whom the Spirit used as his organs. . . The sacred writers impressed their peculiarities on their several productions as plainly as though they were the subjects of no extraordinary influence." (Baker, 39-40)

- Norman L. Geisler (*Secretary/Musical Instrument*)—"The mode of operation by which the Holy Spirit worked with the authors in order to assure an infallible and inerrant product is a matter of much speculation among theologians. The mystery remains inscrutable, but the process is intelligible and the parameters are definable.

  Two factors define the limits within which legitimate speculation may occur: 1) the product is infallible and inerrant; 2) whatever the means used, different personalities, different styles, and the freedom of the authors manifested in their books must be accounted for.

  The first point is known as the doctrine of Scripture and is supported above by numerous references. The second is known from the data of Scripture, clearly manifested in its human characteristics.

Like illustrations of the Trinity, no analogies of scriptural inspiration are prefect, some are better than others, and still others are misleading. Several fall into the latter category.

In particular, two illustrations would be avoided: that of a secretary and that of a musical instrument. Early church fathers were particularly known to use the latter. The problem with these illustrations is that they lend to the false charge that evangelicals believe in mechanical dictation.

The musical instrument illustration is unhelpful because a musical instrument has no free will, no personality, and no literary style — it is an inanimate object, and not an efficient cause of the notes but only an instrumental cause.

The secretary illustration is not much better, because faithful secretaries take dictation. They are not inanimate or non-free instruments, nevertheless, by the very nature of their occupation, they are not creating the material by merely recording it. The words written are not theirs, nor is their personality expressed. This is not true of Biblical inspiration, which, as we have seen employs freedom, style, vocabulary, and personalities of the various Biblical authors to convey God's Word to humankind.

In his noted Theopneustia, Louis Gaussen (1790-1863) uses the illustration of an orchestra conductor. This is somewhat better, since all members of the orchestra are freely participating and expressing their distinctive sounds while the master brings them together in unity and harmony, as does God with the Scriptures. Even here the analogy breaks down, however, since the whole sound is not really the result of each member playing his own solo. Further, instrumentalists make mistakes, while the Bible does not.

Many evangelicals have been content to rely on the providently pre-planned personalities model, whereby God preplanned the lives, styles, and vocabularies of the various Biblical authors so that they would freely choose to write the correct thing in the right way at the right time, which God, by preordained divine concurrence, has determined would be their part of His Word. While it is no doubt true, even this does not account for the whole story. For one thing, it does not explain how free will fits into the picture. Were the free choices of the various authors causally predetermined? If so, were they really free? Further,

> how could God guarantee that the results would be infallible and inerrant if the authors were free to do otherwise?
>
> While some models are better than others, no matter how good the model is, there always seems to be some mystery left at the very point where there is a divine/human encounter. This is true of the doctrines of predestination and free will as well as the doctrines of how the two natures of Christ relate and the mode of inspiration." (Geisler, Systematic Theology, 178-179)

- As usual, I find Geisler's comments to be the widest ranging and complete. I appreciate the fact that Geisler acknowledges that "no matter how good the model is, there always seems to be some mystery left at the very point where there is a divine/human encounter." This is no doubt true; it is exceedingly difficult to illustrate the supernatural nature of divine inspiration.

- What troubles me is the overall lack of Scriptural support offered by these theologians to justify their positions. To a man, they seem to be more concerned with the freedom of thought, expression, and personality afforded to the human authors than on explaining how they were able to record on paper the very words God wanted written. Apart from some form of dictation, it is difficult to conceive how the standard demanded by the *Plenary Verbal View* of inspiration would have been accomplished. Some of the statements made regarding why dictation is a poor descriptor for how inspiration was accomplished seem very close to arguing for Dynamic Inspiration.

- Moreover, some of the statements quoted above seem to be contrary to the Biblical text itself. For example, Chafer stated, "There is no intimation that God ever dictated any message to a man other than that which Moses transcribed when in Jehovah's presence in the holy Mount" (Baker says something very similar.). All this makes one wonder if Chafer has ever considered the story of Balaam and Balak from Numbers 22-24 (or the other two passages we considered in Lesson 13 in I Kings 13 & John 11) as an example of dictation. Balaam is only allowed to speak the words that God placed in his mouth despite his desired will to do otherwise.

- The quote from Charles Hodge a different person from A.A. Hodge of Warfield and Hodge fame found in Pastor Baker's book is truly puzzling. Hodge stated, "the church has never held what has been stigmatized as the mechanical theory of inspiration." First of all, if one reads between the lines, Hodge reveals that his thoughts on "the mechanical theory of inspiration" are a response to how inspiration had been "stigmatized." This speaks to one of my fundamental contentions, Fundamentalist and Evangelical views on inspiration changed as a result of the controversies with evolutionists, German higher critics, and Modernists in the late 19th and early 20th century. Hodge, writing in 1872, reflects the stigmatism that had been placed upon the notion of dictation by theological liberals during the second half of the 19th century. This stigmatism did not exist thirty years earlier in 1840 when Louis Gaussen wrote *The Divine Inspiration of the Bible* and used the word "dictation" liberally throughout to describe the mechanism by which Plenary inspiration was accomplished (more on Gaussen in Lesson 15).

- Secondly, I find Hodge's statement quoted in the previous point to be a bit misleading. Hodge leaves his readers with the impression that at no point throughout church history was the "mechanical theory of inspiration" ever articulated. Meanwhile, Geisler correctly conveys the fact that the church fathers did use the imagery of a musical instrument to describe how inspiration was accomplished.

- In the next section we will turn our attention to historical articulations of inspiration before the publication of Charles Darwin's *On the Origin of the Species* in 1859.

HISTORIC ARTICULATIONS OF INSPIRATION

- The words "dictate", "dictation", or "*dictare*" in Latin have a long history of being associated with the inspiration of God's word. Please recall from above that Geisler objected to the imagery of a *secretary* or *musical instrument* as illustrations of inspiration because they "lend to the false charge that evangelicals believe in mechanical dictation." In this section we will consider the testimony as to the usage of this imagery for inspiration from the following three eras of church history:

- The Pre-Reformation Fathers
- The Reformers
- Post-Reformation Theologians

Testimony of the Pre-Reformation Fathers

- From very early in church history, the imagery of a musical instrument was used to illustrate how inspiration was accomplished. Please consider the following examples.

    - Justin Martyr (c. 160 AD)—". . . Rather, they presented themselves in a pure manner to the energy of the Divine Spirit, so that the divine plectrum itself could descend from heaven and use those righteous men as an instrument like a harp or lyre. Thereby, the Divine Spirit could reveal to us the knowledge of things divine and heavenly." (Cataloged in Bercot, 601-602)
    - Athenagoras (c. 175 AD)—"We have the prophets as witnesses of the things we comprehend and believe. These were men who declared things about God and the things of God. They were guided by the Spirit of God. . . It would be irrational for us to disbelieve the Spirit from God and to give heed to the mere human opinions. For He moved the mouths of the prophets like musical instruments." (Cataloged in Bercot, 602)
    - Athenagoras (c. 175 AD)—"Prophets were lifted in ecstasy above the natural operations of their minds by the impulses of the Divine Spirit, and they spoke the things with which they were inspired. The Spirit operated through them just as a flute player breaths into a flute." (Cataloged in Bercot, 602)
    - Hippolytus (c. 200 AD)—"These fathers were furnished with the Spirit and they were largely honored by the Word Himself. They were similar to instruments of music. For they had the Word always in union with them, like a plectrum (the small implement by which a lyre was plucked). When moved by Him, the prophets spoke what God willed. For they did not speak of their own

power. Let there be no mistake about that. Nor did they speak the things which pleased themselves." (Cataloged in Bercot, 602)

  o Eusebius quoting Caius (c. 215 AD)—"For this reason, (the heretics) have boldly laid their hands upon the divine Scriptures, alleging that they have corrected them. . . and as to the great audacity implied in this offense, it is not likely that even they themselves can be ignorant. For either they do not believe that the divine Scriptures were dictated by the Holy Spirit (and are thus infidels), or else they think that they themselves are wiser than the Holy Spirit (which makes them demoniacs)." (Cataloged by Bercot, 602-603)

  o Augustine of Hippo (c. 354-430 AD)—"When they write what He has taught and said, it should not be asserted that He did not write it, since the members only put down what they had come to know at the dictation (*dictis*) of the Head. Therefore, whatever He wanted us to read concerning His words and deeds, He commanded His disciples, His hands to write. Hence, one cannot but receive what he reads in the Gospels, though written by the disciples, as though it were written by the very hand of the Lord himself." (quoted by Geisler, *Systematic Theology*, 217)

- Robert D. Preus is the author of Chapter 12, "The View of the Bible Held by the Church: The Early Church Through Luther" found in the book *Inerrancy* edited by Norman L. Geisler. According to Preus, Augustine used the terms inspire and dictate interchangeably in a large variety of contexts. (Geisler, *Inerrancy*, 364)

  o Thomas Aquinas (c. 1125-1274)—"Prophecy is a type of knowledge impressed on the prophet's intellect from a divine revelation; this happens after the manner of education. Now the truth of knowledge is the same in both the student and the teachers since the student's knowledge is a likeness of the teacher's knowledge." (Aquinas, *Summa Theologica*)

- Geisler offers the following commentary on this quotation from Aquinas, "Unlike the mechanical illustration used by many of his predecessors (such as God playing on a musical instrument), Aquinas provided new insight into the process of inspiration. Just as a teacher activates the potential of the student for knowledge, so God (the Primary Cause) activates the potential of man (the secondary cause) to know what He desires to reveal to him. Thus, the prophet is not a puppet or even a secretary but a human learner. And, like a human teacher, God only activates in the prophet what he has the potentiality to receive in terms of his own capacities, culture, language, and literary forms." (Geisler, *Systematic Theology*, 219)

- The nuanced articulation of inspiration offered by Aquinas notwithstanding, there is ample evidence that the Church Fathers, from very early in church history and stretching through the Medieval Period, conceived of dictation as being the primary means by which inspiration was accomplished.

WORKS CITED

Aquinas, Thomas. *Summa Theologica*.

Baker, Charles F. *A Dispensational Theology*. Grand Rapids, MI: Grace Bible College Publications, 1971.

Bercot, David W. *Dictionary of Early Christian Beliefs*. Peabody, MS: Hendrickson Publishers, 1998.

Chafer, Lewis Sperry. *Systematic Theology Vol. I*. Dallas, TX: Dallas Theological Seminary, 1947.

Enns, Paul. *The Moody Handbook of Theology*. Chicago, IL: Moody Press, 1989.

Geisler, Norman L. *Inerrancy*. Grand Rapids, MI: Zondervan, 1980.

Geisler, Norman L. *Systematic Theology: In One Volume*. Minneapolis, MN: Bethany House, 2011.

Lesson 15

DIVINE DICTATION: THE MECHANISM OF INSPIRATION? PART 2

INTRODUCTION

- During Lesson 14 we began looking at the topic of whether or not Divine Dictation is an appropriate descriptor for how *Plenary Verbal Inspiration* i.e., the inspiration of every word, was accomplished.
- The following four verses from the book of Numbers (also see Lesson 13) were used as the jumping off point to begin this discussion.

- - Numbers 22:38 — "And Balaam said unto Balak, Lo, I am come unto thee: have I now any power at all to say any thing? the word that God putteth in my mouth, that shall I speak."
  - Numbers 23:5— "And the LORD put a word in Balaam's mouth, and said, Return unto Balak, and thus thou shalt speak."
  - Numbers 23:12 — "And he answered and said, Must I not take heed to speak that which the LORD hath put in my mouth?"
  - Numbers 23:16 — "And the LORD met Balaam, and put a word in his mouth, and said, Go again unto Balak, and say thus."

- These verses in Numbers seem to imply the notion of dictation; God placed His word into the mouth of Balaam thereby causing Balaam to utter forth only those words that God gave him to speak.
- The notion of Mechanical or Divine Dictation as a descriptor for how *Plenary Verbal Inspiration* was accomplished has fallen on hard times in the past 150 years or so but this was not always the case. In this lesson we want to continue our consideration of whether or not dictation is an appropriate Scriptural descriptor to explain how inspiration was accomplished.
- In order to accomplish this task, I outlined the following three points for our consideration in Lesson 14: first, survey what modern theologians have said regarding the notion of dictation; second, consider historic articulations of inspiration before the publication of Darwin's *On the Origin of the Species* in 1859; last, and most importantly, we will consider the Bible's testimony concerning itself.
- In Lesson 14 we accomplished our first objective by surveying what modern theologians have said about the notion of dictation in their Systematic Theology books. Time, however, would not allow us to conclude our consideration of the historical articulations of inspiration before the publication of *On the Origin of the Species* in 1859. Please recall that I had broken point two up into the following time periods:

  - The Pre-Reformation Fathers
  - The Reformers
  - Post-Reformation Theologians

- During Lesson 14 we only had time to consider the writings of the Pre-Reformation Fathers. In doing so, we saw that the words "dictate", "dictation", or *"dictare"* in Latin have a long history of being associated with the inspiration of God's word. Please see Lesson 14 for the pertinanet citations from the Pre-Reformation Fathers.

- Robert D. Preus is the author of Chapter 12, "The View of the Bible Held by the Church: The Early Church Through Luther" found in the book *Inerrancy* edited by Norman L. Geisler. According to Preus, Augustine used the terms 'inspire' and 'dictate' interchangeably in a large variety of contexts. (Geisler, *Inerrancy*, 364)

- There is ample evidence that the Pre-Reformation Fathers, from very early in church history and stretching through the Medieval Period, conceived of dictation as being the primary means by which inspiration was accomplished.

- We will now turn our attention to finishing our consideration of historic articulations of inspiration by looking at our final two time periods: 1) the Reformers and 2) Post-Reformation Theologians.

HISTORIC ARTICULATIONS OF INSPIRATION CONTINUED

Testimony of the Reformers

- The arrival of the Reformation may have changed a lot of things, but an explanation of how inspiration was accomplished was not one of them. Explicit as well as implicit examples of dictation being used as a descriptor for inspiration abound in the writings of the Reformers.

    o Martin Luther (1483-1546)—"He is called a prophet who has received his understanding directly from God without further intervention, into whose mouth the Holy Ghost has given the words.

> > For He (the Spirit) is the source, and they have no other authority than God... Here (2 Sam. 23:2, "The Spirit of the Lord spake to me, and His word was in my tongue") it becomes too marvelous and soars too high for me..." (Geisler, *Systematic Theology*, 223)
> > - "The Holy Scriptures are the Word of God, written and (I might say) lettered and formed in letters, just as Christ is the eternal Word of God veiled in human nature." (Quoted in Geisler, *Inerrancy*, 377)
> > - "The very order of the words found in Scripture are intentionally arranged by the Holy Spirit. Thus, not merely the phrases and expression in Scripture are divine but their very words and their arrangements." (Quoted in Geisler, *Inerrancy*, 377-378)
> > - "The prophets do not set forth statements that they have spun up in their own mind. What they have heard from God Himself... they proclaim and set forth." (Quoted in Geisler, *Inerrancy*, 378)

- While Martin Luther did not explicitly use the word dictation, the concept is present in his thinking when he uttered statements like: "The very order of the words found in Scripture are intentionally arranged by the Holy Spirit. Thus, not merely the phrases and expression in Scripture are divine but their very words and their arrangements."

> > - John Calvin (1509-1564)—"He commanded also that the prophecies be committed to writing and be accounted part of His Word. To these at the same time histories were added, also the labour of the prophets, but composed under the Holy Spirit's dictation... Yet they were not to do this except from the Lord, that is, with Christ's Spirit going before them and in a sense dictating their words...They were sure and genuine penmen of the Holy Spirit, and their writings are therefore to be considered oracles of God..." (*Institutes of the Christian Religion* IV.viii.8f;cf.I.vi.2)
> > - "In order to uphold the authority of Scripture, he (Paul) declares it to be divinely inspired: for if it be so, it is beyond all controversy that man should receive it with reverence... Whoever then wishes to profit in the Scriptures, let him first of all lay down as a settled point this — that the law and the prophecies are not teaching (*doctrinam*) delivered by the will of man, but dictated (*dictatum*) by the Holy Ghost... Moses and the prophets did not utter at random

what we have from their hand, but, since they spoke by divine impulse, they confidently and fearlessly testified as was actually the case, that it was the mouth of the Lord that spoke...We owe to the Scripture the same reverence which we owe to God, because it proceeded from Him alone." (*Calvin, Commentary on II Timothy*)

- It should be noted that John Calvin as a principal disciple of Augustine, followed him in using the terms dictation and inspiration interchangeably. Modern theologians have spilled much ink trying to convince modern readers that Calvin did not mean what he clearly appears to be teaching.

Testimony of Post-Reformation Theologians

- Johnathan Edwards (1703-1758)—"God had designed the meaning which the penman never thought of, which he makes appear these ways: by his own interpretation, and by his directing the penman to such a phrase and manner of speaking, that has a much more exact agreement and consonancy with the thing remotely pointed to, than with the thing meant by the penman." (Quoted in Geisler, *Inerrancy*, 405)

- Moses, then, was so intimately conversant with God and so continually under the divine conduct, it cannot be thought that when he wrote the history of the creation and the fall of man, and the history of the church from the creation, that he should not be under the divine direction in such an affair. Doubtless he wrote by God's direction, as we are informed that he wrote the law and the history of the Israelitish church." (Quoted in Geisler, *Inerrancy*, 405)

- "Ministers are not to make those things that seem right to their own reason a rule in their interpreting a revelation, but the revelation is to be the rule of its own interpretation; i.e., the way that they must interpret Scripture is not to compare the dictates of the Spirit of God in his revelation with what their own reason says, and then to force such an interpretation as shall be agreeable to those dictates, but they must interpret the dictates of the Spirit of God by comparing them with other dictates of Scripture.

>>> (Minkema & Bailey, *Reason, Revelation and Preaching: An Unpublished Ordination Sermon by Jonathan Edwards*, 27.)

- o Noah Webster (1785-1843)—in his famous Dictionary published in 1828, Webster defined the verb "dictate" as: "1) To tell with authority; to deliver, as an order, command, or direction; as, what God has dictated, it is our duty to believe; 2) To order or instruct what is to be said or written; as, a general dictates orders to his troops; 3) To suggest; to admonish; to direct by impulse on the mind. We say, the spirit of God dictated the messages of the prophets to Israel. Conscience often dictates to men the rules by which they are to govern their conduct."

- In seeking to define the word "dictate," Webster attached to the process whereby the spirit of God delivered "the messages of the prophets to Israel" to the English definition. This very fact speaks to widespread use of the word in this fashion before the controversies of the latter half of the 19th century.

  - o Louis Gaussen (1840)—uses the term "dictation" at least 23 times in the first four chapters of his classic book *Theopneustia (The Divine Inspiration of the Bible)* to describe the process by which inspiration was accomplished. Please consider the following sampling:
    - "Well, then, so it is with the Bible. It is not, as some will have it, a book which God employed men, whom he had previously enlightened, to write under his auspices. No — it is a book which he dictated to them; it is the word of God; the Spirit of the Lord spake by its authors, and His words were upon their tongues." (Guassen, 49)
    - "Is it possible that a book at once so sublime and so simple can be the word of man? was asked of the philosophers of the last century by one who was himself too celebrated a philosopher. And all its pages have replied, No — it is impossible; for every where, traversing so many ages, and whichever it be of God — employed writers that hold the pen, king or shepherd, scribe or fisherman, priest or publican, you every where perceive that one same Author, at a thousand years' interval, and that one same eternal Spirit, has conceived and dictated all." (Gaussen, 57)

- "It ought already to be fully acknowledged, that all that part of Scriptures at least called PROPHECY, whatever it be, has been completely dictated by God; so that the words as well as the thought have been given by him." Gaussen, 67)

- "These psalms were to such a degree all dictated by the Holy Ghost, that the Jews, and the Lord Jesus Christ himself, called them by the name of THE LAW; all their utterances had the force of law; their smallest words were from God. . . The whole Old Testament then is, in a scriptural sense of the expression, a WRITTEN PROPHECY. It is plenarily inspired therefore by God. . ." (Gaussen, 71)

- "His wish (Paul's) is, that every one of them, if he have really received the Holy Ghost, should employ the gifts he has received in acknowledging that the things that he wrote unto them were the commandments of the Lord; and so fully convinced is he that what he writes is dictated by inspiration of God, that, after having dictated ORDERS to the churches. . ." (Gaussen, 81)

- "All these sacred books, without exception are the word of the Lord. ALL SCRIPTURE says St. Paul, is INSPIRED BY GOD. . . in the apostle's idea, all without exception, in each and all of the books of the Scriptures, is dictated by the Spirit of God." (Gaussen, 127)

- "And just as we believe, because it tells us so, that Jesus Christ is God, and that He became man; so also we believe that the Holy Ghost is God, and that He dictated the whole of the Scriptures." (Gaussen, 139)

- "If it was God himself that dictated the letter of the sacred oracles, that is a fact past recall; and no more can the copies made of them, than the translations given to us of them, undo that first act." (Gaussen, 165)

  o So, we see from these quotes that Gaussen used the terms "plenary" and "dictation" interchangeably when referring to inspiration. In addition to using the term "dictation," Gaussen employs the musical instrument imagery utilized by the early church as well as frequently noting the numerous passages in the Old Testament where God placed his words upon the tongue of the prophet as illustrations for how inspiration was accomplished.

- Lastly, regarding Gaussen, he has no problem with using the terminology "dictation" while at the same time making allowances for the variety in personality and literary style exhibited by the human authors (interested parties are encouraged to read the whole of Chapter 1 Part V on the "Individuality of Sacred Writers").
  - "The individuality of the sacred writers, so profoundly stamped on the books they have respectively written, seems to many impossible to be reconciled with a plenary inspiration. No one, say they, can read the Scriptures without being struck with the differences in language, conception, and style, discernible in their authors; so that even were the titles of the several books to give us no intimation that we were passing from one to another, still we should almost instantly discover from the change of their character, that we had no longer to do with the same writer, but that a new personage had taken the pen. Who could read the writings of Isaiah and Ezekiel, of Amos and Hosea, of Zephaniah and Habakkuk, of Jeremiah, and Daniel and proceed to the study of Paul and Peter, or of John, without observing, with respect to each of them, how much his view of the truth, his reasoning, and his language, have been influenced by his bias, his condition in life, his genius, his education, his recollections — all circumstances, in short that have acted upon his outer and inner man?" (Gaussen, 38)
- Charles Hodge (1872)—"The church has never held what has been stigmatized as the mechanical theory of inspiration. The sacred writers were not machines. Their self-consciousness was not suspended; nor were their intellectual powers superseded. Holy men spake as they were moved by the Holy Ghost. It was men, not machines; not unconscious instruments, but living, thinking, willing minds, whom the Spirit used as His organs. . . The sacred writers impressed their peculiarities on their several productions as plainly as though they were the subjects of no extraordinary influence." (Hodge, 156-157)
- B.B. Warfield & A.A. Hodge (1881)—coauthored an article for the April, 1881 issue of *The Presbyterian Review* titled "Inspiration" in which they stated the following, in part, regarding inspiration.
  - "The human agency, both in the histories out of which the Scriptures sprang, and in their immediate composition and inscription, is everywhere apparent, and gives substance and form to the entire collection of writings. It is not merely in

the matter of verbal expression or literary composition that the personal idiosyncrasies of each author are freely manifested by the untrammelled play of all his faculties, but the very substance of what they write is evidently for the most part the product of their own mental and spiritual activities. This is true except in that comparatively small element of the whole body of sacred writing, in which the human authors simply report the word of God objectively communicated, or as in some of the prophecies they wrote by Divine dictation. As the general characteristic of all their work, each writer was put to that special part of the general work for which he alone was adapted by his original endowments, education, special information, and providential position. Each drew from the stores of his own original information, from the contributions of other men, and from all other natural sources. Each sought knowledge, like all other authors, from the use of his own natural faculties of thought and feeling, of intuition and of logical inference, of memory and imagination, and of religious experience. Each gave evidence of his own special limitations of knowledge and mental power and of his personal defects, as well as of his powers. Each wrote upon a definite occasion, under special historically grouped circumstances, from his own stand-point in the progressively unfolded plan of redemption, and each made his own special contribution to the fabric of God's Word." (Warfield & Hodge, 225-260)

- "We believe that the great majority of those who object to the affirmation that Inspiration is verbal, are impelled thereto by a feeling, more or less definite, that the phrase implies that Inspiration is, in its essence, a process of verbal dictation, or that, at least in some way, the revelation of the thought, or the inspiration of the writer, was by means of the control which God exercised over His words. And there is the more excuse for this misapprehension because of the extremely mechanical conceptions of Inspiration maintained by many former advocates of the use of this term "verbal." This view, however, we repudiate as earnestly as any of those who object to the language in question. At the present time the advocates of the strictest doctrine of Inspiration, in insisting that it is verbal, do not mean that in any way the thoughts were inspired by means of the words, but simply that the divine superintendence, which we call Inspiration, extended to the verbal expression of the thoughts of the sacred writers, as well as to the thoughts themselves, and that, hence, the Bible considered as a record, an utterance in words of a divine revelation, is the Word of God to us. Hence, in all the affirmations of Scripture of every kind, there is no more error in the words of the original autographs than in the thoughts they were chosen to express. The thoughts and words are both alike human, and, therefore, subject to human limitations, but the divine superintendence and guarantee extends to the one as much as the other." (Warfield & Hodge, 225-260)

- In 1948, some 27 years after his death in 1921, Warfield's *The Inspiration and Authority of the Bible* was published posthumously. Henry Krabbendam summarizes Warfield's teaching on inspiration in an essay titled "B.B. Warfield vs. G.C. Berkouwer on Scripture" for Geisler's 1980 publication *Inerrancy* (see Chapter 14). Krabbendam summarizes Warfield's position as follows:

    o   "Since Warfield characterized Scripture as being not so much a human product breathed into by the Spirit as a divine product breathed out by God through the instrumentality of human authors, the question becomes pressing as to how he envisioned the relationship of the divine and the human with regard to Scripture. . . Warfield rejects the so-called mechanical theory of Scripture production, in which inspiration is conceived as dictation and the human writers regarded as implements rather than instruments and as pens rather than penmen. He marshals several arguments against the mechanical theory by showing that Scripture is fully man's word. First, he points to the numerous times the New Testament refers to Scripture in terms of its human authors (e.g., Matt. 22:24; Mark 12:19; John 12:39; Rom. 11:9). Second, he points out that passages of the Old Testament are quoted in the New Testament as being spoken by men, even if these men were "in the Spirit" (see Mark 12:36). Third he emphasizes the obvious marks of human authorship, such as peculiarities and differences in vocabulary and style.

    Although Warfield rejects the dictation theory, he is just as critical of the opposite extreme, which in his position is the more common error, namely the exclusion of the divine factor from the origin and nature of Scripture. While Scripture is fully man's word, it is not a purely human book.

In rejecting both extremes — Scripture as a purely divine or as a purely human book — Warfield does not opt for the solution of its being partly divine and partly human. The Bible is not divided between two factors that are mutually exclusive, so that the one limits the other and the entrance of the one spells the exit of the other. No, the evidence that shows that Scriptures both as the Word of God and the word of man leads to the conclusion that the Bible is simultaneously the divine utterance of God and the product of man's effort Warfield writes:

> The human and divine factors in inspiration are conceived as flowing confluently and harmoniously to the production of a common product. Over every word of Scriptures is it to be affirmed, in turn, that it is God's word and that it is man's word. All the qualities and divinity and humanity are to be sought and found in every portion and element of the Scripture. While, on the other hand, no quality inconsistent with either divinity or humanity can be found in any portion or element of Scripture.

The concept, in which the Bible is regarded as both a human product in every part and every word and a divine product to the smallest detail, Warfield calls *concursus*. Both the divine and the human elements form the inseparable constituents of one simple uncompounded product in which the human coloration and variety, as well as the divine perfection and infallibility, are acknowledged. Thus Warfield holds that, according to the Word of God and the doctrine of the church;

> By special, supernatural, extraordinary, influence of the Holy Ghost, the sacred writers have been guided in their writing in such a way, as while their humanity was not superseded, it was yet so dominated that their words became at the same time the words of God, and thus, in every case and all alike, absolutely infallible.

> Warfield emphasizes that the concept of *concursus* is not unique to the relationship of the divine and the human factors with regard to the origin and nature of Scripture. He points out that the same relationship obtained with regard to the act of faith as both a work of God and an activity of man.
>
> It must be evident by now that Warfield holds to the plenary verbal inspiration of the Scriptures as the Word of God, and that by virtue of that inspiration they are fully true, fully authoritative, fully infallible, and fully inerrant." (Geisler, *Inerrancy,* 426-428)

- There can be no doubt that the understanding of inspiration had changed since the mid-19th century.

CONCLUSION

- The careers of Charles Hodge, A.A. Hodge, and B.B Warfield transpired during a time of great doctrinal controversy especially as it related to the origin and authority of the Bible. Even the Wikipedia entry for Warfield acknowledges this point when it states,

  o "Much of Warfield's work centered upon the Bible's "inspiration" by God — that while the authors of the Bible were men, the ultimate author was God himself. The growing influence of modernist theology denied that the Bible was inspired, and alternative theories of the origin of the Christian faith were being explored." (Wikipedia)

- During the thirty years between the publication of Gaussen's *Divine Inspiration* in 1840 and Charles Hodges' *Systematical Theology* in 1871 the theological landscape had changed drastically. The intervening thirty years saw the publication of *On the Origin of the Species* by Charles Darwin, the growth and influence of German Higher Criticism, and the resulting theological liberalism of the Modernists.

In response to the controversy, these men and their contemporaries altered many Protestant doctrines in an attempt to answer their critics. The doctrine of inspiration is one such example.

- It has only been in the last 150 years or so that the notion of Divine Dictation has fallen out of favor among professional theologians. For most of the history of the dispensation of grace, Christian thinkers, theologians, and philosophers had no problem with viewing dictation as the means by which inspiration was accomplished.

- The final arbiter in this debate, as with all theological debates, should be "what saith the Scriptures?" We will turn our attention to this in the next lesson.

WORKS CITED

Bercot, David W. *Dictionary of Early Christian Beliefs*. Peabody, MS: Hendrickson Publishers, 1998.

Calvin, John. *Institutes of the Christian Religion IV*. http://www.Biblestudytools.com/history/calvin-institutes-christianity/book4/.

Calvin, John. *Commentary on II Timothy*. http://www.studylight.org/commentaries/cal/view.cgi?bk=54.

Gaussen, Louis. *The Divine Inspiration of the Bible*. Grand Rapids, MI: Kregel Publications, 1971.

Geisler, Norman L. *Inerrancy*. Grand Rapids, MI: Zondervan, 1980.

Geisler, Norman L. *Systematic Theology: In One Volume*. Minneapolis, MN: Bethany House, 2011.

Hodge, Charles. *Systematic Theology Volume I*. http://www.ntslibrary.com/PDF%20Books%20II/Hodge%20-%20Systematic%20Theology%20I.pdf.

Hodge, A.A. & Benjamin Warfield. "Inspiration" in *The Presbyterian Review* 6 (April 1881), pp. 225-60.

Minkema, Kenneth J. & Richard A. Bailey, eds., "Reason, Revelation and Preaching: An Unpublished Ordination Sermon by Jonathan Edwards," *The Southern Baptist Journal of Theology* 3/2 (1999) 27.

Lesson 16

DIVINE DICTATION: THE MECHANISM OF INSPIRATION? PART 3

INTRODUCTION

- In Lesson 15, we concluded our consideration of the historical articulations of inspiration before the publication of *On the Origin of the Species* in 1859. In doing so, we concluded that, before the controversies of the latter half of the 19th century, dictation or the imagery of a musician playing an instrument was a perfectly acceptable way of explaining the mechanism by which *Plenary Verbal Inspiration* was accomplished.

- Therefore, having concluded our investigation of the first two points on this topic we are now ready to look at the third. In Lesson 14, I told you that we were going to study the following three points regarding Divine Dictation:

- o Study what modern theologians have said regarding the notion of dictation (Lesson 14).
- o Consider historic articulations of inspiration before the publication of Darwin's *On the Origin of the Species* in 1859 under the following three categories.
  - The Pre-Reformation Fathers (Lesson 14)
  - The Reformers (Lesson 15)
  - Post-Reformation Theologians (Lesson 15)
- o Consider the Bible's testimony concerning itself. (Lessons 16 & 17)

- In this lesson we will begin our consideration of the third and final point regarding Divine Dictation i.e., the Bible's testimony concerning itself. As I said at the end of Lesson 14, the Bible is to be our final arbiter in answering this question. The fact that a host of Christian theologians and philosophers throughout church history have used dictation to describe how inspiration was accomplished is meaningless if the notion is not substantiated by scripture.

DICTATION: WHAT SAITH THE SCRIPTURE?

- In seeking to answer this question, we will study the following three subpoints:

  - o Testimony of the Lord Jesus Christ
  - o Testimony of the Law and the Prophets
  - o Testimony of the Apostle Paul

Testimony of the Lord Jesus Christ

- Matthew 22:29-31 — "Jesus answered and said unto them, Ye do err, not knowing the scriptures, nor the power of God. For in the resurrection they neither marry, nor are given in marriage, but are as the angels of God in heaven. But as touching the resurrection of the dead, have ye not read that which was spoken unto you by God, saying," (quotes Exodus 3:6)

    o   Who wrote Exodus 3:6? Moses. Jesus asks them, "have ye not read that which was spoken unto you by God." He said (paraphrased), "It's not just what Moses said, or wrote, but it is what God said to you." Christ says that what Moses wrote in Exodus 3 was spoken unto them by God. God spoke through Moses.

- Luke 24:44-46 —"And he said unto them, These *are* the words which I spake unto you, while I was yet with you, that all things must be fulfilled, which were written in the law of Moses, and *in* the prophets, and *in* the psalms, concerning me. Then opened he their understanding, that they might understand the scriptures (*graphē*), And said unto them, Thus it is written, and thus it behooved Christ to suffer, and to rise from the dead the third day:"

    o   The word translated "scriptures" in verse 45 is the same word translated "scripture" in II Timothy 3:16; *graphē*. The Lord Jesus Christ called all three parts of the Hebrew Bible the Law, the Prophets, and the Psalms (our Old Testament), "Scripture". Therefore, our Lord's attitude toward the entire Old Testament was that all of it was scripture and inspired by God.

- In the book of Hebrews, the Law, the prophets, and Psalms are all said to be the words of the Holy Spirit.

- Hebrews 3:7 — "Wherefore (as the Holy Ghost saith, To day if ye will hear his voice," [quotation of Psalm 95]

    o   The writer of Hebrews quotes Psalms chapter 95. So, in the book of Hebrews you are told that words in the book of Psalms are really the words of the Holy Spirit. When you read the book of Psalms, you are reading what the Holy Spirit said.

- Hebrews 9:8 — "The Holy Ghost this signifying that the way into the holiest of all was not yet made manifest while as the first tabernacle was yet standing:"

    o   The writer of Hebrews is talking about the regulations written down back in the books of Moses, (in the book of Exodus), about the tabernacle. Moses wrote some things down, that the book of Hebrews now tells you was really God the Holy Spirit signifying.

    Who wrote Exodus? The writer of the book of Hebrews says that the Holy Spirit wrote it. So when someone tells you that God the Holy Spirit says something to you, and they quote a verse of scripture, they are being scriptural; and so are you when you do it. The word of God is God's word. Don't you forget that! When you speak it, you are speaking with the authority of Almighty God; and when you face it, you are facing Almighty God.

- Hebrews 10:15-16 — "*Whereof* the Holy Ghost also is a witness to us: for after that he had said before, This *is* the covenant that I will make with them after those days, saith the Lord, I will put my laws into their hearts, and in their minds will I write them;" [quotes Jeremiah 31:31-34]

    o   The author of Hebrews is saying that the Holy Spirit is the one who spoke in Jeremiah 31:31-34. So the Holy Spirit is said to be the speaker in the Psalms, the Law, and the Prophets.

Testimony of the Law and the Prophets

- Exodus 4:28-31— "And Moses told Aaron all the words of the LORD who had sent him, and all the signs which he had commanded him. And Moses and Aaron went and gathered together all the elders of the children of Israel: And Aaron spake all the words which the LORD had spoken unto Moses, and did the signs in the sight of the people. And the people believed: and when they heard that the LORD had visited the children of Israel, and that he had looked upon their affliction, then they bowed their heads and worshipped."

    o   God puts the words into the mouths of Moses and Aaron. The words they spoke are the words that God put in their mouths.

- Exodus 19:25-20:1 — "So Moses went down unto the people, and spake unto them. 20:1) And God spake all these words, saying, . . ."

    o   When Moses spake to them, he gave them the words that God gave him to say.

- Exodus 24:4 — "And Moses wrote all the words of the LORD, and rose up early in the morning, and builded an altar under the hill, and twelve pillars, according to the twelve tribes of Israel."
- Numbers 11:24 — "And Moses went out, and told the people the words of the LORD, and gathered the seventy men of the elders of the people, and set them round about the tabernacle."

    o   Notice what Moses did – he told the people the words of the LORD. He got the words from the LORD and then he communicated them to the people.

- Numbers 22:38 — "And Balaam said unto Balak, Lo, I am come unto thee: have I now any power at all to say any thing? the word that God putteth in my mouth, that shall I speak."

    - Once again, here is a man who spake even though it was going against his will, and against his desires, to say what he said. "The word that God putteth in my mouth, that shall I speak." He said, "I do not have any choice; that's all that will come out of my mouth because I am God's spokesman."

- II Samuel 23:1-2 — "Now these *be* the last words of David. David the son of Jesse said, and the man *who was* raised up on high, the anointed of the God of Jacob, and the sweet psalmist of Israel, said, The Spirit of the LORD spake by me, and his word *was* in my tongue."

    - Now, that is some claim to inspiration. David is a man who was conscious of what was going on, "The Spirit of God spake by me, and his word was in my tongue." Turn to the New Testament and notice the attitude of the New Testament writers about what David said. What does the Lord Jesus think about that? Does he think David is a little overzealous? *Is that a hyper view of inspiration, David? You should not feel that way.*

- Mark 12:35-36 — "And Jesus answered and said, while he taught in the temple, How say the scribes that Christ is the Son of David? For David himself said by the Holy Ghost, The LORD said to my Lord, Sit thou on my right hand, till I make thine enemies thy footstool (Psalm 110:1)."

    - Jesus says that when David wrote down Psalm 110:1, he did it by the Holy Spirit. Jesus just confirmed the method of inspiration outlined in II Samuel 23. Christ is not the only one to do this with respect to the writings of David. Consider Peter's statement in Acts 1.

- Acts 1:16 — "Men *and* brethren, this scripture must needs have been fulfilled, which the Holy Ghost by the mouth of David spake before concerning Judas, which was guide to them that took Jesus."

    o Who wrote Psalm 41? David did; it is a Psalm of David. But, whom does the verse say spoke it? The verse says the Holy Spirit by the mouth of David spoke it. Well, then who spoke it? David wrote it down, but what he wrote down was what God the Holy Spirit spoke through him. Do you see how strong that thing is?

    o E.W. Bullinger states the following regarding Acts 1:16, "It was David's "mouth," and David's pen, David's vocal organs, and David's hand; but they were not David's words. They were the words "which the Holy Ghost spake before concerning Judas." David knew nothing about Judas, David could not possibly have spoken anything about Judas. David's "mouth" spake concerning Ahithophel; but they were the words "which the Holy Ghost spake concerning Judas."

    David was "a prophet": and, being a prophet, he "spake as he was moved by the Holy Ghost" (2 Peter 1:21). Hence, in Psalm 16, he spake concerning the resurrection of the Lord Jesus (Acts 2:30,31). In the same way he "spake before concerning Judas." (Bullinger, 2)

- Jeremiah 1:4-9 — "Then the word of the LORD came unto me, saying, 5) Before I formed thee in the belly I knew thee; and before thou camest forth out of the womb I sanctified thee, *and* I ordained thee a prophet unto the nations. Then said I, Ah, Lord GOD! behold, I cannot speak: for I *am* a child. But the LORD said unto me, Say not, I *am* a child: for thou shalt go to all that I shall send thee, and whatsoever I command thee thou shalt speak. Be not afraid of their faces: for I *am* with thee to deliver thee, saith the LORD. Then the LORD put forth his hand, and touched my mouth. And the LORD said unto me, Behold, I have put my words in thy mouth."

- Jeremiah 5:14 — "Wherefore thus saith the LORD God of hosts, Because ye speak this word, behold, I will make my words in thy mouth fire, and this people wood, and it shall devour them."

- Jeremiah 6:18-19 — "Therefore hear, ye nations, and know, O congregation, what *is* among them. 19) Hear, O earth: behold, I will bring evil upon this people, *even* the fruit of their thoughts, because they have not hearkened unto my words, nor to my law, but rejected it."

    o Jeremiah has given the people the revelation, the words of God in God's own words, and when they reject what Jeremiah says, God said, "You rejected me!" God is equal to his word.

- Jeremiah 36:1-8 — "And it came to pass in the fourth year of Jehoiakim the son of Josiah king of Judah, *that* this word came unto Jeremiah from the LORD, saying, Take thee a roll of a book, and write therein all the words that I have spoken unto thee against Israel, and against Judah, and against all the nations, from the day I spake unto thee, from the days of Josiah, even unto this day. It may be that the house of Judah will hear all the evil which I purpose to do unto them; that they may return every man from his evil way; that I may forgive their iniquity and their sin. Then Jeremiah called Baruch the son of Neriah: and Baruch wrote from the mouth of Jeremiah all the words of the LORD, which he had spoken unto him, upon a roll of a book. And Jeremiah commanded Baruch, saying, I *am* shut up; I cannot go into the house of the LORD: Therefore go thou, and read in the roll, which thou hast written from my mouth, the words of the LORD in the ears of the people in the LORD'S house upon the fasting day: and also thou shalt read them in the ears of all Judah that come out of their cities. It may be they will present their supplication before the LORD, and will return every one from his evil way: for great *is* the anger and the fury that the LORD hath pronounced against this people. And Baruch the son of Neriah did according to all that Jeremiah the prophet commanded him, reading in the book the words of the LORD in the LORD'S house."

    o Jeremiah dictates to his secretary, Baruch, the words of the LORD. There is not any way to describe that except with the word dictation. So you do not have to be afraid of the word "dictation." The words come out of Jeremiah's mouth; Baruch writes them down, and then the scripture says (by inspiration in verse 8) that the words that he read are God's words. Jeremiah is writing down the revelation of God in God's own words and they are equal to God. When Jeremiah speaks, God speaks. There is no difference.

- Ezekiel 2:1-2 — "And he said unto me, Son of man, stand upon thy feet, and I will speak unto thee. And the spirit entered into me when he spake unto me, and set me upon my feet, that I heard him that spake unto me."

    o   The spirit comes in and Ezekiel begins to get the revelation.

- Ezekiel 3:10-11 — "Moreover he said unto me, Son of man, all my words that I shall speak unto thee receive in thine heart, and hear with thine ears. And go, get thee to them of the captivity, unto the children of thy people, and speak unto them, and tell them, Thus saith the Lord GOD; whether they will hear, or whether they will forbear."

    o   "God gave Ezekiel the words to say, and he went out and gave them to the people. Go preach it Ezekiel, and whether they get it or they do not, you go tell them my words.

    Turn to the book of Revelation and you will see a similar kind of a thing. In fact the way you understand Revelation 1 is by understanding Ezekiel 2. Revelation 1:10-11 "I was in the Spirit *[like Ezekiel was]* on the Lord's day, *[transported up into the future day of the Lord]*, and heard behind me a great voice, as of a trumpet, Saying, I am Alpha and Omega, the first and the last: *[the Lord Jesus]* and, What thou seest, write in a book, and send *it* unto the seven churches which are in Asia; unto Ephesus, and unto Smyrna, and unto Pergamos, and unto Thyatira, and unto Sardis, and unto Philadelphia, and unto Laodicea." He says to write these things in a book. What is John writing in a book? He is writing what God shows him, and what God gives him. He instructs him to write down the revelation of God and to write it down in God's very own words.

    Look at Revelation 22. John writes it down. Do not fail to understand what is going on in this passage. Revelation 22:18,19 – "For

> I testify unto every man that heareth the words [the individual words] of the prophecy of this book, If any man shall add unto these things, God shall add unto him the plagues that are written in this book: And if any man shall take away from the words of the book of this prophecy, God shall take away his part out of the book of life, and out of the holy city, and *from* the things which are written in the book." The words that John wrote down were the words that God gave him to write down. That is the Bible's attitude toward inspiration." (Jordan, MSS 101, Lesson 4)

- Acts 3:18, 21 — "But those things, which God before had shewed by the mouth of all his prophets, that Christ should suffer, he hath so fulfilled . . . Whom the heaven must receive until the times of restitution of all things, which God hath spoken by the mouth of all his holy prophets since the world began."

  - God shewed by the mouth of all his prophets? In other words, God was speaking by the mouth of those prophets. It is pretty obvious what is being said. When those prophets spoke, it was God speaking through them. If you just read the Bible and take what the Bible writers and speakers say about inspiration, you do not have much problem understanding that the scripture came right out of the mouth of God and that God has made his word equal to himself.

  - Regarding Acts 3:18 Dr. Bullinger wrote, "The particular "things" referred to here are "that Christ should suffer"; but the assertion is comprehensive and includes all other things "showed" by God.

    Note, that it was God who, before, had showed them. It was the same God who had fulfilled them. The "mouth" was the mouth of "all His prophets," but they were not the prophets' words. They were the words of God." (Bullinger, 2)

- Luke 1:67, 70 — "And his father Zacharias was filled with the Holy Ghost, and prophesied, saying, . . . As he spake by the mouth of his holy prophets, which have been since the world began:"

- - o   Zacharias speaks by the filling of the Holy Spirit. And what does he say? He says that God has spoken by the mouth of his holy prophets in verse 70. There is no doubt about what these verses mean when it comes to the issue of inspiration. Go back and read about some of these prophets. The prophets were the mouthpiece of God, speaking/writing only those things which God had placed in their mouths.

- In the next chapter we will consider our third subpoint on The Testimony of Paul

WORKS CITED

Bullinger, E.W. *How to Enjoy the Bible: A Guide to Better Understanding and Enjoyment of God's Word*. Grand Rapids, MI: Kregel Publications: 1990.

Jordan, Richard. *Manuscript Evidence 101*. Grace School of the Bible.

DIVINE DICTATION: THE MECHANISM OF INSPIRATION? PART 4

INTRODUCTION

- In Lesson 14, I told you that we were going to study the following three points regarding Divine Dictation:

    o Study what modern theologians have said regarding the notion of dictation (Lesson 14).
    o Consider historic articulations of inspiration before the publication of Darwin's *On the Origin of the Species* in 1859 under the following three categories:

- The Pre-Reformation Fathers (Lesson 14)
- The Reformers (Lesson 15)
- Post-Reformation Theologians (Lesson 15)
  - Consider the Bible's testimony concerning itself. (Lessons 16 & 17)

- Last week, in Lesson 16, we began looking at the third and final point regarding Divine Dictation i.e., the Bible's testimony concerning itself. In doing so, I outlined the following three sub-points under which we would consider the Bible's testimony concerning itself.

  - Testimony of the Lord Jesus Christ
  - Testimony of the Law and the Prophets
  - Testimony of the Apostle Paul

- This morning, in Lesson 17, we will look at the final sub-point regarding the Testimony of the Apostle Paul and end with some concluding remarks regarding the issue of Divine Dictation.
- Remember, just because a host of Christian theologians and philosophers throughout church history have used dictation to describe how inspiration was accomplished, it is meaningless if the notion is not substantiated by scripture.

DICTATION: WHAT SAITH THE SCRIPTURE?

Testimony of the Apostle Paul

- Acts 22:14-15 — "And he said, The God of our fathers hath chosen thee, that thou shouldest know his will, and see that Just One, and shouldest hear the voice of his mouth. For thou shalt be his witness unto all men of what thou hast seen and heard."

- o What did Paul hear? He heard the words of Christ's mouth. He had direct revelations from the Lord Jesus Christ.

- Acts 28:25 — "And when they agreed not among themselves, they departed, after that Paul had spoken one word, Well spake the Holy Ghost by Esaias the prophet unto our fathers," (quotes Isaiah 6:9-10)

  - o Who spoke Isaiah 6? When you go back there and read it you are reading what the Holy Spirit spoke. God breathed it! The thing that he wrote down back there came out of the mouth of God Almighty. God dictated the words of Isaiah 6 through the penmanship of Isaiah so that the very words that Isaiah wrote down were the very words that God determined should be written down. So, what Isaiah 6 says is what God said. So, when you are dealing with Isaiah 6, you are not dealing with Isaiah, you are dealing with God.

- Galatians 1:1-12 — "But I certify you, brethren, that the gospel which was preached of me is not after man. For I neither received it of man, neither was I taught *it*, but by the revelation of Jesus Christ."

  - o Read the verse closely, it was not *by* the revelation from Christ, not just something sent to him, but it was the revelation *of* Jesus Christ. In other words, the Lord revealed himself to Paul and spoke with Paul face-to-face just like he did with Moses. He put his words in Paul's mouth, and Paul went out to preach and write those things down.

- I Corinthians 14:37 — "If any man think himself to be a prophet, or spiritual, let him acknowledge that the things that I write unto you are the commandments of the Lord."

- I Timothy 6:2-3— ". . . These things teach and exhort. If any man teach otherwise, and consent not to wholesome words, *even* the words of our Lord Jesus Christ, and to the doctrine which is according to godliness;"

  - o The words that Paul wrote down in I Timothy were the very words of the Lord Jesus Christ. Paul's words were the words of the glorified Christ. Not only are these passages from the pen of the Apostle Paul strong with regard to Pauline authority, but they are also strong in regard to the doctrine of inspiration. The words of Christ to us today are found in Paul's epistles. Paul's epistles are not made up of Paul's interpretation of the things that Christ gave him. It is not just Paul's interpretation of the ministry of Christ, but you have the very words of the Lord Jesus Christ given to Paul and written down for you and for me.

- II Corinthians 13:3 — "Since ye seek a proof of Christ speaking in me, which to you-ward is not weak, but is mighty in you."

  - o That is something, isn't it? Who is speaking in Paul? Christ is speaking in Paul. The words that Paul speaks came from Christ.

- I Corinthians 7:12, 25— "But to the rest speak I, not the Lord: If any brother hath a wife that believeth not, and she be pleased to dwell with him, let him not put her away. . . Now concerning virgins I have no commandment of the Lord: yet I give my judgment, as one that hath obtained mercy of the Lord to be faithful."

  - o Here is one example from the pen of Paul where he says that he is speaking to the Corinthians "not the Lord." Yet, what Paul wrote to them is considered scripture. This is evident by the very fact that it was included in the book of I Corinthians.
  - o Later, in I Corinthians 14 Paul states the following:

- I Corinthians 14:37 — "If any man think himself to be a prophet, or spiritual, let him acknowledge that the things that I write unto you are the commandments of the Lord."

○ Paul did not say, "Everything I wrote unto you were the commandments of the Lord accept that part in chapter 7 where I offered my own judgement." No, everything Paul wrote to the Corinthians was to be taken as the commandments of the Lord even the part where Paul offered his own judgement in chapter 7.

○ I Corinthians 5:9 — Paul wrote other things to the Corinthians that did not qualify as scripture because they were not written by inspiration of God. Consequently, they are not found in the cannon because they were not inspired. Yet, Paul's judgment recorded in I Corinthians 7 is.

○ Therefore, Paul's judgement in I Corinthians 7 would be subject to all the verses we have studied regarding inspiration (II Timothy 3:16, II Peter 1:21). How can that be the case? Paul, based on a mind that had been stirred by God the Holy Spirit and saturated with the words of God through the process of inspiration, was able to, out of that mind, write something that the Holy Spirit considered scripture.

○ This is not hard to see when one considers the context of I Corinthians 7. In verse 1, Paul begins to address the Corinthians with respect to the questions they had written to him about.

- I Corinthians 7:1 — "Now concerning the things whereof ye wrote unto me: It is good for a man not to touch a woman."

○ In seeking to answer their questions, Paul references the teachings of the Lord during his earthly ministry regarding divorce and remarriage in verses 10 and 11 when he states:

- I Corinthains 7:10-11 — "And unto the married I command, yet not I, but the Lord, Let not the wife depart from her husband: But and if she depart, let her remain unmarried, or be reconciled to her husband: and let not the husband put away his wife."

○ The statement recorded in verses 10 and 11 does not go beyond the teaching offered by Christ in Matthew 5:32, 19:6-9; Mark 10:11-12, or Luke 16:18 on the subject of divorce and remarriage. In verse 12 and following, Paul expands upon the teaching of the Lord during his earthly ministry by offering instructions regarding divorce and remarriage not found in the gospels. Thus, it makes sense to view Paul's statement in verse 12, "speak I, not the Lord" as a statement regarding the specific nature and more complete nature of the content revealed to him on the subject of divorce and remarriage as it relates to the body of Christ. In other words, Paul is not saying that he is just speaking and offering his own judgment, rather he is referring to the further revelation committed to him with respect to the questions raised by the Corinthians.

- I Corinthians 7:40 — the Spirit of God in Paul was able to bear witness to the authenticity of Paul's judgement. In other words, Paul's judgment was completely congruent with the mind of God the Holy Spirit on the matter.

- So here is an example, where God the Holy Spirit is able to record God's word out of the mind, experience, and vocabulary of the Apostle Paul. This brings to mind what we studied about inspiration in Job 32:8 (But *there is* a spirit in man: and the inspiration of the Almighty giveth them understanding.). The book of Luke stands out as another example of this type of phenomena.

  - Luke 1:1-4 — "Forasmuch as many have taken in hand to set forth in order a declaration of those things which are most surely believed among us, Even as they delivered them unto us, which from the beginning were eyewitnesses, and ministers of the word; It seemed good to me also, having had perfect understanding of all things from the very first, to write unto thee in order, most excellent Theophilus, That thou mightest know the certainty of those things, wherein thou hast been instructed."

- Luke did not just write the book of Luke out of his own understanding from having interviewed the eyewitnesses alone. Rather, the Holy Spirit reached into the research that Luke had conducted to draw out and set forth in writing via the process of inspiration the Holy Spirit's inspired history. The Holy Spirit used the knowledge gleaned from Luke's research to state the history in God's own words.

- What's going on in I Corinthians 7 is very similar to what we saw last week in Lesson 16 where the Old Testament claims that Moses said something unto Israel (Exodus 3:1-6) while the New Testament clearly states that God said that unto Israel (Matthew 22:31). I Corinthians 7 states that Paul said something or offered his judgement while I Corinthians 14 says that what Paul wrote in chapter 7 was the commandment of the Lord. The only difference is that in I Corinthians we see the example occurring within the same book, not across the testaments.

- o Verses like I Corinthians 7:12, 25, and those few like it, do not disqualify the notion of divine dictation. They fit the pattern exhibited across the whole of Scripture where a thing attributed to a human writer/speaker in one place is elsewhere attributed to God himself in another. Paul was able to write out of the supernatural understanding that God had given him and still have what was written qualify as inspired scripture. This could not be said for Paul's first epistles addressed to the Corinthians, referred to in I Corinthians 5:9.

THE WORD AND THE WORDS

- Finis Dake stated, "The Bible writers say 3,808 times that they were writing the words of God."

- According to Dr. E.W. Bullinger, "The Word of God is thus for those "that believe." The "*Word*" as a whole; and the "*words*" of which it is made up. They cannot be separated." (Bullinger, 3)

  - o Jeremiah 15:16 — "Thy words were found, and I did eat them; and thy word was unto me the joy and rejoicing of mine heart: for I am called by thy name, O LORD God of hosts."
  - o John 17:8, 14 — "For I have given unto them the words which thou gavest me; . . . I have given them thy word; and the world hath hated them, because they are not of the world, even as I am not of the world."

- While Bullinger does not use the term dictation or offer any theories with respect to how it was accomplished, he just believed it. He believed it to be the *word* of God made up of the *words* of God. Bullinger did believe that all the *words*, every single one came from God and without them one would not have the *Word* of God.

- Bullinger concludes his "Preliminary Remarks" to *How to Enjoy the Bible* with the following words:

    - "With these introductory remarks we shall proceed to divide what we may call our essential and fundamental principles of Bible study into two parts:
        - First, those connected with THE "WORD" as a whole; and
        - Second: those connected with THE "WORDS" of which the Word is composed." (Bullinger, 6)

- John 8:58 — "Jesus said unto them, Verily, verily, I say unto you, Before Abraham was, I am."

    - The Lord Jesus Christ hung the doctrine of his deity on the tense of one verb. The Jehovah God of the Old Testament is the Jesus Christ of the New Testament. Jesus means "Jehovah Saviour". And Jesus built that whole doctrine on the tense of a verb, not just the verb but the tense.

- John 10:34-35 — "Jesus answered them, Is it not written in your law, I said, Ye are gods? If he called them gods, unto whom the word of God came, and the scripture cannot be broken;"

    - Christ hinges an argument about his being the son of God, and he states that they do not have any right to argue with him about calling himself the Son of God if the scripture called them gods. He takes that one word of Psalm 82 and builds his case on it. That is how carefully the Lord Jesus Christ considered the authority of that book down to one word, one phrase. The verb tense is even important and not only that but the very number of the noun is important.

- Galatians 3:16 — "Now to Abraham and his seed were the promises made. He saith not, And to seeds, as of many; but as of one, And to thy seed, which is Christ."

    - The whole argument of this passage is that God used the singular, and not the plural, of the noun. I am saying that the Bible writers make an entire point and depend upon one phrase, or the tense of the verb, or a single word in a passage, or the number of the noun. That is how minutely close God calls it. The words are important, not just the phrases, or the concepts, or the idea, or the sense and the flow.

CONCLUDING THOUGHTS ON DICTATION

- Based upon the verses we have considered in Lessons 16 and 17, it seems reasonable to conceive that God accomplished the inspiration of His *Word* by dictating the *words* to human authors.
- In Lesson 3 of Manuscript Evidence 101 Brother Jordan states the following regarding dictation before he touches upon the verses contained in this lesson:

    - "God dictated the words of the scripture through human authors. In other words, God reaches into the library of their vocabulary in such a way that the very words they used were the very words God had determined they would use from eternity past. That is where you take into account the human element. You take into account the fact that it is not a sterile kind of a thing – the writers were not glorified stenographers who had no part in it. God reaches into the library of their vocabulary; he reaches into their personality, and their circumstances, and he writes the words out through that.

        Now, there are limitations on inspiration that we will study in future lessons, and you will see all the nuances of this. But the point that Paul is making in 2 Timothy 3:16 is that what is written on that page are the words that God Almighty put there.

> Some of you people are writing with pens. Some of you are writing with pencils. You write with different instruments. What you write down takes on the character of the personality of that instrument. I have two pens in my pocket, and one has a finer tip than the other. The tip determines the way the characters look in large measure. You can write with a fountain pen or a ball-point pen, and you will notice a difference when you write with them.
>
> The different characteristics of the instrument that is writing are there as God dictates the words out, but God Almighty is responsible for the words that are recorded. That means that whatever the scripture says, God says, and that is important!" (Jordan, MSS 101 Lesson 3)

- In Lesson 2 we covered the following presuppositions with respect to the word of God.

    o God exists. (Psalms 14:1)

    o God has magnified his *word* above his own name. (Psalms 138:2)

    o God's *Word* is eternally settled in heaven. (Psalms 119:89)

    o God, through the process of inspiration, has communicated his *word* to mankind. (I Timothy 3:16 and II Peter 1:21)

    o God's *words* were written down so that they could be made eternally available to men. (Isaiah 30:8, I Peter 1:23)

    o God promised to preserve those *words* that he inspired. (Psalm 12:6-7)

- In determining whether dictation is an appropriate descriptor for how inspiration was accomplished one must consider the following questions:

    o Which one of the Biblical presuppositions listed above would the notion of dictation undermine?

    o What attribute of God or aspect of His fundamental nature and character does the notion of dictation overthrow?

- - What passage of scripture falsifies (proves false) the dictation view of inspiration?
  - Are there passages that suggest that God dictated his word to the human authors (see passages cited above)?

- So then, why should we let a group of unbelieving critics who deny all the presuppositions identified above talk us out of a particular view of inspiration?

- In seeking to save the doctrine of inspiration from how it had been "stigmatized" by its critics, modern Theologians failed to adequately meet the critics' accusations. The critics claim the Bible is not of divine origins and cite the "human elements" as their proof. If God created humans, he can certainly use their individual styles and vocabulary to record his word. How does changing the definition of dictation or just backing away from it all together solve the critics' accusations of the Bible not being a divine book? The real issue is, is there a God to dictate? (Contributed by Nathan Kooienga)

- When we consider the Genesis creation account along with the account in the first chapter of John and Colossians 1:17, we meet a God that creates and sustains all things (besides Himself), *ex nihilo* (out of nothing). We are confronted with a terribly powerful and wise being. Is it possible to approach this topic with the idea of it being too large a task for God to dictate His word? Do we really want to say God had no idea what had transpired in the lives of these writers? No! David wrote how well God knew him in the 139th Psalm. David tells us God knew everything about him even to his very thoughts. Likewise, God knew these men intimately, for he created them and sustained them, in being, from moment to moment. If this is an accurate picture of the God we serve, then we must listen to God's words to Job (Job 38:4), "where wast thou when I laid the foundations of the earth? Declare, if thou hast understanding." How can we side with the critics and say the creator cannot use his creation to complete His will as He pleases? Again, God's word recorded by Jeremiah (32:27) "Behold, I am the LORD, the God of all flesh: is there anything too hard for me?" In my opinion The God of the Bible, the creator of the cosmos is capable of dictating his book while using "human elements". If God chose to do it this way that is his prerogative, who are we to say he cannot? He is an awesome God and not prone to writer's block. (Contributed by Nathan Kooienga)

- When one combines these presuppositions with the verses we studied in this lesson regarding how inspiration was accomplished it is not hard to see why many throughout church history conceived of *Plenary Verbal Inspiration* (or just *Verbal Inspiration*) as having been accomplished through the mechanism of dictation. How else does God take his eternally settled upon word and communicate it to human authors without error? I see no problem with viewing God as having accomplished the inspiration of every word (*Plenary Verbal View*) through a process of dictation.

WORKS CITED

Bullinger, E.W. *How to Enjoy the Bible: A Guide to Better Understanding and Enjoyment of God's Word.* Grand Rapids, MI: Kregel Publications: 1990.

Jordan, Richard. *Manuscript Evidence 101.* Grace School of the Bible.

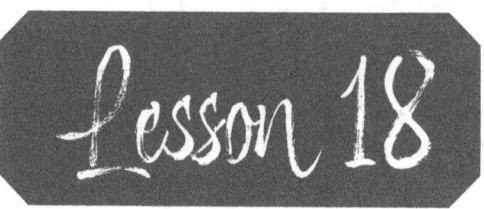

GOD'S DESIGN IN INSPIRATION

INTRODUCTION

- Thus far we have considered the following points regarding the doctrine of inspiration.

    o Considered the various views of inspiration: *Natural, Dynamic, Partial* (*Spiritual-Rule-Only*), *Existential,* and *Plenary Verbal* (Lesson 11)

    o Identified the *Plenary Verbal View* as the correct position. (Lessons 11 and 12)

    o Recognized Potential Pitfalls of the Plenary Position (Lesson 12)

    - Words Not the Men — the main issue with inspiration is the words on the page not what happened to the human authors.

- Preservation Secures the Plenary Position — Plenary Verbal inspiration is meaningless without Preservation.
- Plenary Verbal on Inspiration but Dynamic on Translation— it is inconsistent to hold to the inspiration of every word (Plenary Verbal) only to turn around and advocate for a Dynamic Philosophy of translation.

o Studied Passages Proving the Plenary Position (Lesson 13)
  - Self-authenticating Nature of Inspiration — the Bible self-authenticates its own claim of inspiration.
  - Words Not the Men: Practical Examples— demonstrated practically that the issue in inspiration is the words that are written down and not the men (I Kings 13, John 11, and Numbers 22-24)

o Considered whether or not Dictation is a scripturally approached descriptor to describe how Plenary Verbal Inspiration was accomplished (Lessons 14-17)
  - Divine Dictation and Modern Theologians— the notion of dictation is almost universally rejected as false by modern Evangelical scholarship.
  - Historic Articulations of Inspiration— the words "dictate", "dictation", or "dictare" in Latin have a long history of being associated with the inspiration of God's word.
    - The Pre-Reformation Fathers
    - The Reformers
    - Post-Reformation Theologians

Dictation: What Saith the Scripture?—God dictated the words of the scriptures through human authors.

  - Testimony of the Lord Jesus Christ
  - Testimony of the Law and the Prophets
  - Testimony of the Apostle Paul

- In this Lesson we want to begin considering God's design in inspiration. In other words, what was God seeking to accomplish by inspiring every word of scripture? Simply stated, God's design in inspiration was to make the written word equal with the living Word, the Lord Jesus Christ.

- The scriptures see no difference between the written word of God and the living Word, Jesus Christ. The same attributes that are applied to the scriptures are applied to the Lord Jesus Christ in your Bible. The Bible sees no difference between the two.
- God attributes his own attributes to his word, so that when you deal with God's word you are dealing with God Himself.

GOD'S ATTRIBUTES AND THE WRITTEN WORD

- There is no difference between what God says and what the scriptures say.

    o   Roman 9:17 — "For the scripture saith unto Pharaoh, Even for this same purpose have I raised thee up, that I might shew my power in thee, and that my name might be declared throughout all the earth."

- Romans 9:17 is a quotation of Exodus 9:16. If you go back and look at the context of Exodus 9 it says, "Thus saith the LORD God of the Hebrews" in verse 13. Exodus 9 says that Jehovah God said that unto Pharaoh, but Romans 9 says that "scripture saith unto Pharaoh." That is an illustration of the power and the authority of the written word of God. It can be used interchangeably with Jehovah God. God the Holy Spirit wrote both verses.
- God attributes His own attributes to His word.

    o   Galatians 3:8 — "And the scripture (*graphē*), foreseeing that God would justify the heathen through faith, preached before the gospel unto Abraham, *saying*, In thee shall all nations be blessed."

- Does God possess the ability to foresee the future? Yes. Paul gives an attribute of God to the scripture – "The scripture, foreseeing that God would justify the heathen . . ." The written word of God has the ability to foresee the future. It foresees that God is going to justify the heathen, and therefore it says it "preached before the gospel unto Abraham."
- Tell me something? Did Abraham have a Bible? No, Abraham did not have a Bible. Five hundred years passed before Moses ever wrote any of that stuff down. He did not have a Bible. Therefore, the scripture is doing something that cannot be done. Abraham did not have a Bible to preach to him. So, how could the scripture preach to him? God preached to him! And Paul says that the scripture did it!
- Do you know what Paul is saying? He is saying that the scripture and God are one. They are equal. Now that is how close that connection is between them. You just cannot get around the connection; it is that close. If that book is not that close to God and it is not God's word, then the whole thing is just a bunch of baloney; it's a lie.

THE EQUALITY OF THE LIVING AND WRITTEN WORD

- In *How to Enjoy the Bible*, Dr. E.W. Bullinger sees no difference between the Living Word, the Lord Jesus Christ and the written word, i.e., the word of God.

    o "When we speak of the "*Word*" we can never separate the Living Word, the Lord Jesus Christ; and the written word, the Scriptures of Truth.

    Each of these is called the "Word," because the Greek word *Logos* is used of both.

    Logos means the spoken or written word, because it makes manifest, and reveals to us the invisible thoughts.

    It is used of Christ, the Living Word, because He reveals the invisible God. "No man hath seen God at any time; the only begotten Son, He being in the bosom of the Father, This one [hath] declared [Him]" (John 1:18).

> This is why Christ is called "The Word of God," because He makes known, reveals, and explains the Father...
>
> This is why the Scriptures are called "the Word of God," because they make known the Father and the Son, by the Holy Spirit, the author of the Word.
>
> Christ is "the Way" to the Father (John 14). He makes God known to us in all His attributes, will, and words. "I have given them Thy Word." It is always "THY Word" (John 17:8, 14, 17)." (Bullinger, 7-8)

- John 1:1 — in your Bible there is a connection between the written and the living Word that you do not want to miss. *They are both called the "word of God"*

    o Revelation 19:13 — "And he *was* clothed with a vesture dipped in blood: and his name is called The Word of God."

    o Hebrews 4:12 — "For the word of God *is* quick, and powerful, and sharper than any twoedged sword, piercing even to the dividing asunder of soul and spirit, and of the joints and marrow, and *is* a discerner of the thoughts and intents of the heart."

- The living Word, (the Lord Jesus Christ), and the written word are both called by the same name. They have the same title given to them. The reason for that is that the connection between the living Word and the written word of God is absolutely astounding – the two are complete and inseparable.

- Bullinger goes on to identify the following three manifestations of the Word: 1) The Incarnate Word, 2) The Written Word, and 3) The Preached Word.

    o "Christ reveals the Father. The Scripture reveals Christ. The Spirit reveals both in the written and in the preached Word (1 Cor. 12:7, 8).

How wonderfully does this magnify the preached Word; and show the solemnity of the charge in 2 Timothy 4:2, "Preach the Word."

It shows how small and worthless are all the schemes, tricks and contrivances of present-day evangelists and mission preachers with their ever-new fashions and modern methods, when we see what a high and dignified place God has given to the Preached Word.

How careful should we be that nothing in our manner or matter should lower that dignity, or imply in the slightest degree that the Written Word has lost any of its power; or needs any handmaids or helpmeets.

"I HAVE GIVEN THEM THY WORD" (John 17:14) is the all-sufficient assurance of the Lord Jesus Christ, speaking to the Father. He did not say I have given them Aids to devotion. He did not say I have given them a Hymn-book, or I have given them thy Word AND something else.

He did not give anything instead of, or in addition to, that Word. And that being so, we are assured that the Word which He gave is all-sufficient, in itself, to accomplish all the purposes of God.

The Word that is preached makes known the Written Word; the Word that is written makes known Christ the Living Word; and Christ makes known God our Father." (Bullinger, 8-9)

- "Hence it is, that the same things are stated of both the Living and the Written Word, as it is well put by Joseph Hart:

> The Scriptures and the Word
> Bear one tremendous name,
> The Living and the Written Word
> In all things are the same." (Bullinger, 9)

- In Grace School of the Bible, Pastor Jordan illustrates this point thusly:

o "Now listen people that book (your Bible), is not God. I just had to put my Bible aside because it is coming all apart. You understand that the book is not God. You can scribble on your Bible; you can tear it up and it will fall apart; it will wax and decay. God Almighty will never do any of those things. You can throw your Bible in a mud hole, but you cannot throw God in a mud hole.

But, having said all of that, I will tell you that the closest thing you will ever come to God himself on this earth is that book. That is why that book is important to you. That is why you study it and become friends with it, and that is why it is different from any other book. It is the word of God, and it is so closely connected with the living God. The only contact that you have with the Lord Jesus Christ outside of the pages of that book is on an inner-subjective level (it is inside of you), on a spirit level. Therefore, God has given you that written word in order to be able to evaluate, by an objective standard in black and white, those subjective experiences that you have. Your Bible is an objective standard by which to measure everything." (Jordan, MMS 101)

Similar Declarations regarding the Living Word and the Written Word

- The following is a citation from E.W. Bullinger's book *How To Enjoy the Bible*. I elected to center justify it to accentuate the parings.

"His name is called THE WORD OF GOD," Revelation 19:13.
They "pressed upon Him to hear THE WORD OF GOD," Luke 5:1.

The Prince of PEACE, Isaiah 9:6.
The Gospel of PEACE, Romans 10:15.

Jesus said,..."No man cometh unto the Father, but BY ME," John 14:6.
"Make me to go in the PATH of Thy Commandments," Psalms 119:35.

"Jesus saith unto him, I am THE WAY," John 14:6.
"Teach me, O Lord, THE WAY of Thy statutes," Psalms 119:33.

"I am...THE TRUTH," John 14:6.
"Thy Word is TRUTH," John 17:17.
Christ—"Full of grace and TRUTH," John 1:14.
"All Thy Commandments are TRUTH," Psalms 119:151.

"These things saith He...that is TRUE," Revelation 3:7.
"The Judgments of the Lord are TRUE," Psalms 19:9.

"Jesus Christ. This is the true God, and eternal LIFE," 1 John 5:20.
"Holding forth the Word of LIFE," Philippians 2:16.

"A bone of Him shall not be broken," John 19:36.
"The scripture cannot be broken," John 10:35.

"I am the Living Bread...if any man eat of this Bread he shall LIVE for ever," John 6:51.
"Man shall not LIVE by bread alone, but by every Word of God," Luke 4:4.

"With Thee is the FOUNTAIN OF LIFE," Psalms 36:9.
"Thy Law...is a FOUNTAIN OF LIFE," Proverbs 13:14.

Jesus said, "I am the LIGHT of the World," John 8:12.
David said, "Thy Word is a LIGHT unto my path," Psalms 119:105.

"The Life was the LIGHT," John 1:4.
"The Law is LIGHT," Proverbs 6:23.

"Thou art my LAMP, O Lord," 2 Sam 22:29.
"Thy Word is a LAMP unto my feet," Psalms 119:105.

"I, saith the Lord, will be unto her a wall of FIRE," Zechariah 2:5.
"Is not My Word like as a FIRE? saith the Lord," Jeremiah 23:29.

"The Light of Israel shall be for a FIRE," Isaiah 10:17.
"I will make My Words in thy mouth FIRE," Jeremiah 5:14.

"To you which believe, He is PRECIOUS," 1 Peter 2:7.
"Exceeding great and PRECIOUS Promises," 2 Peter 1:4.

"My beloved is...chiefest among ten THOUSAND," Song of Solomon 5:10.
"The Law of Thy mouth is better unto me than THOUSANDS of gold and silver," Psalms 119:72.

"His Mouth is most SWEET," Song of Solomon 5:16.
"How SWEET are Thy Words unto my taste," Psalms 119:103.

"His Name shall be called WONDERFUL," Isaiah 9:6.
"Thy Testimonies are WONDERFUL," Psalms 119:129.

"Christ, the POWER OF GOD," 1 Corinthians 1:24.
"The Gospel is the POWER OF GOD," Romans 1:16.

Lord, "Thou art GOOD, and doest Good," Psalms 119:68.
"GOOD is the Word of the Lord," Isaiah 39:8.

"Ye have known Him that is FROM THE BEGINNING," 1 John 2:13.
"Thy Word is true FROM THE BEGINNING," Psalms 119:160.

"From Everlasting to EVERLASTING Thou art God," Psalms 90:2.
"The righteousness of Thy Testimonies is EVERLASTING," Psalms 119:144.

"Thy throne, O God, is FOR EVER AND EVER," Hebrews 1:8.
"Thy testimonies,...Thou hast founded them FOR EVER," Psalms 119:152.

"The Lord shall ENDURE for ever," Psalms 9:7.
"The Word of the Lord ENDURETH for ever," 1 Peter 1:25.

"Christ ABIDETH for ever," John 12:34.
"The Word of God...ABIDETH for ever," 1 Peter 1:23.

"Worship Him that LIVETH for ever," Revelation 4:10.
"The Word of God LIVETH for ever," 1 Peter 1:23.

Christ's Kingdom "shall STAND FOR EVER," Daniel 2:44.
"The Word of our God shall STAND FOR EVER," Isaiah 40:8.

The STONE..."on whomsoever it shall fall, it will grind him to powder," Luke 20:18.

"Is not my Word...saith the Lord, like a HAMMER that breaketh the rock in pieces?" Jeremiah 23:29.

Christ, "A STUMBLING Stone," Romans 9:33.
They "STUMBLE at the Word," 1 Peter 2:8.

"Lo, I am with you ALWAY, even unto the end of the world," Matthew 28:20.
"Thy commandments...are EVER WITH ME," Psalms 119:98.

"Christ may DWELL in your hearts by faith," Ephesians 3:17.
"Let the Word of Christ DWELL in you richly," Col 3:16.

Christ said, "ABIDE in me, and I IN YOU," John 15:4.
"If... my Words ABIDE in you," John 15:7.

"Hereby we know that He ABIDETH in us," 1 John 3:24.
"The Word of God ABIDETH in you," 1 John 2:14.

Christ called, "FAITHFUL and true," Revelation 19:11.
"Thy Testimonies...are very FAITHFUL," Psalms 119:138.

"Out of His mouth goeth a sharp SWORD," Revelation 19:15.
"The Word of God...is sharper than any two-edged SWORD," Hebrews 4:12. Probably refers to both the Living Word and the written Word.

"The Lord TRIETH the Righteous," Psalms 11:5.
"The Word of the Lord TRIED him," Psalms 105:19.

Christ a "TRIED Stone," Isaiah 28:16.
"The Word of the Lord is TRIED," Psalms 18:30.
(Bullinger, 9-11)

Similar Affects Attributed to the Living Word and the Written Word

We are "BORN OF God," 1 John 5:18.
"BORN...by the Word of God," 1 Peter 1:23.

"BEGOTTEN...by...Jesus Christ," 1 Peter 1:3.
BEGOTTEN...through The Gospel," 1 Corinthians 4:15.

"The Son QUICKENETH whom He will," John 5:21.
"Thy Word hath QUICKENED me," Psalms 119:50.

"You hath he QUICKENED who were dead," &c., Ephesians 2:1.
"Thy Precepts...with them thou hast QUICKENED me," Psalms 119:93.
"He that eateth me, even he shall LIVE by me," John 6:57.
"Desire the sincere milk of The Word, that ye may GROW thereby," 1 Peter 2:2.

"Christ hath made us FREE," Galations 5:1.
"The Truth shall make you FREE," John 8:32.

"The Blood of Jesus Christ...CLEANSETH us from all sin," 1 John 1:7.
"YE are CLEAN through the Word which I have spoken," John 15:3.

Christ "is able also to SAVE them to the uttermost that come unto God by Him," Hebrews 7:25.
"Receive...the engrafted Word, which is able to SAVE your souls," James 1:21.

"SANCTIFIED in Christ Jesus," 1 Corinthians 1:2.
"SANCTIFIED by the Word of God and prayer," 1 Timothy 4:5.

"SANCTIFIED through the offering of the body of Jesus Christ once for all," Hebrews 10:10.
"SANCTIFY them through THY TRUTH. Thy Word is truth," John 17:17.

> "Christ Jesus, who of God is made unto us WISDOM,"
> 1 Corinthians 1:30.
> "The Holy Scriptures...able to make thee WISE unto salvation," 2 Timothy 3:15.
>
> Christ "HEALED them," Matthew 4:24.
> "He sent His Word and HEALED them," Psalms 107:20.
>
> "Striving according to His Working which WORKETH in me mightily," Colossians 1:29.
> "The Word of God which effectually WORKETH also in you that believe," 1 Thessalonians 2:13.
>
> "The Lord Jesus Christ...shall JUDGE the quick and the dead," 2 Timothy 4:1.
> "The Word that I have spoken...shall JUDGE him," John 12:48.
>
> "I will go unto God, my exceeding Joy," Psalms 43:4.
> "Thy Word was unto me the JOY and rejoicing of my heart," Jeremiah 15:16.
> (Bullinger 11-12)

- Bullinger follows up the preceding lists of similarities between the Living and written Word with the following comments.

    o "Thus we see that the Living Word and the Written Word cannot be separated. And we can understand also why they cannot be separated in the preaching of the Word.

    To preach the Written Word without preaching Christ is not preaching at all. Neither is it done in the power of the Spirit.

    When Paul went to Thessalonica, he ("as his manner was") "reasoned with them out of the SCRIPTURES" (not as is done to-day, out of the newspapers, or out of the preacher's own head or experience); but he did not end there. We are immediately told that this preaching consisted in "opening and setting forth that CHRIST (the Living Word) must needs have suffered, and risen again from the dead, and that this Jesus, whom I preach unto you, is Christ (the Messiah)" (Acts 17:1-3).

> If the Living Word and the Written Word cannot be separated, we learn that in sitting down to the study of the Word and Words of God it is to hear His voice, to choose that "better part"; to sit at Jesus' feet, and hear HIS word (Luke 10:39)." (Bullinger, 13)

- Brother Jordan offered the following summation regarding God's design in inspiration:

  o "The living Word, (the Lord Jesus Christ), and the written word are that close. God attributes his own attributes to his word, and the reason for that is that he is demonstrating that word to be the final authority. It is what he says. *When you are dealing with God's word, you are dealing with God himself.* And if you are going to deal with God, you will have to deal with his word. That is God's design and inspiration." (Jordan. *MSS 101*, Lesson 1)

- Once again, we see that the Bible is not like any other book. God attributes his own attributes to his word. That is why we need to take Satan's policy of evil against God's Word, outlined in Lessons 2 and 3 seriously.

WORKS CITED

Bullinger, E.W. *How to Enjoy the Bible: A Guide to Better Understanding and Enjoyment of God's Word.* Grand Rapids, MI: Kregel Publications: 1990.

Jordan, Richard. *Manuscript Evidence 101.* Grace School of the Bible.

Lesson 19

THE LIVING WORD'S ATTITUDE TOWARD THE WRITTEN WORD

INTRODUCTION

- In Lesson 18 we studied that God's design in inspiration was to make the written word equal with the Living Word, the Lord Jesus Christ.
- First, we noted that God attributes His own attributes to His word. According to Galatians 3:8, the scriptures, like God, can see the future and therefore preached unto Abraham before God's written Word even existed.
- Second, we studied the absolute equality between the Living Word (the Lord Jesus Christ) and the written word (the scriptures). In doing so, we looked at 39 pairs of verses where similar declarations are made regarding the Living and Written Word and fifteen pairs of passages that attribute similar effects to Christ and the scriptures.

- In the end, we considered the following statement from Brother Jordan regarding God's design in inspiration:

    - "The living Word, (the Lord Jesus Christ), and the written word are that close. God attributes His own attributes to His word, and the reason for that is that He is demonstrating that word to be the final authority. It is what He says. *When you are dealing with God's word, you are dealing with God Himself.* And if you are going to deal with God, you will have to deal with His word. That is God's design and inspiration." (Jordan. *MSS 101*, Lesson 1)

- Today, in this Lesson, we want to consider the attitude of the Lord Jesus Christ (the Living Word) toward the written Word. In other words, what did the Lord Jesus Christ believe about the Old Testament Scriptures?

THE TESTIMONY OF THE LORD JESUS CHRIST

- As we consider the testimony of the Living Word toward the written word, I would like to do so under the following four sub-points:

    - Attitude Toward the Words Themselves
    - General Declarations Regarding Scripture
    - Critical Theories of Old Testament Authorship
    - Advanced Authentication of the New Testament

Attitude Toward the Words Themselves

- Jesus Christ believed that every word in the Bible was the Word of God. He even believed the very words in the Bible.
- Matthew 22:29-32 — "Jesus answered and said unto them, Ye do err, not knowing the scriptures, nor the power of God. For in the resurrection they neither marry, nor are given in marriage, but are as the angels of God in heaven. But as touching the resurrection of the dead, have ye not read that which was spoken unto you by God, saying, I am the God of Abraham, and the God of Isaac, and the God of Jacob? God is not the God of the dead, but of the living."

    - o "The point is that the whole argument turns on the fact that God says, "I am." It is the tense of the verb that is important. He does not say, "I was a God of the living when they were alive." He says, "I am, right now, the God of the living." Then the implication is that Abraham, who is dead, is included in the verse. It says, "I am". Right now, in the present tense, God is the God of Abraham, so Abraham must be alive. Isaac must be alive, and Jacob must be alive. That is the issue that is being dealt with, and the whole thing turns on the tense of that verb – present tense." In short, Jesus Christ believed every word of scripture." (Jordan, MSS 101, Lesson 5)

- Matthew 22:41-46 — "While the Pharisees were gathered together, Jesus asked them, Saying, What think ye of Christ? whose son is he? They say unto him, *The Son* of David. He saith unto them, How then doth David in spirit call him Lord, saying, The LORD said unto my Lord, Sit thou on my right hand, till I make thine enemies thy footstool? If David then call him Lord, how is he his son? And no man was able to answer him a word, neither durst any *man* from that day forth ask him any more *questions*."

    - o "Jesus hangs the Pharisees on one word. David called Him Lord. Well, how can Jesus be David's son and his Lord? He takes that one word and builds a question on it. The Lord Jesus Christ believed the very words of the Bible."

- My point is that Christ believed the Old Testament to be the very words of God, and He divided between them. The attitude of Christ is that the words are the very words of God.
- Luke 4:16-21 — notice what Jesus does as he reads from Isaiah 61:1-2 in the synagogue in Nazareth.

Isaiah 61:1-2	Luke 4:18-19
1) The Spirit of the Lord GOD *is* upon me; because the LORD hath anointed me to preach good tidings unto the meek; he hath sent me to bind up the brokenhearted, to proclaim liberty to the captives, and the opening of the prison to *them that are* bound; 2) To proclaim the acceptable year of the LORD, and the day of vengeance of our God; to comfort all that mourn;	18) The Spirit of the Lord *is* upon me, because he hath anointed me to preach the gospel to the poor; he hath sent me to heal the brokenhearted, to preach deliverance to the captives, and recovering of sight to the blind, to set at liberty them that are bruised, 19) To preach the acceptable year of the Lord.

- In Luke 4, Jesus stopped reading at the comma in Isaiah 61:2, closed the book, gave it back to the minister, and said unto them "this day is this scripture fulfilled in your ears." What did Jesus just do? He rightly divided between His first and second comings. That is how precise Christ was in His attitude and handling of the scriptures (*graphē*).
- Matthew 4:4 — "But he answered and said, it is written, Man shall not live by bread alone, but by every word that proceedeth out of the mouth of God."
- When you believe that your Bible is entirely comprised of the words of God that places you in some pretty good company. We need to have the same attitude toward the scriptures that our Lord had.

General Declarations Regarding Scripture

- John 10:35 — *Jesus Asserted Its Unbreakability.* He said, ". . . the scripture cannot be broken." Geisler believes that this is equivalent to claiming that the Bible is infallible.
- Matthew 4:3-10 — *Jesus Affirmed Its Divine Authority.* When the Lord Jesus Christ was tempted, He answered Satan every time with the words "it is written." He just kept coming back with verses. He recognized that the power, spiritually, is in the book, in the words of God.
- Matthew 26:24, 54 — *Jesus Fulfilled Prophecy.* Jesus Christ not only believed the very words of scripture; He not only acknowledged the power of scripture, but He also fulfilled the prophecies of scripture. He is fulfilling the prophecies of the scripture. He has come to do exactly what they say must be done.

  - Matthew 27:46 — Christ quotes Psalm 22:1 in fulfillment of the scriptures.

- Matthew 5:17-18 — *Jesus Affirmed Its Imperishability.* Jesus came to fulfill the Law and the Prophets, i.e., to do what they said needed to be done. He recognized their authority in that regard, and He also verified their truthfulness. Jesus Christ never one time questioned the Old Testament. He always quoted it in such a way as to endorse it, and He endorsed it as verbally inspired.
- Matthew 15:3, 6 — *Jesus Declared Their Ultimate Supremacy.* The Bible is exalted above all human instruction.
- Matthew 22:29 and John 17:17 — *Jesus Affirmed Their Factual Accuracy.* In short, the Bible is wholly true and without error.
- Mark 13:19 — *Jesus Affirmed Their Scientific Accuracy.* Even on the highly debated matter of the origin of the world and mankind, Jesus insisted on the truthfulness of scripture. (Geisler, 197-202)

- Matthew 19:4-5 — Jesus believed that God created Adam and Eve "at the beginning."

Critical Theories of Old Testament Authorship

- There are 66 chapters in Isaiah. The first 39 chapters in Isaiah are a unit, and chapters 40 through 66 are another unit. It is interesting that Isaiah has 66 chapters just like your Bible has 66 books. It is also interesting that whoever wrote the book of Isaiah knew right where to make the break – after the 39th chapter.
- There are 39 books in the Old Testament. Also, the first 39 chapters of Isaiah talk about the judgment on the nation Israel and the captivity and that kind of thing. Then John the Baptist shows up in chapter 40 of the book of Isaiah. Isaiah 40:3 – "The voice of him that crieth in the wilderness, Prepare ye the way of the LORD, make straight in the desert a highway for our God." Isn't it interesting that Isaiah 1:2 says, "Hear, O heavens, and give ear, O earth", which refers to the heaven and the earth just like Genesis does? There are 39 chapters, and then there is a break, and then you begin in chapter 40 and see a verse quoted about John the Baptist. Then you read chapter 66 and you conclude with the new heaven and the new earth. The book of Isaiah is like a capsule of the Bible. The second half of the book is about the restoration – what God is going to restore.
- There is a view out there called *Deutero-Isaiah* (*Deutero* means two) which maintains that one Isaiah wrote the first 39 chapters, and that an entirely different Isaiah wrote chapters 40 through 66. This view was posited by the German Rationalists and Higher Critics.
- John 12:37-38 — "But though he had done so many miracles before them, yet they believed not on him: That the saying of Esaias the prophet might be fulfilled, which he spake, Lord, who hath believed our report? and to whom hath the arm of the Lord been revealed?"

  - Verse 38 is a quotation from Isaiah 53:1. According to Christ in John 12:38, Isaiah the prophet wrote Isaiah 53, and Isaiah 53 is in the second section of the book. So, I know if there are two authors to Isaiah, I know that Isaiah the prophet wrote the second section in spite of the fact that some people say that he wrote the first and editors wrote the second.

- John 12:39-41 — "Therefore they could not believe, because that Esaias said again, He hath blinded their eyes, and hardened their heart; that they should not see with *their* eyes, nor understand with *their* heart, and be converted, and I should heal them. These things said Esaias, when he saw his glory, and spake of him."

    o   Verse 40 is a quote from Isaiah 6:10, the first section of Isaiah. Yet the Lord Jesus Christ said that it was spoken by Esaisas. So did the Lord Jesus Christ believe the *Deutero-Isaiah* theory? No, Jesus says in John 12 that Isaiah the prophet wrote the first part of the book of Isaiah, and Isaiah the prophet also wrote the second part of the book of Isaiah.

- As with the *Deutero-Isaiah* theory, there are many who question whether or not Moses wrote Genesis through Deuteronomy. In fact, these people say that Moses could not even write. I have never quite understood how they figured that out, since Moses was trained in the School of the Egyptians and had all of heir wisdom according to Acts 7:22.
- Supporters of the Graph-Wellhausen Theory maintain that Genesis through Deuteronomy were written by five different authors J, E, P, D, R. The Jehovah passages, the passages where God is called by the name of Jehovah, are written by "J". The passages where God is called by the name of Elohim are written by "E". The priestly passages are written by "P". The Deuteronomic passages, the law passages, are written by "D". "R" is a redactor or an editor that put all this stuff together.
- John 5:45-47 — "Do not think that I will accuse you to the Father: there is *one* that accuseth you, *even* Moses, in whom ye trust. For had ye believed Moses, ye would have believed me: for he wrote of me. But if ye believe not his writings, how shall ye believe my words?"

    o   The Lord Jesus Christ believed that Moses wrote all five books.

- Jesus Christ verifies the authenticity of the following Old Testament figures and narratives. Christ believed these events as having occurred in history:

    - God created Adam and Eve — Matthew 19:4-5
    - The birth of Seth — Luke 3:38
    - Marriage before the flood — Luke 17:27
    - The days of Noah and the flood — Matthew 24:37-38
    - Noah's son Shem and his descendants — Luke 3:35-36
    - The birth of Abraham — Luke 3:34
    - Sodom and Gomorrahh — Luke 17:29-32
    - Moses and the burning bush — Matthew 12:26; Luke 20:37
    - Israel ate manna in the wilderness — John 6:31-51
    - The brazen serpent — John 3:14
    - Jonah was swallowed by a whale — Matthew 12:40
    - David wrote the Psalms ascribed to him — Matthew 22:43-45
    - Daniel was a prophet not a mere historian — Matthew 24:15; Mark 13:14
    - The slaying of Zechariah — Matthew 23:35 (Geisler, 197-202)

Advanced Authentication of the New Testament

- In John 16, Jesus gave an advanced announcement concerning the inspiration of the New Testament. The New Testament had not been written when Jesus Christ was on the earth, and yet He gives a pre-authenticating announcement about the New Testament. This is a very important passage for us to grasp.
- John 16:12-14 — "I have yet many things to say unto you, but ye cannot bear them now. Howbeit when he, the Spirit of truth, is come, he will guide you into all truth: for he shall not speak of himself; but whatsoever he shall hear, *that* shall he speak: and he will shew you

things to come. He shall glorify me: for he shall receive of mine, and shall shew *it* unto you."

- - o "The Lord Jesus Christ pre-announced the coming of the Holy Spirit in such a way that guarantees the authenticity and genuineness of the New Testament. There are two words that you need to remember: authenticity and genuineness. "Authenticity" means "truthfulness, and accuracy". When we say that the scriptures are authentic, we mean that they are true, and they are accurate. "Genuineness" means "the scriptures are written by who they say they were written by". The genuineness of Genesis means that Moses really wrote it. The authenticity of Genesis means that what is written is true and accurate." (Jordan, MSS 101, Lesson 5)

- John 16:13 — "Howbeit when he, the Spirit of truth, is come, he will guide you into all truth: for he shall not speak of himself; but whatsoever he shall hear, *that* shall he speak: and he will show you things to come."

  - o Notice how Christ guarantees the authenticity and the genuineness of the New Testament.

- John 14:26 — "But the Comforter, *which is* the Holy Ghost, whom the Father will send in my name, he shall teach you all things, and bring all things to your remembrance, whatsoever I have said unto you."

  - o You want to be able to get John 16:12, 13 and John 14:26 together. So when those men, (Matthew, Mark, Luke, and John), begin to write down the gospel account, Jesus Christ has already given assurance of the fact that the Holy Spirit is going to bring to remembrance those things. There is a pre-authentication of the gospel records. We can now look back and see how He was given a statement that preannounced and guaranteed the authenticity of those books. This passage is very important in understanding that the New Testament books were pre-authenticated.

FINAL THOUGHTS

- You need to remember that Jesus Christ never one time questioned the Old Testament. He always quoted it in such a way as to endorse it. When he endorsed it, he endorsed it as verbally inspired. Remember these three things and fix them in your mind.

    - Christ never questioned the Old Testament.
    - Christ always quoted it in such a way as to endorse it.
    - Christ endorsed it as verbally inspired.

- There are only three possibilities concerning that testimony of Christ to scripture:

    - "*Number One* — there are errors in the scripture, but Jesus did not know about them; so He really is not God. (And if He is not God, you can just throw the whole Bible out the window, and we can stop studying right now.)"
    - "*Number Two* — there are errors, and Jesus Christ knew about them, and He covered them up. (Well, then He is not holy, and He would not be a suitable or sufficient Savior.)"
    - "*Number Three* — there are not any errors and that it is God's word; and when you are dealing with the Bible, you are dealing with God Himself. This is the one we opt for. (Jordan, *MMS 101*)"

WORKS CITED

Geisler, Norman L. *Systematic Theology: In One Volume.* Minneapolis, MN: Bethany House, 2011.

Jordan, Richard. *Manuscript Evidence 101.* Chicago, IL: Grace School of the Bible.

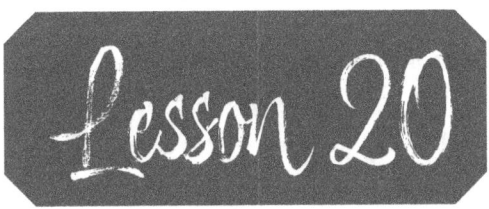

THE NEW TESTAMENT WRITER'S ATTITUDE TOWARD THE WRITTEN WORD

INTRODUCTION

- Last week, in Lesson 19, we looked at the attitude of the Living Word (the Lord Jesus Christ) toward the written Word. In doing so we observed the following:

    o   Jesus Christ believed that every word in the Bible was the word of God.

    o   Jesus Christ verifies the historical authenticity of Old Testament figures and events.

- - Jesus Christ gave advanced authentication for the New Testament.
  - Jesus Christ never one time questioned the Old Testament. He always quoted it in such a way as to endorse it as verbally inspired.

- Given the testimony of the Living Word toward the written Word we concluded Lesson 19 by noting the following three options:

  - *Number One* — there are errors in the scripture, but Jesus did not know about them; so He really is not God. (And if He is not God, you can just throw the whole Bible out the window, and we can stop studying right now.)
  - *Number Two* — there are errors, and Jesus Christ knew about them, and He covered them up. (Well, then He is not holy, and He would not be a suitable or sufficient Savior.)
  - *Number Three* — there are not any errors and that it is God's word; and when you are dealing with the Bible, you are dealing with God himself.

- Having established a firm understanding of our Lord's thoughts regarding the scriptures we will now turn our attention to ascertaining the attitude of the writers of the New Testament toward the written Word. We will do this by considering the following two points:

  - New Testament writers affirm the Old Testament
  - New Testament writers on the New Testament

NEW TESTAMENTS WRITERS AFFIRM THE OLD TESTAMENT

- The writers of the New Testament give ample evidence that the Old Testament is exactly what it claims to be — the inspired Word of God.

- The Old Testament is quoted in the New Testament about 250 times, and it is alluded to approximately 850 times. There are only five books in the Old Testament that are not quoted in the New Testament – Esther, Ezra, Nehemiah, Ecclesiastes, and Song of Solomon. All of the other books are quoted and/or alluded to in the New Testament. The New Testament writers view the Old Testament as authoritative and authentic.

- The Apostle Paul cited the Old Testament over and over again. In Romans 4, Paul talks about Abraham, and he never questions whether or not Abraham believed God, or that his faith was counted unto him for righteousness. Paul just accepted it as true.

- In Romans 9 Paul talks about Isaac, Esau, Jacob, and Pharaoh as well as Sodom and Gomorrah. In Romans 3, he quotes Psalms 14, Psalms 5, Psalm 140 and he says that they are all scripture. Paul never questions or denies the Old Testament; rather, he quotes it in such a way so as to affirm it.

- The following is a list of Old Testament persons and events affirmed by the New Testament writers. Please note that this list excludes examples from the four gospels made by Christ. Please see Lesson 19 for a list of Old Testament historical verifications found in the narrative of the four gospels.

    - Creation of the universe (Genesis 1)—Colossians 1:16
    - Creation of Adam and Eve (Genesis 1-2)—I Corinthians 11:8-9; 15:45; I Timothy 2:13
    - God resting on the seventh day (Genesis 1)—Hebrews 4:3-4
    - Marriage of Adam and Eve (Genesis 2)—I Corinthians 6:16; Ephesians 5:31

- The temptation of Eve (Genesis 3)—II Corinthians 11:3; I Timothy 2:14
- The disobedience of Adam (Genesis 3)—Romans 5:12-19
- The sacrifices of Cain and Abel (Genesis 4)—Hebrews 11:4
- The murder of Abel by Cain (Genesis 4)—I John 3:12; Jude 11
- The birth of Seth (Genesis 4)—Luke 3:38
- The translation of Enoch to heaven (Genesis 5)—Hebrews 11:5
- Marriage before the flood (Genesis 6)—Luke 17:27
- The preservation of Noah and his family (Genesis 8-9)—I Peter 3:20; II Peter 2:5
- The call of Abraham (Genesis 12-13)—Hebrews 11:8
- Tithes to Melchizedek (Genesis 14)—Hebrews 7:1-3
- Justification of Abraham (Genesis 15)—Romans 4:3
- Ishmael (Genesis 16)—Galatians 4:21-26
- Promise of Isaac (Genesis 17)—Hebrews 11:18
- Abraham's sojourn (Genesis 20)—Hebrews 11:9
- Birth of Isaac (Genesis 21)—Acts 7:8
- Offering of Isaac (Genesis 22)—Hebrews 11:17
- Exodus through the Red Sea (Exodus 14)—I Corinthians 10:1-2
- Provision of Manna (Exodus 16-17)—I Corinthians 10:3-5
- Fall of Jericho (Joshua 6)—Hebrews 11:30
- Miracles of Elijah (I Kings 17-18)—James 5:17-18
- Three Hebrew youths in the fiery furnace (Daniel 3)—Hebrews 11:34
- Daniel in the lion's den (Daniel 6)—Hebrews 11:33 (Geisler, 201-202)

NEW TESTAMENT WRITERS ON THE NEW TESTAMENT

- The New Testament views itself as scripture. The New Testament writers view other New Testament authors as writing scripture. In other words, they viewed them as inspired and writing with equal authority.

- II Peter 3:1-2 — "This second epistle, beloved, I now write unto you; in *both* which I stir up your pure minds by way of remembrance: 2) That ye may be mindful of the words which were spoken before by the holy prophets, and of the commandment of us the apostles of the Lord and Saviour:"

  - o   Peter says (paraphrased), "I want you to remember what the Old Testament prophets said as well as what I and the other apostles have commanded." He does not consider that there was any gap between them, but total equality. In other words, Peter considered what he was saying as equal with the Old Testament.

- II Peter 3:15-16— "And account *that* the longsuffering of our Lord *is* salvation; even as our beloved brother Paul also according to the wisdom given unto him hath written unto you; As also in all *his* epistles, speaking in them of these things; in which are some things hard to be understood, which they that are unlearned and unstable wrest, as *they do* also the other scriptures, unto their own destruction."

  - o   Peter calls everything Paul wrote in "all his epistles" scripture or *graphē*. When the New Testament writers look out and see the other authors writing books, they say, "Hey, that is scripture too." They recognize what is going on. They know and recognize each other's books. There is a process whereby they are able to authoritatively identify which books are authoritative and authentic.

- I Timothy 5:18—"For the scripture (*graphē*) saith, Thou shalt not muzzle the ox that treadeth out the corn. And, The labourer *is* worthy of his reward." As we have already seen in Lesson 13, this verse is comprised of quotations from both the Old and New Testaments.

- o Deuteronomy 25:4—"Thou shalt not muzzle the ox that treadeth out the corn."
- o Matthew 10:10 and Luke 10:7—"The labourer *is* worthy of his reward."

- Now, do you see what Paul did? He quoted a passage out of Deuteronomy, (the words of Moses), and then he quoted a passage out of the Gospels (the words of Christ), and he called them both scripture. Paul did not make any distinction between them. So, they are both scripture—the Old Testament and the New Testament. Paul considers Luke 10 just as authoritative as Deuteronomy 25. That is important for you to realize, so you understand that Paul and the other New Testament writers consider their writings as equally inspired as the rest of the word of God.
- I Thessalonians 4:8 — "He therefore that despiseth, despiseth not man, but God, who hath also given unto us his holy Spirit."

    - o In other words, if you despise what Paul is telling you, you despise what God said.

- I Thessalonians 4:15 — "For this we say unto you by the word of the Lord, …"

    - o "That expression "by the word of the Lord" denotes a special and specific prophetic announcement, and it is used repeatedly in the Old Testament to describe God's word coming unto someone and then going out through them.

        Let's look at a couple of verses. There is a formula that denotes a specific and special prophetic announcement – God's word. Paul is very conscious of the fact that he is giving out more than just his own word and that he is giving out God's word.

> Genesis 15:1 – "AFTER these things the word of the LORD came unto Abram in a vision, saying . . ."
>
> Do you see that? The word of the LORD comes to Abraham in a vision and gives him the communication. There are a number of passages like this, but I just picked out a couple samples for you.
>
> II Samuel 7:4 – "And it came to pass that night, that the word of the LORD came unto Nathan, saying . . ."
>
> Do you see that formula—"the word of the LORD?" It has to do with a prophetic announcement. Paul knew what he was doing when he used that expression.
>
> I Kings 12:22 – "But the word of God came unto Shemaiah the man of God, saying." The word came to him.
>
> Now, you can run other references in the Old Testament and see the significance of what Paul is doing in 1 Thessalonians 4:15 when he says, "For this we say unto you by the word of the Lord." He is saying, "What I am writing to you people here is God Almighty's communication to you." Paul is conscious of what he is doing.
>
> By the way, 1 Thessalonians is probably Paul's first epistle (if not his first, then it is his second). But his very first epistles bear the highest claim to inspiration of any of them. He makes the highest claim to inspiration right at the beginning of his writing ministry. Paul starts out right at the beginning knowing what he is doing." (Jordan, MSS 101, Lesson 5)

- I Timothy 6:3 — "If any man teach otherwise and consent not to wholesome words, *even* the words of our Lord Jesus Christ, and to the doctrine which is according to godliness;"

    o I Timothy 6 is a passage about Paul's authority as the apostle of the Gentiles, but it also shows you his estimation of the scripture. In Chapter 6 Paul is talking about what he had written in the book of I Timothy. It is obvious that Christ's words were coming from Paul's mouth, and he was conscious of that fact.

- II Corinthians 13:3 — Since ye seek a proof of Christ speaking in me, which to you-ward is not weak, but is mighty in you.

- o The words of Jesus Christ were coming from Paul's mouth, and he was conscious of that.

- II Thessalonians 3:6, 14 — "Now we command you, brethren, in the name of our Lord Jesus Christ, that ye withdraw yourselves from every brother that walketh disorderly, and not after the tradition which he received of us... And if any man obey not our word by this epistle, note that man, and have no company with him, that he may be ashamed."

  - o Paul is commanding them in the name of the Lord Jesus Christ to do some things; and he says that if the man does not "obey our word by this epistle" (i.e., the epistle that he is in the process of writing), that they are to have no company with him.

CONCLUSION

- Considering the evidence, the choice is clear: either the Bible or the critics? What the Bible affirms the critics deny.
- If Jesus is the Son of God, then the Bible is the Word of God, including what it says about the historical events listed in Lessons 19 and 20.
- On the contrary, if the Bible is not the Word of God, then Christ is not the Son of God. The Words of God, the Living and the written, are tied together.

WORKS CITED

Geisler, Norman L. *Systematic Theology: In One Volume.* Minneapolis, MN: Bethany House, 2011.

Jordan, Richard. *Manuscript Evidence 101.* Grace School of the Bible.

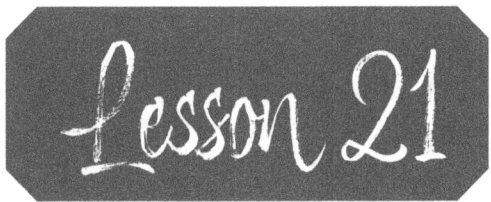

INTERNAL EVIDENCE OF INSPIRATION: UNDESIGNED COINCIDENCES

Brother Craig Holcom's lesson on Undesigned Coincidences from July 27, 2014 was used as a basis to write this lesson.

INTRODUCTION

- Since Lesson 18 we have been looking at the close connection between the Living Word (the Lord Jesus Christ) and the written Word, i.e., the Scriptures. In doing so we considered the attitude of the Living Word toward the written Word (Lesson 19) as well as the attitude of the New Testament writers toward the Scriptures (Lesson 20).

- In our day, the Word of God is being attacked on all fronts. For example, the authenticity of the Biblical books is routinely questioned. For instance, critics have questioned who really wrote the gospels. Consider the following case in point; critics of God's word will say things like "the gospels are just forgeries". They weren't really written by the actual disciples of Jesus; they were written much later than the first century. They are for the most part just made-up stories like the Lord of the Rings or the Narnia stories.

- While this type of attack on the veracity of God's word is nothing new, they began in earnest a couple hundred years ago with the advent of German Higher Criticism and the writings of Friedrich Schleiermacher (1768-1834).

- Over the last two centuries, Christian philosophers and theologians have sought to counter the arguments made by the opponents of the divine origin of Scriptures. As we have seen, some, certainly not all, of the answers offered by Christian academia have not been helpful or productive and have altered the understanding of basic Christian doctrine amongst the faithful (Inspiration & Inerrancy).

- One area where Christian apologetics has shined brightest is in its presentation of the internal evidence of the Bible's divine origin.

- In this lesson we want to begin a consideration of the internal evidence found within scripture that speaks to having been inspired by God. Under the general category of internal evidence for inspiration I would like to consider the following points:

    o Undesigned Coincidences
    o Fulfilled Prophecy

- In this lesson we will use the notion of *Undesigned Coincidences* (*UC*) to demonstrate the reliability of the Bible. This discussion will extend to:

    o The authenticity of the books — they were written by who they claim to have been written by.

- o The genuineness of the books — they are trustworthy history, an accurate presentation of the material they report.

- In seeking to accomplish this task, we will first consider what *UC* are and then consider examples of them from both the four Gospels and the Pauline Epistles.

WHAT IS AN *UNDESIGNED COINCIDENCE*?

- In our day, the notion of *UC* as a defense of the Bible's divine nature has been championed loudly by Dr. Timothy McGrew, a professor of Philosophy at Western Michigan University.
- Dr. McGrew has produced a nine-part lecture series on the reliability of the Bible in addition to participating in websites devoted to Christian Apologetics such as Apologetics315.com
- While McGrew uses the notion of *UC* in his defense of the veracity of the Bible, he was not the first to do so. Earlier Christian thinkers and theologians to use *UC* in support of the Bible's truthfulness include:

    - o William Paley — English Clergyman and Apologist: 1743-1805
        - *Horae Paulinae* (1790)
    - o John James Blunt — English Anglican:1794-1855
        - *Undesigned Coincidences in the Writings Both of the Old and New Testament : An Argument of Their Veracity : With an Appendix, Containing Undesigned Coincidences Between the Gospels and Acts, and Josephus* (1851)
    - o Edmund Bennett — American Lawyer: 1824-1898
        - *The Four Gospels From a Lawyer's Standpoint* (1899)

- According to William Paley, *UC* are markers of the authenticity of scripture and validate its reliability.

- "The very particularity of St. Paul's epistles; the perpetual recurrence of names of persons and places; the frequent allusion to the incident of his private life, and the circumstances of his condition and history; and the connection and parallelism of these with the same circumstances in the Acts of the Apostles, so as to enable us, for the most part, to confront them one with another; as well as the relations which subsist between the circumstances, as mentioned or referred to in the different Epistles — afford no inconsiderable proof of the genuineness of the writings, and the reality of the transactions. For as no advertency is sufficient to guard against slips and contradictions, when circumstances are multiplied, and when they are liable to be detected by contemporary accounts equally circumstantial, an imposter, I should expect, would either have avoided particulars entirely, contenting himself with doctrinal discussion, moral precepts, and general reflections; or if, for the sake of imitating St. Paul's style, he should have thought it necessary to intersperse his composition with names and circumstances, he would have placed them out of the reach of comparison with the history." (Paley, 168)

- In short, *UC* provide us with evidence for the reliability and truthfulness for what the Biblical writers report in a way that made up stories or simply copies of made up stories or forgeries claiming to report events not really witnessed could not provide.

- Dr. McGrew states the following regarding *UC*:

    - "Sometimes two works by different authors (for example Acts, which was written by Luke, and the Pauline epistles) interlock in a way that would be very unlikely if one were copied from the other or both were copied from a common source. For example, one book may mention in passing a detail that answers a question raised by the other. The two records fit together like pieces of a jigsaw puzzle.

        Fictions and forgeries aren't like that. Why would a forger leave loose ends, unanswered questions? And how could a forger control what another writes to make it interlock with what you have written? But this is what we expect to find when both writers are talking about real historical events that they both are familiar with." (McGrew)

- When we see parallel passages in the N.T. we usually simply see one as filling in a few more details not supplied in the other account. But sometimes they supply much more than that, especially when we find details in passages that are not even in the same context as another passage.

- When considering *UC* it is important to keep in mind that we have the luxury of possessing a completed Bible. We have all twenty-seven New Testament books bound together in one book. Consequently, we sometimes miss or don't think about things like these *UC*. Bear in mind that the New Testament books were not originally bound together in one book. Rather they were twenty-seven separate books written by eight to nine different men. That is what makes the cumulative force of this argument for the genuineness of the Bible so strong.

UNDESIGNED COINCIDENCES IN THE GOSPELS

- Regarding why there are four gospel accounts and not more or less, Christians have typically stated the following:

    o   Each presents a different quality of Christ's character: 1) Matthew as King, 2) Mark as Suffering servant, 3) Luke as the Son of Man, and 4) John as Deity.

    o   Via all four gospels we get a full picture of who Christ is through the four different accounts.

- While these are valid points, there is more. As stated above, when we compare them, they provide us with evidence for the reliability and truthfulness of what they report in a way that made up stories or simply copies of made up stories or forgeries claiming to report events not really witnessed could not provide.

- Critics of the New Testament claim that the Gospels are just copies of made up stories. They will say things like, Matthew just copied Mark and made up some stuff of his own to go along with it. Like if we went and bought a copy of the Grand Rapids press and then bought another copy to verify what we read in the first copy. Consequently, the critics will tell us that we can't use the gospels as separate independent witnesses.

- Dr. McGrew disagrees. He maintains that by noting the *UC* in the gospel narratives we build a case that "the Gospel authors were well informed and habitually truthful."

UC #1 – Waiting to be Healed

- Matthew 8:14-16— so if the people believed that Jesus could heal them, why did they wait till evening? If you were sick would you want to wait to get in to see a Doctor?

- Mark 1:21, 29-32 — Mark tells the same story, but he gives us this detail in verse 21, "straightway on the sabbath day..." The reason the people waited till evening in Matthew 8 is because they were waiting for the Sabbath to end.

- So, do you see here how these accounts interlock? Was Matthew simply copying from Mark? No, why would he leave out this detail. Was Mark copying Matthew? No, Matthew doesn't even include the detail.

UC#1 Mark Explains Matthew

Matthew ←──────────── Mark

Luke   John

FROM THIS GENERATION FOR EVER

- So, a skeptic could come along and say, "Well Matthew could have copied from Mark and just left out that little detail. While this admittedly could be the case in one instance, if we have numerous instances like this, it builds the case that it is more than just accidental. It builds a case of cumulative force, which makes it ridiculous to claim accident or forgery.

UC#2 – Tell No Man

- Luke 9:28-36 — why did they tell "no man in those days any of those things which they had seen?"
- Mark 9:9-10 — so Mark gives us the command whereas Luke gives us what they did while offering no explanation for it. Luke just leaves the reader with a curious reaction on the part of the disciples.

UC#2 Mark Explains Luke

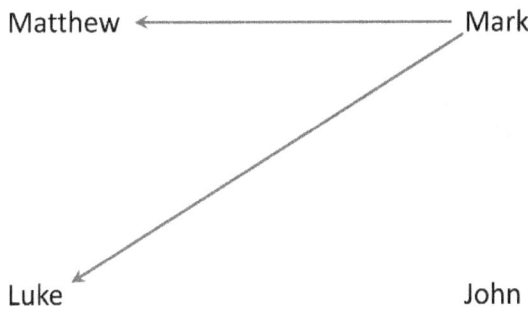

UC#3 – The Feeding of the 5,000

- Mark 6:31, 39 — Mark's account of the feeding of the 5,000 gives two details that the other gospel writers do not.

- Verse 31—...many were coming and going and they had no leisure so much as to eat.
- Verse 39 — And he commanded them to make all sit down by companies upon the green grass.
- Why would Mark say this about the "green grass" given the following image?

About that green grass ...

- John 6:4 — John tells us that the context for the feeding of the 5,000 was during the Passover season. Passover is in the midst of the growing season, the only time of year when there would have been "much green grass" spoken of in Mark. In addition, this also explains the reason "Many were coming and going, and they had no leisure so much as to eat." The first century Jewish historian Josephus stated there may have been as many as one million pilgrims in Jerusalem at Passover. Even if he is exaggerating, there must have been a mass of people and this explains this detail given in Mark.

- o So now we have Mark explaining something found in Matthew and Luke and we have John explaining something found in Mark.

- Notice the way this is happening? Mark doesn't tell us why there were many people coming and going. John doesn't tell us that there were many coming and going, but he gives us the explanation for it. See how the accounts interlock in this *undesigned* manner?

UC#3 John Explains Mark

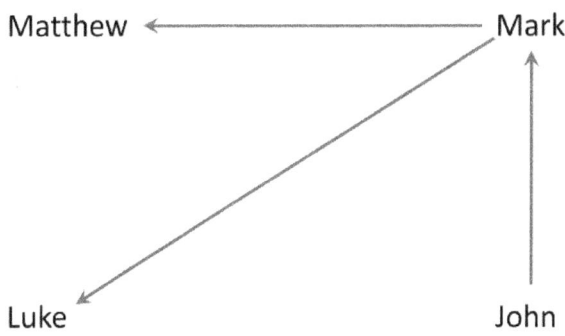

UC#4 – Events in Herod's Place

- Matthew 14:1-2 — two questions arise here that are not answered by Matthew. First, why would Herod be talking to his servants about this? Does this seem a bit odd? Someone of Herod's stature discussing something of this nature with servants? Second, how would Matthew know what Herod was talking about in his Palace?
- Luke 8:3— Luke, in a totally different context, when talking about women who ministered to Jesus mentions "Joanna, the wife of Chuza, Herod's steward. Here we see in a totally different context, a totally undesigned interlocking of Luke and Matthew.

UC#4 Luke Explains Matthew

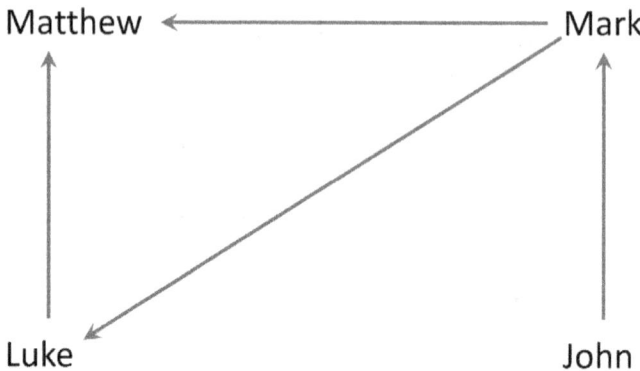

- Would anyone think Luke would have made up this information about Joanna in a totally different context just to explain Matthew? Don't miss what's happening, each of the gospels is explaining things in other gospels in a non-deliberate, undesigned way that gives them the mark of truth.

UC#5 – Mighty Works in Bethsaida

- Matthew 11:21 — what are the mighty works Matthew is talking about? For Chorazin the Bible doesn't tell us. But for Bethsaida we may find an answer. Wouldn't that be fortunate for us?
- John 6:5 — why Phillip? Philip is not really a major character.
- Luke 9:10-11 — in Luke, Bethsaida is the setting for the feeding of the 5,000.
- John 12:21 — look at the interlocking of Luke and John. Luke doesn't mention Philip in this context at all. Meanwhile, John doesn't mention Bethsaida as the setting of the miracle. Only by putting the two accounts together can we understand why Jesus speaks to Phillip in John 6. We see that John and Luke interlock.

- As to the mighty works done in Bethsaida in Matthew 11 one needs Luke 9 to learn that Bethsaida was where the feeding of the 5,000 took place. Also note that Matthew gives the account of the feeding of the 5,000 in chapter 14, after the woes are pronounced in Matthew 11. This is on account of the fact that Matthew arranges things thematically rather than chronologically. By comparing Luke, who arranges his account chronologically, we find that the feeding of the 5,000 took place before the woes were pronounced. Luke explains and informs Matthew.

UC#5 Luke Explains Matthew & John

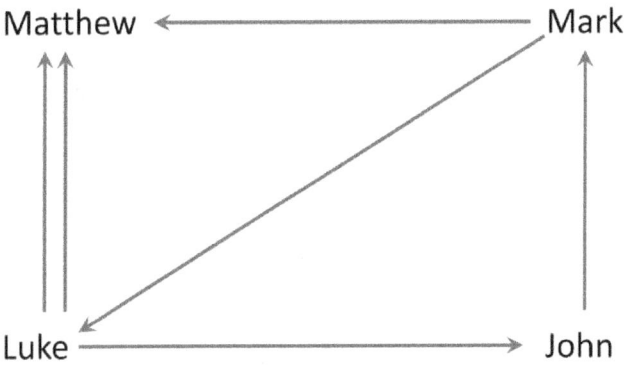

UC#6 – I Will Destroy This Temple

- Mark 14:58, 15:29 — In Mark 14 the Jews, before the high priest, at Jesus' trial, make the accusation "we heard Him say I will destroy this temple"... Later in chapter 15, they mockingly throw this accusation at Jesus while on the cross. There is nothing in the synoptic Gospels (Matthew, Mark, or Luke) that could have been the pretext for this accusation.

- John 2:18-19 — the Jews don't get what He is talking about. John gives the original statement but not the accusation; the synoptic gospels give us the accusation but not the original statement. Only by putting the two together do we get the whole picture.

UC#6 John Explains Mark

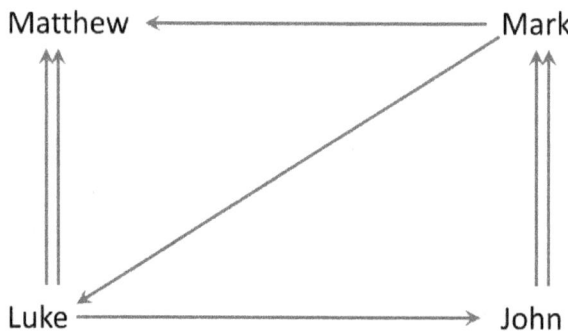

UC#7 – Jesus Questions Peter

- John 21:15 — this example is interesting because the context is after the resurrection. So a mark of authenticity here would be extremely important. Notice carefully the content of what Christ asks Peter: "do you love me more than these…" Without a context, Christ's question seems challenging and mean. The context is not found in John.
- Matthew 26:33 — Matthew records this boast although John does not. Also remember right after this Peter denies knowing the Lord three times. Another connection between John and the synoptic gospels is where Christ asks the question three times and the synoptics where Peter denies Christ.

UC#7 Matthew Explains John

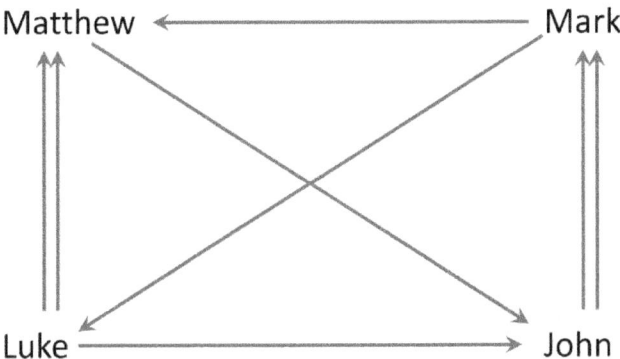

UC#8 – Jews Accusation Against Jesus

- Luke 23:2-4 — the Jews make this grave accusation against Jesus, "He is claiming to be a king." The Jews want Jesus put to death for blasphemy, but why would Pilate care about that? Pilate was probably blasphemer himself. So, they bring this charge that would be a clear violation of Roman law. Christ claiming to be king.

- But look at Pilate's response. Christ admits to the charge and Pilate says "I find no guilt in this Man." The Jews had to have been highly annoyed at this point. So why does Pilate find no guilt?

- John 18:33-38 — Pilate asks, "are you king of the Jews?" Jesus answers "my kingdom is not of this world". Pilate surmises this is a spiritual kingdom (i.e. make believe). Pilate thus pronounces "I find no fault in this Man". Only by comparing Luke and John do we get the full story.

UC# 8 John Explains Luke

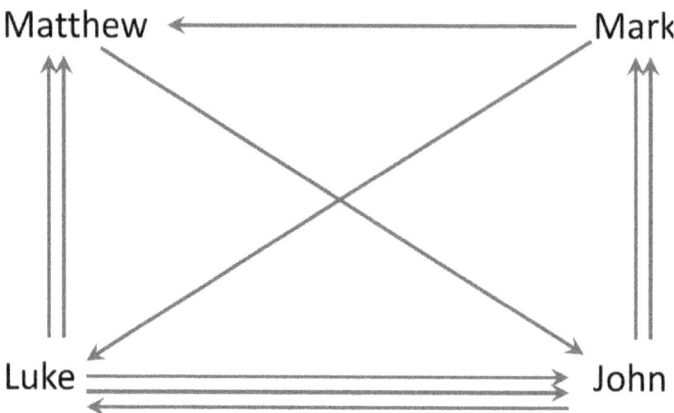

CONCLUSION

- "We are not left merely to guess what forgery looks like. The gnostic "gospels" of the second century afford us a clear illustration of how writers of the time who were forging a document on the basis of documents already known make use of their material. Thus, the "Gospel of Peter" is studded with phrases that sound like they have been lifted directly from the canonical Gospels:

    o And one of them brought a crown of thorns and put it on the head of the Lord. (cf. Mark 15:17)
    o And they brought two malefactors, and they crucified the Lord between them. (cf. Luke 23:32-33)
    o And in that hour the veil of the temple in Jerusalem was rent in twain. (cf. Mark 15:38)
    o But who shall roll away for us the stone …? (cf. Mark 16:3)

- o Whom seek ye? Him that was crucified? He is risen and gone. (cf. Mark 16:6)

The degree of verbal similarity between the Synoptic Gospels and the "Gospel of Peter" is high precisely because the forger — and he must be a forger, for he is writing long after Peter's death — wants to create a certain effect. He wants to give a ring of authenticity to the text he is manufacturing in order to ensure its favorable reception in a community where the established texts carry high prestige." (McGrew, Undesigned Coincidences: Part 3)

- Notice there is at least one line between all the gospels. Critics make a big deal about which gospel was written first, who copied from who etc. The force of this evidence is that it doesn't matter. This evidence points to independent testimony. The gospels are four separate witnesses giving accurate truthful accounts of actual historical events.
- These *UC* serve as internal proof of the Bible's inspiration. Only a book written under divine inspiration would exhibit characteristics such as these.

WORKS CITED

Holcom, Craig. *Undesigned Coincidences*. Grand Rapids, MI: Grace Life Bible Church, July 27, 2014.

McGrew, Timothy. Undesigned Coincidences: Part 3. http://christianapologeticsalliance.com/2013/09/29/undesigned-coincidences-part-3/

Paley, William. *The Complete Works of William Paley*. Philadelphia, PA: Crissy & Markley, 1830.

RESOURCES BY DR. TIMOTHY MCGREW

Undesigned Coincidences Series of articles by Dr. Timothy McGrew on Apologetics315.com

Video series by Dr. Timothy McGrew on the Apologetics315 YouTube page.

- Who Wrote the Gospels?
- External Evidence for the Truth of the Gospels
- Internal Evidence for the Truth of the Gospels, Part 2
- Alleged Historical Errors in the Gospels (Matthew & Mark)
- Alleged Historical Errors in the Gospels (Luke & John)
- Alleged Contradictions in the Gospels
- Alleged Contradictions in the Gospels, Part 2
- The Resurrection of Jesus

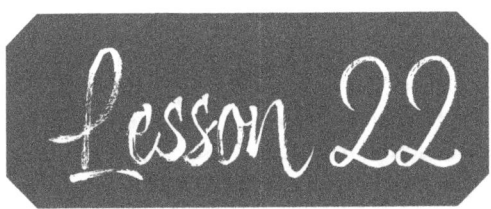

INTERNAL EVIDENCE OF INSPIRATION: UNDESIGNED COINCIDENCES, PART 2

INTRODUCTION

- Last week in Lesson 21 we began looking at the internal evidence of inspiration. Under the general category of internal evidence for inspiration I said that we would consider the following points:

    o   Undesigned Coincidences
    o   Fulfilled Prophecy

- Last week, with the help of William Paley, Dr. Timothy McGrew, and Craig Holcom we studied the general concept of *Undesigned Coincidences* (*UC*) and looked at examples found in the four gospels. In doing so we concluded:

    - This evidence (*UC* in the gospels) points to independent testimony. The gospels are four separate witnesses giving accurate truthful accounts of actual historical events. These *UC* serve as internal proof of the Bible's inspiration. Only a book written under divine inspiration would exhibit characteristics such as these.

- This morning I want to consider some examples of *UC* in Paul's epistles. This seems prudent given the fact that our assembly believes that Paul is the apostle of the Gentiles for the current dispensation of grace.

UNDESIGNED COINCIDENCES IN THE PAULINE EPISTLES

- In his *Horae Paulinae* (1790), William Paley examines the Book of Acts, on the one hand, and the Pauline epistles, on the other, with a view to showing how each might illustrate the other. Paley's *Horae Paulinae* was the first work to explore this sort of argument in detail. Paley's object is to show the numerous correspondences between the Pauline epistles and the book of Acts.

- "Paley stresses, in the first chapter of the *Horae Paulinae*, that the indirectness, the evident undesignedness, is what makes these coincidences significant. The information that makes the passages from the epistles interlock with the history is dropped casually and naturally into the narrative. By contrast, although there is a very close verbal parallel between Paul's description of the last supper in I Corinthians 11:24-25 and the words of institution in Luke 22:17-20, this coincidence might easily be explained by the hypothesis that one of the sources is copied from the other. That is not to say that either author actually did copy from the other. But when the points of coincidence are too obvious, the correspondence might have been forged after the historical work became well known, or vice versa." (McGrew, Undesigned Coincidences: Part 2)

- "If there were only a small number of undesigned coincidences, we might shrug them off as statistical noise. After all, in a large box of jigsaw puzzle pieces taken at random, one piece, from many different puzzles, someone searching with great patience might find a few pairs that fit together (more or less) by sheer accident. But when a large number of pieces fit together, sometimes in clusters, the chance explanation rapidly becomes absurd. That is why, to appreciate the force of the argument from undesigned coincidences, we must have the patience to work through multiple examples. But the picture that emerges when we take the time to do this will amply repay us for the labor and study we bestow on the project." (McGrew, Undesigned Coincidences: Part 2)

Pauline UC#1 — I am of Paul and I am of Apollos

- I Corinthians 1:12, 3:6 — both of these verses suggest that Apollos had been at Corinth; the second also suggests that Paul had preceded him there.
- Acts 18:19, 23, 26; 19:1—"after his first visit to Greece, Paul went from Corinth to Ephesus, where he left his companions Priscilla and Aquila; he returned to Palestine, stopping in Jerusalem, and then went north into Asia Minor (Acts 18:19, 23), ultimately making his way back to Ephesus. It is during the period of these later travels that Apollos comes on the scene, being instructed in Ephesus by Priscilla and Aquila (Acts 18:26) and passing from them over to Achaia, where "he greatly helped those who through grace had believed" (Acts 18:27). We might have inferred from this alone that Apollos went to Corinth on this trip, but we need not stop here, as we find that Paul came back to Ephesus at the very time that Apollos was in Corinth (Acts 19:1)." (McGrew, Undesigned Coincidences: Part 2)

Pauline UC#2 – Letters of Commendation

- There is a further point of coincidence, equally indirect, between this passage of Acts and an expression Paul uses when remonstrating with the Corinthians in his second epistle.
- II Corinthians 3:1-2
- Acts 18:27 — as it happens, the book of Acts provides the clue to Paul's language; for when Apollos, having been instructed by Priscilla and Aquilla, made his own trip to Corinth, "the brothers encouraged him and wrote to the disciples to welcome him" (Acts 18:27).

"What should we infer from the way that the book of Acts interlocks with the Corinthian epistles? The examples we have looked at here offer us some evidence that the authors of each were well informed and habitually truthful. That falls short of a demonstration, of course, but all historical evidence falls short of mathematical demonstration. The case is a *prima facie* one, and it would be strengthened if we found other, similar arguments with respect to these texts. Paley gives a dozen for each of these epistles." (McGrew, Undesigned Coincidences: Part 2)

Pauline UC#3 – Contribution for the Poor Saints at Jerusalem

- "One of the benefits of having both Paul's letters and a history of Paul's activities (the book of Acts) from another hand is that we are able to compare points of contact across the two genres. Their overlap is all the more valuable since they appear to have been written largely or wholly independently of one another, with very little verbal similarity at any point.
- What should we expect from such material, if each is independently grounded in the facts? With luck, and if the material is extensive, we should be able to find multiple instances where the documents refer

to the same people or events. Of course, we should not expect the history and the letters to correspond point-for-point; in the nature of the case, there will be much in the letters that would be out of place in the history, while the history — in keeping with the historical standards of the times — may organize material conceptually rather than chronologically and may compress or pass over some incidents in the course of the narration. And occasionally, the correspondences may cross over several letters, creating a network of related passages that cannot with any plausibility be dismissed as fabrication or forgery." (McGrew, Undesigned Coincidences: Part 3)

- Romans 15:25-26 — here we have three points of interest all in the same passage in one of the letters: a collection being take up in Macedonia, a similar collection in Achaia, and Paul's plan to travel to Jerusalem to take this aid to the saints there.
- Acts 20:2-3 — we find Paul on the way back to Palestine, but there is not a word about a contribution.
- Acts 24:17-19 — Paul mentions that he came to bring alms to his countrymen, but there is no mention of where the monies come from.
- The points of correspondence are so indirect that there is no suspicion of copying here. Two other passages from the letters enable us to fill out the picture.
- I Corinthians 16:1-4 — we see that there was a contribution being collected at Corinth, the capital of Achaia, for the Christians of Jerusalem.
- II Corinthians 8:1-4, 9:2 — we find the churches of Macedonia introduced as already engaged in a collection for this very purpose.
- "Thus all of the circumstances brought together in those two verses in Romans are corroborated by a number of other passages in the history of Acts and in the Corinthian epistles. And each of these, by some hint in the passage, or by the date of the writing in which the passage occurs, can be fixed at a particular time — a period toward the close of Paul's second missionary journey.

Does this conformity, scattered and indirect, with not a whiff of verbal similarity, look like forgery on one part or on the other? Or rather, does each passage stand perfectly naturally in connection with its own context? If so, the suggestion that such a coincidence is the effect of design is most improbable." (McGrew, Undesigned Coincidences: Part 3)

- "The book of Acts and the Pauline epistles are verbally independent; their interconnections are indirect. That is what makes their harmonies so impressive as evidence that both give us substantially truthful representations of real events." (McGrew, Undesigned Coincidences: Part 3)

Pauline UC#4 – Greet Priscilla and Aquila

- "There are certain parts of Paul's letters that we typically pass over in silence. The long lists of greetings, in particular, are flyover territory for expository preachers. "Greet Asyncritus, Phlegon, Hermes, Patrobas, Hermas…" The congregation is probably snoring already. And yet such passages can, on occasion, furnish us with beautiful examples of coincidence without design." (McGrew, Undesigned Coincidences: Part 4)
- Romans 16:3-4—"first, the fact that this greeting appears in the epistle to the *Romans* suggests that Prisca and Aquila are inhabitants of that city." (McGrew, Undesigned Coincidences: Part 4)
- Acts 18:2 — so Priscilla and Aquila were originally inhabitants of Rome, perhaps recently returned once the expulsion under Claudius ceased to be enforced. This is one point of coincidence." (McGrew, Undesigned Coincidences: Part 4)
- Acts 18:3, 18—"again, from Acts 18, we find that Paul stayed with them (18:3), and when he left, they departed with him (18:18). From this, it would be a fair inference that they were fellow workers with him, though only Paul's greeting in Romans makes this fact explicit." (McGrew, Undesigned Coincidences: Part 4)
- Acts 18:12-17—"third, Paul says that they "laid down their own necks" for his sake. How so? See Acts 18:12-17, where Paul is dragged before the Roman tribunal and Sosthenes is beaten by the mob. If Aquila and Prisca were Paul's fellow workers Christ Jesus in Corinth,

it is clear that they, too, were exposed to dangers." (McGrew, Undesigned Coincidences: Part 4)

- "Fourth, Paul indicates that the churches of the Gentiles give thanks for them. Given the themes of the entire letter, this singling out of the Gentiles seems to have more than ordinary significance. And going back to Acts 18:2, we find that Aquila was a Jew, expelled from Rome when the emperor Claudius, exasperated with riots in the Jewish quarter that had something to do with a fellow named "Chrestus" (a common Roman misspelling of "Christus"), decided to evict the Jews. Yet they were working with Paul, who in this very city declared that he was turning from the Jews to the Gentiles and from that time forward conducted a highly effective mission among them (18:5-11). So Prisca and Aquila, though Jews, took part in the ministry to the Gentiles. And that is how they earned the thanks of the Gentile churches." (McGrew, Undesigned Coincidences: Part 4)

- Romans 16:1 — *why commend a servant of the church at Cenchrea?* Paul is writing, apparently, from Corinth. Perhaps Cenchrea is, then, in the neighborhood of Corinth.

- Acts 18:18 — we find from the book of Acts that Paul himself, upon leaving Corinth, visited Cenchrea.

- "Thus the apparently barren lists of greetings furnish us with numerous points of indirect correspondence — consistency and even harmony, but without verbal borrowing — with the events in the historical narrative of Acts." (McGrew, Undesigned Coincidences: Part 4)

Pauline UC#5 – The Life and Journeys of Timothy

- I Corinthians 4:17 — Paul explains that he has sent Timothy unto the Corinthians. From that passage alone, however, we cannot tell whether he has sent him *before* the letter or *with* it, in which case the language of "sending" would be anticipation of the act.

- I Corinthians 16:10-11 — makes it plain that Paul had sent Timothy before writing the letter, as he speaks of Timothy's arrival as something independent from their receipt of the letter itself.

- "But the comparison of these two passages raises an interesting question. If Timothy had been sent first, why should he not arrive first? And if he arrived first, what use would it be to send, after the fact, instructions on how they were to receive him?

    The only plausible resolution is that Timothy, though sent first, must have taken some indirect route to Corinth. The fastest method of travel from Ephesus, where Paul was writing, to Corinth would be to take a ship; with a fair wind, the journey between these two cities on opposite sides of the archipelago can be made in a very short time." (McGrew, Undesigned Coincidences: Part 6)

- Acts 19:21-22—"we discover that Timothy, when he left Ephesus, took the land route, and went up through Macedonia. Here once again we have the characteristic of undesigned coincidences that neither the historical account nor the letters could plausibly be said to have been written up from the other. The letter does not mention Timothy's journey through Macedonia at all; the book of Acts does not mention Paul's letter. But what we find in the book of Acts is the only plausible way of reconciling those stray comments Paul makes in the letter." (McGrew, Undesigned Coincidences: Part 6)

- "It is not always so in historical work. Jortin's *Life of Erasmus*, for example, is framed almost entirely from Erasmus's letters, and for just that reason it gives us virtually nothing that cannot be found in the letters themselves. There is much parallel material between the letters and Jortin's biography, but there is no *interlocking*. The coincidences do not qualify as *undesigned*." (McGrew, Undesigned Coincidences: Part 6)

- II Timothy 3:15 — clearly, this is a reference to the Jewish scriptures; but Paul gives no clue as to how Timothy, who was not circumcised until after his conversion as a young man (Acts 16:3), had acquired such knowledge.

- Acts 16:1 — his mother made sure he was instructed in the scriptures of her people.

Pauline UC#6 – Acts Was Not Written by Someone Copying Paul's Letters

- "A life as rich in travel and relationships as Paul's was, documented both by his letters and by the history of the book of Acts, affords many opportunities for undesigned coincidences to emerge — so many, in fact, that it is worth pausing to see some of the evidence that Acts was not written by someone who had Paul's letters before him.

  Leafing through II Corinthians, we notice how conspicuous a part is played by Titus. He is named multiple times (see chapters 7 and 8 in particular), and Paul describes him in II Corinthians 8:23 as "my partner and fellow helper concerning you." Yet in the book of Acts, his name does not appear even once. It would be a poor fabricator who could not make more of his material than this. Yet in real historical documents, the omission of some person or event that we could hardly imagine ourselves omitting is quite common.

  Or consider Paul's enumeration of his sufferings in II Corinthians 11:24-25. "Thrice was I beaten with rods"—but only one of those occasions makes it into the history (Acts 16:22). "Thrice I suffered shipwreck; a night and a day I have been in the deep"—what an opportunity to tell a set of dramatic tales! Yet not one of these three is mentioned in the book of Acts, where the one disastrous voyage that is recounted (Acts 27) takes place years after this letter was penned.

  Or compare the account Paul gives of his escape from Damascus in II Corinthians 11:32-33 with the account of the same adventure in Acts 9:23-25. The main facts are the same, but the differences make it perfectly clear that the history was not written up from the letter. In II Corinthians, for example, Paul says that Aretas had the city guarded, though there is no information as to who did the guarding. In Acts, we are told that the Jews kept watch at the gates for Paul, for which they probably needed the leave of the ethnarch; yet Aretas goes unnamed. True, it is not hard to reconcile these statements. *Qui facit per alium, facit per se*, as the saying goes: he who does a thing by another does it himself. But here again, it is not credible to suggest that the author of Acts wrote his history from the letter.

This same manifest independence is visible in I Corinthians as well. Consider all of the problems that the church at Corinth had written about, problems to which Paul replies in 1 Corinthians 7 and 8: problems about marriage, about calling, about the unmarried, about food offered to idols. It is wholly natural that they should make these inquiries of Paul and wholly natural that he should reply to them. Yet in the book of Acts we find no trace of these problems at Corinth, and the one place that the question of food offered to idols is touched upon, the Jerusalem council arguably enjoins something stricter than Paul himself, writing later than that event, imposes (Acts 15:20).

All of these passages provide evidence that the history was written independently of these letters. The numerous coincidences between them, some of which we have already seen in this series and some of which we will be looking at in subsequent installments, are therefore genuinely undesigned. And that is why they provide evidence of their substantial trustworthiness.

One more touch of verisimilitude in 1 Corinthians itself, noted by Paley in his *Horae Paulinae*, though not really an undesigned coincidence, deserves attention. Paul begins chapter 7 with a reference to earlier correspondence now lost: "Now concerning the things whereof ye wrote unto me. . ."

The issues they have raised, however foreign to us, are the sorts of things we can well imagine arising in a young church of the time. But other parts of the letter reveal that there were graver and more embarrassing problems that they had not written about but that Paul had evidently learned of from other sources: bitter quarreling and divisions (1:11, 11:18), sexual immorality (5:1), and lawsuits between members of the church (6:1). What is more natural or probable than that their letter to Paul should speak of the issues that did not reflect poorly on any of them, while rumor carried to Paul's ears ("It is commonly reported ..." 5:1) an account of the more scandalous matters? This manner of dividing the issues Paul addresses would be most improbable in a forgery. It has the ring of truth." (McGrew, Undesigned Coincidences: Part 5)

CONCLUSION

- Please recall from Lesson 21 last week that *UC* demonstrate the reliability of the Bible and demonstrate the following:

    o The authenticity of the books — they were written by who they claim to have been written by.

    o The genuineness of the books — they are trustworthy history, an accurate presentation of the material they report.

- These *UC* serve as internal proof of the Bible's inspiration. Only a book written under divine inspiration would exhibit characteristics such as these.

WORKS CITED

McGrew, Timothy. *Undesigned Coincidences Series.* Apologetics315.com.

INTERNAL EVIDENCE OF INSPIRATION: FULFILLED PROPHECY

INTRODUCTION

- In Lesson 22 we continued our consideration of the internal evidence of inspiration by looking at Undesigned Coincidences between the book of Acts and the Pauline epistles.

- Previously, I said that we would be looking at two primary categories of internal evidence for the Bible's inspiration: 1) Undesigned Coincidences, and 2) fulfilled prophecy. Having completed our cursory study (much more could be said) of Undesigned Coincidences we are now ready to turn our attention to a consideration of fulfilled prophecy.

OUR PROPHETIC GOD

- Fulfilled prophecies give clear attestation to the hand of God in human history and are some of the most important evidence we have for the divine origin and inspiration of the Bible. The Bible is the only religious document in existence that provides more than two thousand prophecies that validate its historical claims. Biblical prophecy deals with everything from the Lord Jesus Christ, the nation Israel, Gentile nations (Babylon, Persia, Greece, and Rome), cities (Tyre), and people (Nebuchadnezzar and Cyrus). (Story, 37)

- Other religions have, of course, made prophetic claims, but in no other religion in the world has prophecy been fulfilled so completely and so accurately as what is recorded in the Bible.

- Many believe that the issue of fulfilled prophecy is the single greatest Divine apologetic.

- Isaiah 46:9-10 — "Remember the former things of old: for I *am* God, and *there is* none else; *I am* God, and *there is* none like me, Declaring the end from the beginning, and from ancient times *the things* that are not *yet* done, saying, My counsel shall stand, and I will do all my pleasure:"

    o God almighty has the capacity to declare from the beginning the things "not yet done." God's ability to do this stems from the fact that, as God, He knows the "end from the beginning." Whatever, God declares "shall stand" i.e., it will come to pass.

- Numbers 23:19 — "God *is* not a man, that he should lie; neither the son of man, that he should repent: hath he said, and shall he not do *it*? or hath he spoken, and shall he not make it good?"

    o If God would be wrong about something, He declared in advance He would not be God. What makes God God is the fact that He knows the end from the beginning and cannot lie or be wrong about anything He declares. God's knowledge is infinite, and His word cannot be broken (John 10:35).

- Isaiah 48:3, 5 — "I have declared the former things from the beginning; and they went forth out of my mouth, and I shewed them; I did *them* suddenly, and they came to pass. . . I have even from the beginning declared *it* to thee; before it came to pass I shewed *it* thee: lest thou shouldest say, Mine idol hath done them, and my graven image, and my molten image, hath commanded them.»

  - God's ability to predict an event in advance and have it come to pass as it was foretold is what sets God apart from the man-made gods of the Gentiles. Furthermore, not only does God possess the capacity to declare the end from the beginning, He had the audacity to set forth His predictions in writing. The issue of fulfilled prophecy is not only one of the greatest proofs for the existence of God, it is also serves as strong internal evidence for inspiration.

- Deuteronomy 13:1-5, 18:20-22

  - "God issues strong decrees concerning the use or misuse of prophecy and the identification of true and false prophets. God instructed Israel to put to death anyone who prophesied on any authority other than God's — even if his prophecy came to pass. Moreover, if a prophecy did not come to pass, even if it was spoken in the name of the Lord, that person was to be put to death as a false prophet." (Story, 37)

OLD TESTAMENT PROPHECIES FULFILLED IN CHRIST

- "The Old Testament, written over a one-thousand-year period, contains nearly three hundred references to the coming Messiah." (McDowell,

164) The fact that all three hundred of these prophesies were fulfilled in Jesus Christ establishes solid internal confirmation of inspiration.

- Not only was the Old Testament written over a 1,000-year time span but it was also completed at least 250 years before the advent of Christ. According to the traditional view of the Septuagint (which I am not necessarily endorsing), the Greek translation of the Hebrew Old Testament dates its origin to about 250 B.C. When one considers that a complete Hebrew Old Testament must have predated its translation into Greek, the date for the completion of the Old Testament is pushed back even further into antiquity. 450 B.C. is the date accepted by most conservative scholars for the completion of the Old Testament. Therefore, suffice it to say that there was at least a 400-year gap (many times longer) between the prophecies concerning the coming of the Messiah and their fulfilment in the advent of Christ.

- In his book *The New Evidence That Demands a Verdict,* Josh McDowell catalogues 61 Old Testament prophecies that were fulfilled in the person of Jesus Christ during his first advent. Time and space will not permit an exhaustive investigation of all 61 prophecies in this lesson. Interested parties are encouraged to obtain a copy of McDowell's book and look at pages 168 through 192.

- For our purposes we will consider the following ten prophetic utterances fulfilled in the person of Jesus Christ.

Born at Bethlehem

Prophecy	Fulfillment
Micah 5:2 — But thou, Bethlehem Ephratah, *though* thou be little among the thousands of Judah, *yet* out of thee shall he come forth unto me *that is* to be ruler in Israel; whose goings forth *have been* from of old, from everlasting.	Matthew 2:1 — Now when Jesus was born in Bethlehem of Judaea in the days of Herod the king, behold, there came wise men from the east to Jerusalem, Also see Luke 2:4-7 & John 7:42

- God eliminated all the cities of the world, save one, for the entrance of his Son into the world. Jesus was born in precisely the place that the prophet predicted.

Preceded by a Messenger

Prophecy	Fulfillment
Isaiah 40:3 — "The voice of him that crieth in the wilderness, Prepare ye the way of the LORD, make straight in the desert a highway for our God." Also see Malachi 3:1	Matthew 3:1-3 — "In those days came John the Baptist, preaching in the wilderness of Judaea, And saying, Repent ye: for the kingdom of heaven is at hand. For this is he that was spoken of by the prophet Esaias, saying, The voice of one crying in the wilderness, Prepare ye the way of the Lord, make his paths straight." Also see Luke 1:17 & John 1:23

- John the Baptist was the fulfillment of Isaiah 40:3 according to Matthew, Luke, and John.

Entrance into Jerusalem on a Donkey

Prophecy	Fulfillment
Zechariah 9:9 — "Rejoice greatly, O daughter of Zion; shout, O daughter of Jerusalem: behold, thy King cometh unto thee: he *is* just, and having salvation; lowly, and riding upon an ass, and upon a colt the foal of an ass."	Luke 19:35-37 — "And they brought him to Jesus: and they cast their garments upon the colt, and they set Jesus thereon. And as he went, they spread their clothes in the way. And when he was come nigh, even now at the descent of the mount of Olives, the whole multitude of the disciples began to rejoice and praise God with a loud voice for all the mighty works that they had seen;" Also see Matt. 21:6-7

Betrayed By a Friend

Prophecy	Fulfillment
Psalm 41:9 — "Yea, mine own familiar friend, in whom I trusted, which did eat of my bread, hath lifted up *his* heel against me." Also see Psalm 55:12-14	Matthew 10:4 — "Simon the Canaanite, and Judas Iscariot, who also betrayed him." Also see Matt. 26:49-50 & John 13:21

Betrayed for Thirty Pieces of Silver

Prophecy	Fulfillment
Zechariah 11:12 — "And I said unto them, If ye think good, give *me* my price; and if not, forbear. So they weighed for my price thirty *pieces* of silver."	Matthew 26:15 — "And said *unto them*, What will ye give me, and I will deliver him unto you? And they covenanted with him for thirty pieces of silver."

Silver to be thrown in the House of the LORD

Prophecy	Fulfillment
Zechariah 11:13 — "And the LORD said unto me, Cast it unto the potter: a goodly price that I was prised at of them. And I took the thirty *pieces* of silver, and cast them to the potter in the house of the LORD."	Mathew 27:5 — "And he cast down the pieces of silver in the temple, and departed, and went and hanged himself."

Silver Used to Purchase the Potter's Field

Prophecy	Fulfillment
Zechariah 11:13— "And the LORD said unto me, Cast it unto the potter: a goodly price that I was prised at of them. And I took the thirty *pieces* of silver, and cast them to the potter in the house of the LORD."	Matthew 27:7— "And they took counsel, and bought with them the potter's field, to bury strangers in."

Silent before His Accusers

Prophecy	Fulfillment
Isaiah 53:7— "He was oppressed, and he was afflicted, yet he opened not his mouth: he is brought as a lamb to the slaughter, and as a sheep before her shearers is dumb, so he openeth not his mouth"	Matthew 27:12— "And when he was accused of the chief priests and elders, he answered nothing."

Hands and Feet Pierced

Prophecy	Fulfillment
Psalm 22:16 — "For dogs have compassed me: the assembly of the wicked have inclosed me: they pierced my hands and my feet." Also see Zech. 12:10	John 20:25 — "The other disciples therefore said unto him, We have seen the Lord. But he said unto them, Except I shall see in his hands the print of the nails, and put my finger into the print of the nails, and thrust my hand into his side, I will not believe." Also see Luke 23:33

- Here we see the Roman manner of execution foretold before the Roman Empire even existed.

Numbered with the Transgressors

Prophecy	Fulfillment
Isaiah 53:12— "Therefore will I divide him *a portion* with the great, and he shall divide the spoil with the strong; because he hath poured out his soul unto death: and he was numbered with the transgressors; and he bare the sin of many, and made intercession for the transgressors."	Mathew 27:38— "Then were there two thieves crucified with him, one on the right hand, and another on the left." Also see Mark 15:27-28

FULFILLED PROPHECY AND THE LIFE OF JESUS: ENGINEERED OR LUCKY?

- In the face of the internal evidence of inspiration provided by fulfilled prophecy, skeptics and critics have tried to rescue their enterprise arguing either one of the following in respect to the fulfillment of Messianic prophecies.

    - Engineered Fulfillment
    - Accidental Fulfillment

Engineered Fulfillment

- In 1965, radical New Testament scholar H.J. Schonfield wrote a book titled *The Passover Plot* in which he argued that Jesus was a messianic pretender who conspired to fulfill prophecy in order to substantiate His claims. There are several lines of argumentation that demonstrate the implausibility of Schonfield's thesis:

> o "There is no way that Jesus could have controlled many events necessary for the fulfillment of Old Testament prophecies about the Messiah. For example, He could not control where He was born (Mic. 5:2), how He would be born of a virgin (Is. 7:14), when He would die (Dan. 9:25), what tribe (Gen. 49:10) and lineage He would be from (II Sam. 7:12), or other facts about His life that have corresponded to prophecy.
>
> . . . there is no way short of being supernatural that Jesus could have manipulated the events and people in His life to respond in exactly the way necessary for it to appear that He was fulling all these prophecies, including John's heralding (Matt. 3), His accuser's reactions (Matt. 27:12), how the soldiers cast lots for His garments (John 19:23-24), and how they would pierce His side with a spear (John 19:34).
>
> Indeed, even Schonfield admits that the plot failed when the Romans actually pierced Christ. The fact is that anyone with all this power would have to be divine — the very thing the Passover hypothesis attempts to avoid. In short, it takes a bigger miracle to believe the *Passover Plot* than to accept these prophecies as supernatural." (McDowell, 192-193)

- Belief that the fulfillment of Messianic prophecies was engineered by Christ during his earthly ministry would require belief in a greater supernatural act than simply believing in their organic fulfillment as recorded in the four gospels.

Accidental Fulfillment

- A second argument one might utilize to try and escape the internal evidence for inspiration provided by fulfilled prophecy is coincidence. In other words, Jesus fulfilled all 61 Old Testament prophecies concerning His first advent by accident and happenstance.

- In 1944 a book appeared by Peter Stoner titled *Science Speaks*. Among other things, Stoner's work presented the mathematical probability of the ten prophetic statements we looked at above ever having been fulfilled in one person. The following is a quotation from Stoner's book:

    o "... the chance that any man might have lived down to the present time and fulfilled all eight prophecies [The same ten we looked at above. Stoner combined a few of them.] is 1 in 10^{17}.

    Let us try to visualize this chance. If you mark one of ten tickets, and place all of the tickets in a hat, and thoroughly stir them, and then ask a blindfolded man to draw one, his chance of getting the right ticket is one in ten. Suppose that we take 10^{17} silver dollars and lay them on the face of Texas. They will cover all of the state two feet deep. Now mark one of these silver dollars and stir the whole mass thoroughly, all over the state. Blindfold a man and tell him that he can travel as far as he wishes, but he must pick up one silver dollar and say that this is the right one. What chance would he have of getting the right one? Just the same chance that the prophets would have had of writing these eight prophecies and having them all come true in any one man, from their day to the present time, providing they wrote using their own wisdom.

    Now these prophecies were either given by inspiration of God or the prophets just wrote them as they thought they should be. In such a case the prophets had just one chance in 10^{17} of having them come true in any man, but they all came true in Christ.

    This means that the fulfillment of these eight prophecies alone proves that God inspired the writing of those prophecies to a definiteness which lacks only one change in 10^{17} of being absolute.

    ... Sometimes we weigh our chances in the business world, and say if an investment has nine chances in ten of being profitable, and only one chance in ten of being a failure, it is safe enough for us to make the investment. Whoever heard of an investment that had only one chance in 10^{17} of failure? The business world has no conception of such an investment. Yet we are offered this investment by God. By the acceptance of Jesus Christ as our Savior we know, from only these eight prophecies which lack only 1 chance in 10^{17} of being an absolute proof, that that investment will yield the wonderful dividend of eternal life with Christ. Can anyone be so unreasonable as to reject Jesus Christ and pin his hope of eternal life on such a slim chance as finding the right silver dollar among this great mass, covering the whole state of Texas two feet deep? It does not seem possible, yet every man who rejects Christ is doing just that.

More than three hundred prophecies from the Old Testament which deal with the first advent of Christ have been listed. Every one of them was completely fulfilled by Jesus Christ. Let us see what happens when we take more than eight prophecies.

Suppose we add eight more prophecies to our list, and assume that their chance of fulfillment is the same as the eight just considered. The chance that one man would fulfill all sixteen is $1 \times 10^{28} \times 10^{17}$ or 1 in 10^{45}.

Let us try to visualize this as we did before. Take this number of silver dollars. If you make these into a solid ball, you will have a great sphere with a center at the earth, and extending in all directions more than 30 times as far as from the earth to the sun. (If a train had started from the earth at the time the Declaration of Independence was signed, and had traveled steadily toward the sun at the rate of sixty miles per hour, day and night, it would be about reaching its destination today. But remember that our ball of silver dollars extends thirty times that far in all directions.) If you can imagine the marking of one silver dollar, and then thoroughly stirring it into this great ball, and blindfolding a man and telling him to pick out one dollar, and expect it to be the marked one, you have somewhat of a picture of how absolutely the fulfillment of sixteen prophecies referring to Jesus Christ proves both that He is the Son of God and that our Bible is inspired. Certainly God directed the writing of His Word.

In order to extend this consideration beyond all bounds of human comprehension, let us consider forty-eight prophecies, similar in their human chance of fulfillment to the eight which we originally considered, using a much more conservative number, 1 in 10^{21}. Applying the same principle of probability used so far, we find the chance that any one man fulfilled all forty-eight prophecies to be 1 in 10^{157}.

This is really a large number and it represents an extremely small chance. Let us try to visualize it. The silver dollar, which we have been using, is entirely too large. We must select a smaller object. The electron is about as small an object as we know of. It is so small that it will take 2.5×10^{15} of them laid side by side to make a line, single file, one inch long. If we were going to count the electrons in this line one inch long, and counted 250 each minute, and if we counted day and night, it would take us 19,000,000 years to count just the one-inch line of electrons. If we had a cubic inch of these electrons and we tried to count them, it would take us 1.2×10^{38} years (2×10^{28} times the 6 billion years back to the creation of the solar system).

With this introduction, let us go back to our chance of 1 in 10^{157}. Let us suppose that we are taking this number of electrons, marking one, and thoroughly stirring it into the whole mass, then blindfolding a man and letting him try to find the right one. What chance has he of finding the right one? What kind of a pile will this number of electrons make? They make an inconceivably large volume.

. . . To the extent, then, that we know this blindfolded man cannot pick out the marked electron, we know that the Bible is inspired. This is not merely evidence. It is proof of the Bible's inspiration by God-proof so definite that the universe is not large enough to hold the evidence. Some will say that our estimates of the probability of the fulfillment of these prophecies are too large and the numbers should be reduced. Ask a man to submit his own estimates, and if they are smaller than these we have used, we shall add a few more prophecies to be evaluated and this same number will be reestablished or perhaps exceeded.

Our Bible students claim that there are more than three hundred prophecies dealing with Christ's first advent. If this number is correct, and it no doubt is, you could set your estimates ridiculously low on the whole three hundred prophecies and still obtain tremendous evidence of inspiration.

For example you may place all of your estimates at one in four. You may say that one man in four has been born in Bethlehem: that one of these children in four was taken to Egypt, to avoid slaughter; that one in four of these came back and made his home in Nazareth; that one in four of these was a carpenter; that one in four of these was betrayed for thirty pieces of silver; that one in four of these has been crucified on a cross; that one in four was then buried in a rich man's tomb; yes, even that one in four rose from the dead on the third day; and so on for all of the three hundred prophecies and from them I will build a number much larger than the one we obtained form the forty-eight prophecies.

Any man who rejects Christ as the Son of God is rejecting a fact proved perhaps more absolutely than any other fact in the world." (Stoner, 100-110)

- The accidental fulfillment argument is just as ridiculous as the engineered fulfillment argument if not more so.

CONCLUSION

- The issue of fulfilled prophecy remains one of the strongest apologetic arguments for the existence of God and internal evidence for the inspiration of scripture.

WORKS CITED

McDowell, Josh. *The New Evidence That Demands a Verdict*. Nashville: Thomas Nelson, 1999.

Stoner, Peter. *Science Speaks*. Chicago, IL: Moody Press, 1944.

Story, Dan. *Defending Your Faith: How to Answer the Tough Questions*. Nashville: Thomas Nelson, 1992.

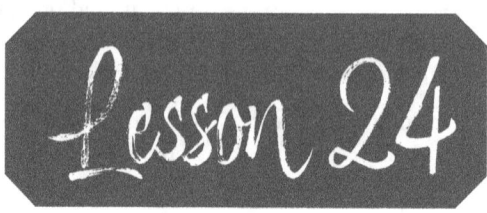

EXTERNAL EVIDENCE OF INSPIRATION: THE HISTORICITY OF THE OLD TESTAMENT

INTRODUCTION

- Way back at the beginning of this class, in Lesson 2, we discussed the difference between an Evidential and Presuppositional approach to the topic of inspiration. Specifically, I stated:

    o "In the weeks and months leading up to the start of class I gave a lot of thought to how I should begin and the best order for covering the material. While I knew I was going to start with the issue of inspiration, originally, I thought I would cover the evidentiary proofs of inspiration first.

As I pondered my options further, I decided that beginning with an evidentialist approach might send the wrong message. I believe that the Bible is the inspired Word of God because that is the Bible's claim for itself. This does not mean that there are no evidentiary proofs that speak to the Bible's inspiration, it just means that we need to base our study on the proper set of assumptions.

- God exists. (Psalms 14:1)
- God has magnified His Word above His own name. (Psalms 138:2)
- God's word is eternally settled in heaven. (Psalms 119:89)
- God, through the process of inspiration, has communicated His Word to mankind. (I Timothy 3:16 and II Peter 1:21)
- God's Words were written down so that they could be made eternally available to men. (I Peter 1:23)
- God promised to preserve that which He inspired. (Psalms 12:6-7)

So, for the purposes of this class, we are going to initially adopt a presuppositional approach that assumes the Bible to be the inspired Word of God at the outset. This assumption is made on account of the FACT that the Bible claims to be inspired by God. After we have learned what the Bible says about itself, we will consider the many evidential proofs that the Bible is, in fact, of divine origin.

I am aware of the division that exists within Christian Apologetics between the presuppositional and evidential approaches. It is my view that both are valid and have a seat at the table. Consequently, throughout the course of this study we will be looking at both. There is ample internal and external evidence that the Bible was given by inspiration of God and is therefore of divine origin." (Ross, Lesson 2)

- After taking some time to get our footing (Lessons 1-10), we have spent the last twelve lessons (Lesson 11-23) studying the Bible's own claim of inspiration as well as the internal evidence that substantiates that claim.

- Now beginning with Lesson 24, I would like to adopt a more evidentialist approach and look at some of the external proofs for inspiration. In order to accomplish this task, I intend to touch upon the following:

    o Historicity of the Old Testament
    o Historicity of the New Testament
    o The Transmission of the Text

- For the remainder of this lesson, we will focus on the first of these three points-the Historicity of the Old Testament.

HISTORICITY OF THE OLD TESTAMENT

- We have already seen in Lessons 19 and 20 that Jesus and the rest of the New Testament authors referred to the most disputed passages of the Old Testament as historical, including the creation of Adam and Eve, Jonah and the whale, and Noah's flood. Indeed, the New Testament writers refer to persons or events from every chapter of Genesis 1-22 and many others from the rest of the Old Testament.

- First, it is important to state at the outset that the purpose of this lesson is not to exhaust this subject. We could easily spend twenty plus lessons just on the topic of the historical reliability of the Old Testament. The amount of available literature that has been written on this topic is as deep as it is wide.

- Unlike the *Book of Mormon* or the Islamic *Quran*, the Bible was not written in a historical vacuum. Consider the following unique features of the Scriptures:

    o Written over a 1,500-year span.

- Written by more than forty authors from every walk of life:

  - Kings, military leaders, peasants, philosophers, fishermen, tax collectors, poets, musicians, statesmen, scholars, and shepherds.

- Written in different places:
  - Moses in the wilderness
  - Jeremiah in a dungeon
  - John while in exile on the isle of Patmos
- Written at different times:
  - David in times of war
  - Solomon in times of peace and prosperity
- Written on three continents:
  - Asia
  - Africa
  - Europe
- Written in three languages:
  - Hebrew
  - Aramaic
  - Greek
- Written in a wide variety of literary styles:
  - Poetry, historical narrative, song, romance, personal correspondence, memoirs, satire, biography, autobiography, law, prophecy, parable, and allegory.
- Despite its diversity, the Bible presents a single unfolding story: God's redemption of human beings.
  - "Contrast the books of the Bible with the compilation of Western classics called the Great Books of the Western World. The Great Books contains selections from more than 450 works by close to 100 authors spanning a period of about twenty-five centuries: Homer, Plato, Aristotle, Plotinus, Augustine, Aquinas, Dante, Hobbes, Spinoza, Calvin, Rousseau,

Shakespeare, Hume, Kant, Darwin, Tolstoy, Whitehead, and Joyce, to name but a handful. While these individuals are all part of the Western tradition of ideas, they often display incredible diversity of views on just about every subject. And while their views share commonalties, they also display numerous conflicting and contradictory positions and perspectives. In fact, they frequently go out of their way to critique and refute key ideas proposed by their predecessors. . . The uniqueness of the Bible shown does not prove that it is inspired. It does, however, challenge any person sincerely seeking truth to consider seriously its unique quality in terms of its continuity." (List amended from McDowell, 3-7)

- The Bible is an historical document of demonstrable accuracy and reliability. It is full of information on the history of the Hebrew people as well as other ancient civilians. In every area in which it can be checked-out: historically, culturally, geographically, and scientifically the Bible has been verified as factual by extra-biblical sources. (Story, 33)
- "Over the past one hundred years, the archaeologist's spade has verified numerous events, customs, cities, and nations mentioned in the Old Testament. At one time many scholars dismissed some of the Old Testament as mythical because they had no outside confirmation of the people, places, or events in doubt. But archaeology has changed all that, demonstrating the Old Testament's reliability on literally hundreds of historical facts." (Story, 36)
- In his 1992 book *Defending Your Faith: How to Answer the Tough Questions*, Christian apologist Dan Story provided the following list of archeological confirmations of the Old Testament. In the intermittent 24 years this list has grown by leaps and bounds.

    o The Ebla Tablets. Since 1974, archeologists have unearthed seventeen thousand tablets at Tell Mardikh in northern Syria. These tablets contain a record of laws, customs, and events from the same area Moses and the patriarchs lived. This discovery helped to disprove the Documentary hypothesis which, in part, claimed that Moses lived before the invention of written language and therefore could not have composed the first five books of the Old Testament. Thus

Bible critics claimed that the Old Testament was written much later (and by many unknown authors) than traditionally thought. However, the Ebla Tablets prove that written language existed at least a thousand years before Moses...

- Archaeology has proven that Israel derives its ancestry from Mesopotamia, as the Bible teaches (Genesis 11:27-12:4)
- Archaeology suggests that the world's languages likely arose from a common origin, as Genesis 11 teaches.
- Jericho, and several other cities mentioned in the Old Testament previously thought to be legendary by skeptics, have now been discovered by archaeologists.
- Bible critics used to claim that the Hittite civilization mentioned in Genesis did not exist at the time of Abraham because there was no record of it apart from the Old Testament. However, archaeology has discovered that it not only existed but it lasted more than 1,000 years. Now you can get a doctorate in Hittite studies from the University of Chicago.
- Social customs and stories in the Old Testament credited to the time of the patriarchs (Abraham, Jacob, and Isaac) are in harmony with archaeological discoveries, casting additional light on the historical accuracy of the Biblical record. (Story, 36)

- See the PowerPoint provided by Bud Chrysler of Chrysler Ministries for further examples.

  - Click here to review the PowerPoint.

CONCLUSION

- Literally thousands of archaeological finds have validated the picture presented in the Old Testament, none have refuted it. Negative higher criticism of the Old Testament, based as it is on philosophical presuppositions and not factual data, has crumbled under the facts of archaeological discoveries. (Geisler, 345) Regarding the historicity of the Old Testament, world-renowned archeologist William F. Albright stated:

- "There can be no doubt that archaeology has confirmed the substantial historicity of the Old Testament tradition." (Albright, 176)

- Nelson Glueck, author of *Rivers in the Desert* has stated:

  - "It can be stated categorically that no archaeological discovery has ever controverted a Biblical reference." (Glueck, 31)

- Norman L. Geisler states the following in his chapter on "The Historicity of the Old Testament" in his *Systematic Theology In One Volume*:

  - "Even usually liberal sources are now admitting the overall historical reliability of the Old Testament. Excerpting from his book, Is the Bible True?, Jeffery L. Sheler notes for U.S. News & World Report:

    In extraordinary ways, modern archaeology has affirmed the historical core of the Old Testament — corroborating key portions of the stories of Israel's patriarchs, the Exodus, the Davidic monarchy, and the life and times of Jesus." (Geisler, 331)

- "In other words, in every instance where the Bible could be checked-out historically against extra-biblical sources, the Bible has always been found accurate in what it reports." (Story, 37)

- Given the fact that the Bible has been proven to be trustworthy in what it reports when checked against extra-Biblical sources it is reasonable to assume that one can trust its spiritual content as well. This would extend to the Bible's internal claim to have been given by inspiration of God.

WORKS CITED

Albright, William F. *Archaeology and the Religion of Israel*. Baltimore, MD: The Johns Hopkins Press, 1953.

Geisler, Norman L. *Systematic Theology: In One Volume*. Minneapolis, MN: Bethany House, 2011.

Glueck, Nelson. *Rivers in the Desert*. New York, NY: Farrar, Strauss & Cudahy, 1959.

McDowell, Josh. *The New Evidence That Demands a Verdict*. Nashville: Thomas Nelson, 1999.

Story, Dan. *Defending Your Faith: How to Answer the Tough Questions*. Nashville, TN: Thomas Nelson Publishers, 1992.

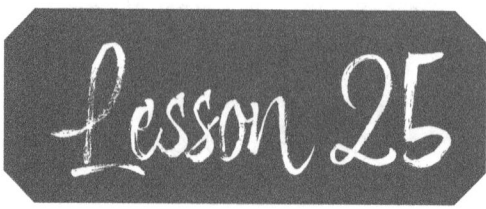

EXTERNAL EVIDENCE OF INSPIRATION: THE HISTORICITY OF THE NEW TESTAMENT

INTRODUCTION

- Last week, in Lesson 24, we began our consideration of the External Evidence of Inspiration by looking at some things regarding the historical reliability of the Old Testament.
- This week, in Lesson 25, we want to do the same with respect to the historicity of the New Testament.
- As with our discussion of the historicity of the Old Testament, our purpose is not to exhaust the amount of available material on the historical accuracy of the New Testament. Rather, our purpose is to

point out some extra-Biblical highpoints that provide external evidence that the New Testament was written by inspiration of God.
- Since the evidence for the historical reliability for the book of Acts is the strongest, we will focus our investigation on a consideration of the Acts of the Apostles.

THE HISTORICITY OF ACTS

- Acts 1:1-2 — "The former treatise have I made, O Theophilus, of all that Jesus began both to do and teach, Until the day in which he was taken up, after that he through the Holy Ghost had given commandments unto the apostles whom he had chosen:"

    o The book of Acts is the second part of a two-part treatise addressed to Theophilus.

- Luke 1:1-3 — "Forasmuch as many have taken in hand to set forth in order a declaration of those things which are most surely believed among us, Even as they delivered them unto us, which from the beginning were eyewitnesses, and ministers of the word; It seemed good to me also, having had perfect understanding of all things from the very first, to write unto thee in order, most excellent Theophilus,"

    o Luke 1:1-3 speaks to the identity of the "former treatise" addressed to Theophilus spoken of in Acts 1:1. Simply stated, Luke was part 1 and Acts was part 2 of a two part "treatise" addressed to Theophilus.

- A careful reading of Luke 1:1-3 ought to highlight the following points: first, Luke interviewed eyewitnesses who were present from the beginning of the events recorded; second, Luke's goal is to present a chronological record of the events as they were commonly believed.

While the Gospel of Luke is written to present Christ as the son of man, it also doubles as a chronological history of the life of Christ. When coupled with Acts, the Gospel of Luke takes its reader from the annunciation of Christ's birth all the way through to Paul's imprisonment in Rome in Acts 28. Considering that Luke did not write by his own will or in his own words, but rather the words of God under the inspiration of the Holy Spirit, the foolishness of doubting these events becomes clear.

- "The date and authenticity of the book of Acts is crucial to the historicity of early Christianity and, thus, to apologetics in general. If Acts was written before AD 70 while the eyewitnesses were still alive, then it has great historical value in informing us of the earliest Christian beliefs." (Geisler, *ST*, 348)

- Furthermore, if Acts was written by Luke, the same author as the Gospel of Luke who was also the travel companion of the Apostle Paul; it would provide a point of contact between the narratives of the earthly ministry of the Lord Jesus Christ and the author of the majority of the New Testament.

    o II Timothy 4:9-11 — Luke was with Paul at the end of his life.

- "If Acts was written by AD 62 (the traditional date), then it was written by a contemporary of Jesus (who died in AD 33). And, if Acts is shown to be accurate history, then it brings credibility to its reports about the most basic Christian beliefs in miracles (Acts 2:22), death (Acts 2:23), resurrection (Acts 2:24, 3:29-32), and ascension of Christ (Acts 1:9-10). Further, if Luke wrote Acts, then his "former treatise" (Acts 1:1), the gospel of Luke, should be extended the same credibility manifested in the book of Acts." (Geisler, *ST*, 348)

Evidence for an Early Date for Acts

- In his book *The Book of Acts in the Setting of Hellenistic History*, Roman historian Colin Hemer offers seventeen reasons for accepting the traditional early date for the authorship of the book of Acts. By extension, Hemer's argumentation also indirectly testifies to the historicity of the book of Luke. Norman L. Geisler believes that Hemer's first five arguments are sufficient to prove that Acts was penned before 62 AD.

- ○ "There is no mention in Acts of the crucial historical event of the fall of Jerusalem in AD 70, which places the Acts before that event.
- ○ There is no hint of the outbreak of the Jewish War in 66 or of any serious deterioration of relations between Romans and Jews, which implies Acts was written before that time.
- ○ There is no hint of the more immediate deterioration of Christian relations with Rome involved in the Neronian persecution of the late 60s.
- ○ There is no hint of the death of James at the hands of the Sanhedrin in c. 62, recorded by Josephus (*Antiquities*, 20.9.1.200)
- ○ Since the apostle Paul was still alive (Acts 28), it must have been written before his death (c. AD 65)." (Geisler, *ST*, 349)

- "By comparison, claiming that Acts was written after AD 62 is like claiming that a book on the life of John F. Kennedy was written after 1963 (when he was assassinated) but never mentions his death; if the event had already occurred, it was too important to omit. In the same way, any book like Acts that was written after the death of the apostle Paul (c. AD 65) or the destruction of Jerusalem (AD 70) would surely have mentioned these momentous events." (Geisler, *ST*, 349)

Luke Was a First-Rate Historian

- In addition to the arguments for early authorship of Acts, Colin Hemer demonstrates that the book was written by a careful historian. According to Hemer, Luke's skill as a historian is demonstrated by his use of the following three categories of knowledge: 1) Common Knowledge, 2) Specialized Knowledge, and 3) Specific Local

Knowledge. For our purposes we will consider examples of Specialized and Specific Local Knowledge.

- Examples of *Specialized Knowledge* include:

    o   Acts 1:12, 19; 3:2, 11 — shows knowledge of the topography of Jerusalem.
    o   Acts 4:6 — Annas is pictured as continuing to have great prestige and to bear the title 'high priest' deposition by the Romans and the appointment of Caiaphas.
    o   Acts 12:4 — gives details on the organization of a military guard.
    o   Acts 13:7 — he correctly identified Cyprus as a proconsular (senatorial) province at this time, with the proconsul resident at Paphos (v. 6)
    o   Acts 16:8 — he acknowledges the part played by Troas in the system of communication.
    o   Acts 17:1 — Amphipolis and Apollonia are known as stations (and presumably overnight stops) on the Egyptian Way from Philippi to Thessolonica.
    o   Acts 27 & 28 — contains many details in the geography and navigational details of the voyage to Rome.

- Regarding *Specific Local Knowledge*, Luke manifests an incredible array of knowledge regarding local places, names, conditions, customs, and circumstances that befit only an eyewitness contemporary of the time and events recorded. Hemer identifies eighty-four facts in the last sixteen chapters of Acts that have been confirmed by extra-Biblical historical and archeological research (*Please note that I reproduced this information without alteration from its source. Any differences in spelling or terminology found in this list when compared against the KJB are the sources not my own*):

    1) the natural crossing between correctly named ports (Acts 13:4-5)

2) the proper port (Perga) along the direct destination of a ship crossing from Cyprus (13:13)

3) the proper location of Lycaonia (Acts 14:6)

4) the unusual but correct declension of the name Lystra (14:6)

5) the correct language spoke in Lystra — Lycaonian (14:11)

6) the gods known to be so associated-Jupiter and Mercurius (14:12)

7) the proper port, Attalia, which returning travelers would use (14:25)

8) the correct order of approach to Derbe and then Lystra from the Cilician Gates (16:1, cf. 15:41)

9) the proper form of the name Troas (16:8)

10) the place of a conspicuous sailors' landmark, Samothracia (16:11)

11) the proper description of Philippi as a Roman colony (16:12)

12) the right location of the river (Gangites) near Philippi (16:13)

13) the proper association of Thyatira as a center of dyeing (16:14)

14) correct designations for the magistrates of the colony (16:22)

15) the proper locations (Amphipolis and Apollonia) where travelers would spend successive nights on this journey (17:1)

16) the presence of a synagogue in Thessalonica (17:1)

17) the proper term "politrarchs" used for the magistrates there (17:6)

18) the correct implication that sea travel is a most convenient way of reaching Athens, with the favoring east winds of summer sailing (14:14-15)

19) the abundant idols in Athens (17:16)
20) the reference to the synagogue in Athens (17:17)
21) the depiction of the Athenian life of philosophical debate in the Agora (17:17)
22) the use of the correct Athenian slang word for Paul, a babbler (*spermologos*, 17:18) as well as the court Areopagus (17:19)
23) the proper characterization of the Athenian character (17:21)
24) an altar to the "unknown god" (17:23)
25) the proper reaction of Greek philosophers, who denied the bodily resurrection (17:32)
26) Areopagite as the correct title for a member of the court (17:34)
27) The Corinthian synagogue (18:4)
28) the correct designation of Gallio as proconsul, resident in Corinth (18:12)
29) the bema (judgment seat), which overlooks Corinth's forum (18:16)
30) the name of Tyrannus as attested from Ephesus in first-century inscriptions (19:9)
31) well-known shrines and images of Diana (19:24)
32) the well-attested "great goddess Diana" (19:27)
33) that the Ephesians theatre was the meeting place of the city (19:29)
34) the correct titled grammateus for the chief executive magistrate in Ephesus (19:35)
35) the proper title of honor "neokoros," authorized by the Romans (19:35)
36) the correct name to designate the goddess (19:37)
37) the proper term for those holding court (19:38)

38) use of the plural anthupatoi, perhaps a remarkable reference to the fact that two men were conjointly exercising the function of proconsul at this time (19:38)

39) the "regular" assembly, as the precise phrase is attested elsewhere (19:39)

40) use of precise ethnic designation, beraiaios (20:4)

41) employment of the ethnic term Asianos (20:4)

42) the implied recognition of the strategic importance assigned to the city of Troas (20:7)

43) the danger of the coastal trip in this location (20:13)

44) the correct sequence of places (20:14-15)

45) the correct name of the city (21:1)

46) the appropriate route passing across the open sea south of Cyprus favored by persistent northeast winds (21:3)

47) the suitable distance between these cities (21:8)

48) a characteristically Jewish act of piety (21:24)

49) the Jewish law regarding Gentile use of the temple area (21:18)

50) the permanent stationing of a Roman cohort at Antonia to suppress any disturbance at festival times (21:31)

51) the flight of steps used by the guards (21:31, 35)

52) the common way to obtain Roman citizenship at this time (22:28)

53) the tribune being impressed with Roman rather than Tarsian citizenship (22:39)

54) Ananias being high priest at this time (23:2)

55) Felix being governor at this time (23:34)

56) the natural stopping point on the way to Cesarea (23:31)

57) whose jurisdiction Cilicia was in at the time (23:34)

58) the provincial penal procedure of the time (24:1-9)

59) the name of Festus, which agrees precisely with that given by Josephus (24:27)

60) the right of appeal as Roman citizens (25:11)

61) the correct legal formula (25:18)

62) the characteristic form of reference to the emperor at the time (25:26)

63) the best shipping lanes at the time (27:5)

64) the common bonding of Cilicia and Pamphylia (27:4)

65) the principal port to find a ship to Italy (27:5-6)

66) the slow passage to Cnidus, in the face of the typical northwest wind (27:7)

67) the right rout to sail in view of the winds (27:7)

68) the locations of Fair Havens and the neighboring site of Lasea (27:8)

69) Fair Havens as a poorly sheltered roadstead (27:12)

70) a noted tendency of a south wind in these climates to back suddenly into a violent northeaster (27:13)

71) the nature of a square-rigged ancient ship, having no option but to drive before a gale (27:15)

72) the precise place and name of this island (27:16)

73) the appropriate maneuvers for the safety of the ship in its particular plight (27:16)

74) the fourteenth night — a remarkable calculation, based inevitably on a compounding of estimates and probabilities confirmed in the judgment of experienced Mediterranean navigators (27:27)

75) the proper term of the time for the Adriatic (27:27)

76) the precise term (Bolisantes) for taking soundings, and the correct depth of the water near Malta (27:28)

77) a position that suits the probable line of approach of a ship released to run before an easterly wind (27:39)

78) the severe liability of guards who permitted a prisoner to escape (27:42)

79) the local people and superstitions of the day (28:4-6)

80) the proper title Publius (28:7)

81) Rhegium as a refuge to await a southerly wind to carry them through the straight (28:13)

82) Appii Forum and Tres Tabernae as correctly placed stopping places on the Appian Way (28:15)

83) appropriate means of custody with Roman soldiers (28:16)

84) the conditions of imprisonment, living at his own expense (28:30-31) (Hemer quoted in Geisler and Turek, 256-259)

Theological Implications of Luke's Accuracy

- The accuracy of the preceding list is quite astounding when one considers that Luke recorded these details without the aid of modern GPS, maps, or nautical charts. Can there be any doubt that Luke was an eyewitness to the events he records or at least possessed access to eyewitness testimony, not to mention the knowledge of the Holy Spirit Himself? In short, Luke's use of geographical details, specialized knowledge of nautical details, and specific local knowledge testify to the historical reliability of his writings.

- "The historicity of the book of Acts is confirmed by overwhelming evidence. Nothing like this amount of detailed confirmation exists for any other book from antiquity. Acts is not only a direct confirmation of the earliest Christian belief in the death and resurrection of Christ but also indirectly of the gospel record, for the same author (Luke) wrote a gospel as well. Further, substantially the same basic events are recorded in two other gospels (Matthew and Mark) and, for that matter, the gospel of John provides the same picture of the most crucial events, namely, the death and resurrection of Christ." (Geisler, ST, 353)

- Simply stated, the historicity of the Book of Acts is confirmed by overwhelming evidence. As one might expect, this reality makes skeptics rather uncomfortable. In the same book that Luke reports eighty-four historically-confirmed details, he also records a total of thirty-five miracles. To make matters worse for the skeptics, many of these miracles are recorded in the second half of the Book of Acts within the same historical narrative that has been verified extra Biblically. For example, Luke records the following Pauline miracles:

- temporarily blinded a sorcerer (13:11)
- cured a man who was crippled from birth (14:8)
- exorcized an evil spirit from a possessed girl (16:18)
- performed many miracles that convinced many in the city of Ephesus to turn from sorcery to Jesus (19:11-20)
- raised a man from the dead who had died after falling out a window during a long-winded lecture (20:9-10)
- healed Publius' father of dysentery, and healed numerous others who were sick on Malta (28:8-9) (Geisler and Turek, 260)

- Dr. Norman Geisler offers the following assessment of the situation, "in light of the fact that Luke has proven accurate with so many trivial details, it is nothing but pure anti-supernatural bias to say he's not telling the truth about the miracles he records." (Geisler and Turek, 260)

CONCLUSION

- "Nothing from antiquity compares with the amount of detailed confirmation that exists for the historical reliability for the Book of Acts. Not only does this offer direct confirmation of the death, burial, and resurrection of Christ, it also indirectly proves the historical reliability of the Gospel of Luke. Paralleling Matthew and Mark, the evidence suggests that all three of the so-called synoptic Gospels were written before 60 A.D., within thirty years after the death of Jesus." (Geisler, *BECA*, 8)

- Much more ink could be spilt here covering the historicity of the rest of the New Testament i.e., the Gospel accounts and the epistles of Paul but, alas, we have neither the time nor the space. Suffice it to say that the historical reliability of the New Testament has been established to such a degree that even the most "ultra-liberal" scholars have been forced to acknowledge that the following points concerning Jesus and Christianity are actual historical facts, according to Dr. Gary Habermas:

    o   Jesus died by Roman crucifixion.
    o   He was buried, most likely in a private tomb.
    o   Soon afterwards his disciples were discouraged, bereaved, and despondent, having lost hope.
    o   Jesus' tomb was found empty very soon after his interment.
    o   The disciples had experiences that they believed were actual appearances of the risen Jesus.
    o   Due to these experiences, the disciple's lives were transformed. They were even willing to die for their belief.
    o   The proclamation of the Resurrection took place very early, from the beginning of church history.
    o   The disciple's public testimony and preaching of the Resurrection took place in the city of Jerusalem, where Jesus had been crucified and buried.
    o   The gospel message centered on the preaching of the death and resurrection of Jesus.
    o   Sunday was the primary day for gathering and worship.
    o   James, the brother of Jesus and a skeptic before this time, was converted when he believed he also saw the risen Jesus.
    o   A few years later, Saul of Tarsus (Paul) became a believer, due to an experience that he also believed was an appearance of the risen Jesus. (Habermas, 9-10)

- It is only a foolish heart attitude that would doubt the historical reliability of the Bible. As we have seen, "if Christians can demonstrate that the Bible is truthful in all areas in which it can be validated, we have before us the most powerful and compelling evidence for the truthfulness of Christianity." (Story, 34) After weighing the evidence, any reasonable person must accept the Bible as God's chosen medium for revealing spiritual truth to humanity. The Bible alone can sustain its truth claims in any area in which it can be investigated; therefore, it is reasonable to trust the Bible in the arena of spiritual truth.

WORKS CITED

Geisler, Norman L. *Baker Encyclopedia of Christian Apologetics*. Grand Rapids: Baker Books, 1999.

Geisler, Norman L, and Frank Turek. *I Don't Have Enough Faith to Be an Atheist*. Wheaton, IL: Crossway Books, 2004.

Geisler, Norman L. *Systematic Theology: In One Volume*. Minneapolis, MN: Bethany House, 2011.

Habermas, Gary. *The Risen Jesus and Future Hope*. Rowman & Littlefield Publishers, 2003.

Hemer, Colin. *The Book of Acts in the Setting of Hellenistic History*. Mohr Siebeck, 1989.

Story, Dan. *Defending Your Faith: How to Answer the Tough Questions*. Nashville, TN: Thomas Nelson Publishers, 1992.

Lesson 26

EXTERNAL EVIDENCE OF INSPIRATION: THE TRANSMISSION OF THE TEXT

INTRODUCTION

- Beginning with Lesson 24, we adopted a more evidentialist approach and began looking at some of the external proofs for inspiration. In order to accomplish this task, I told you that we would consider the following three points:

    o   Historicity of the Old Testament
    o   Historicity of the New Testament
    o   The Transmission of the Text

- In Lessons 24 and 25 we looked at the external evidence for inspiration by studying the historicity of both the Old and New Testaments. There is much more that could be said about the historical reliability of the Bible that is beyond the space I wish to devote to the topic in this class.
- This week we want to consider the third and final point identified above-namely the transmission of the text. Once again, my intention in this lesson is not to exhaust all that could be said about the topic. In fact, as we will see moving forward, a discussion of textual issues will play a big role in this class.
- This morning we will not seek to cast judgment upon any of the manuscript witnesses, rather we will just discuss them in a general sense. In future lessons we will discuss them more critically and seek to identify criteria for distinguishing between sound and unsound manuscripts.
- The very fact that the Bible was copied so extensively speaks to the fact that people believed it to be the word of God and of divine authority. To accomplish our purpose this morning we will touch upon a few points regarding the transmission of both the Old and New Testament.

TRANSMISSION OF THE OLD TESTAMENT

- Romans 3:1-2 — "What advantage then hath the Jew? or what profit is there of circumcision? Much every way: chiefly, because that unto them were committed the oracles of God. For what if some did not believe? shall their unbelief make the faith of God without effect?"

    o One of the reasons God created the nation of Israel was so that they could watch over God's word. The "oracles of God" were committed or entrusted to the nation of Israel.

- Deuteronomy 31:24-28 — "And it came to pass, when Moses had made an end of writing the words of this law in a book, until they were finished, That Moses commanded the Levites, which bare the ark of the covenant of the LORD, saying, Take this book of the law, and put it in the side of the ark of the covenant of the LORD your God, that it may be there for a witness against thee. For I know thy rebellion, and thy stiff neck: behold, while I am yet alive with you this day, ye have been rebellious against the LORD; and how much more after my death? Gather unto me all the elders of your tribes, and your officers, that I may speak these words in their ears, and call heaven and earth to record against them."

> o   The tribe of Levi was given the responsibility to teach Israel the word of God.

- Deuteronomy 10:2-8 — "And I will write on the tables the words that were in the first tables which thou brakest, and thou shalt put them in the ark. And I made an ark of shittim wood, and hewed two tables of stone like unto the first, and went up into the mount, having the two tables in mine hand. And he wrote on the tables, according to the first writing, the ten commandments, which the LORD spake unto you in the mount out of the midst of the fire in the day of the assembly: and the LORD gave them unto me. And I turned myself and came down from the mount, and put the tables in the ark which I had made; and there they be, as the LORD commanded me. And the children of Israel took their journey from Beeroth of the children of Jaakan to Mosera: there Aaron died, and there he was buried; and Eleazar his son ministered in the priest's office in his stead. From thence they journeyed unto Gudgodah; and from Gudgodah to Jotbath, a land of rivers of waters. At that time the LORD separated the tribe of Levi, to bear the ark of the covenant of the LORD, to stand before the LORD to minister unto him, and to bless in his name, unto this day."

> o   Moses places the Ten Commandments into the Ark. In verse 8, who was given the responsibility of taking care of the Ark? The Levites.

- Deuteronomy 31:9-13 — "And Moses wrote this law, and delivered it unto the priests the sons of Levi, which bare the ark of the covenant of the LORD, and unto all the elders of Israel. And Moses commanded them, saying, At the end of every seven years, in the solemnity of the year of release, in the feast of tabernacles, When all Israel is come to appear before the LORD thy God in the place which he shall choose, thou shalt read this law before all Israel in their hearing. Gather the people together, men, and women, and children, and thy stranger that is within thy gates, that they may hear, and that they may learn, and fear the LORD your God, and observe to do all the words of this law: And that their children, which have not known any thing, may hear, and learn to fear the LORD your God, as long as ye live in the land whither ye go over Jordan to possess it."

- o The Levites were given the responsibility of copying and teaching the Word.

- Ezra 7:6-7 — "This Ezra went up from Babylon; and he was a ready scribe in the law of Moses, which the LORD God of Israel had given: and the king granted him all his request, according to the hand of the LORD his God upon him. And there went up some of the children of Israel, and of the priests, and the Levites, and the singers, and the porters, and the Nethinims, unto Jerusalem, in the seventh year of Artaxerxes the king."

- o Ezra was a member of the tribe of Levi. He was a ready scribe and an expert in the Law of Moses. He was part of the group of People who God had established for the handling of the Word of God.

- Ezra 7:10-11 — "For Ezra had prepared his heart to seek the law of the LORD, and to do it, and to teach in Israel statutes and judgments. Now this is the copy of the letter that the king Artaxerxes gave unto Ezra the priest, the scribe, even a scribe of the words of the commandments of the LORD, and of his statutes to Israel."

- o Ezra made copies of the Word of God.

- My point is that God did not simply allow his Word to be handled and copied by anyone. In the Old Testament He established a specific group of men (the Levitical priesthood) whose job it was to see to the care and copying of the Word of God.
- The Levitical scribes knew they were duplicating God's word, so they went to incredible lengths to prevent error from creeping into their work. The whole process of copying the Bible was controlled by strict religious rituals and the scribes carefully counted every line, word, syllable, and letter to ensure accuracy.
- Prior to the discovery of the Dead Sea Scrolls in 1947, the oldest existing Old Testament manuscript was the Masoretic Text (the Hebrew text supporting the KJB) which dates from around 900 AD.
- Among the manuscripts found in the Dead Sea Scrolls were fragments and two copies of the book of Isaiah. The copies of the book of Isaiah were dated to around 150 BC-almost one thousand years older than the Masoretic Text.
- A comparison of the two sources proved to be word for word identical with our standard Hebrew Bible in more than 95% of the text. The 5% variation consisted chiefly of obvious slips of the pen and variations in spelling.
- In addition to being historical confirmation of the Biblical doctrine of Preservation (not just of the thoughts but of the very words themselves), these facts also serve as strong external evidence of the inspiration of those words.

TRANSMISSION OF THE NEW TESTAMENT

- There is also much evidence to support the reliability and inspiration of the New Testament. Let's consider the following three areas:

    o Early Eyewitness Testimony
    o Short Time Gap
    o Number of Available Witness

Early Eyewitness Testimony

- The New Testament writers were either eyewitnesses themselves or interviewed eyewitnesses to the events they recorded.

    o Luke 1:2 — "Even as they delivered them unto us, which from the beginning were eyewitnesses, and ministers of the word;"

    o I Corinthians 15:4-8 — "And that he was buried, and that he rose again the third day according to the scriptures: And that he was seen of Cephas, then of the twelve: After that, he was seen of above five hundred brethren at once; of whom the greater part remain unto this present, but some are fallen asleep. After that, he was seen of James; then of all the apostles. And last of all he was seen of me also, as of one born out of due time."

    o II Peter 1:16 — "For we have not followed cunningly devised fables, when we made known unto you the power and coming of our Lord Jesus Christ, but were eyewitnesses of his majesty."

- We convict people in a court of law every day in this nation based on the testimony of eyewitnesses.

FROM THIS GENERATION FOR EVER

- The New Testament documents are written within 35 years of the events recorded. No other religious or secular document from antiquity can make such a claim.

    o   Luke 1 — Acts 1 — Acts 28

Short Time Gap

- Many other religious documents have tremendous time spans between when they were transmitted orally and when they were eventually written down. For example, the sayings of Buddha were not recorded until 500 years after his death.

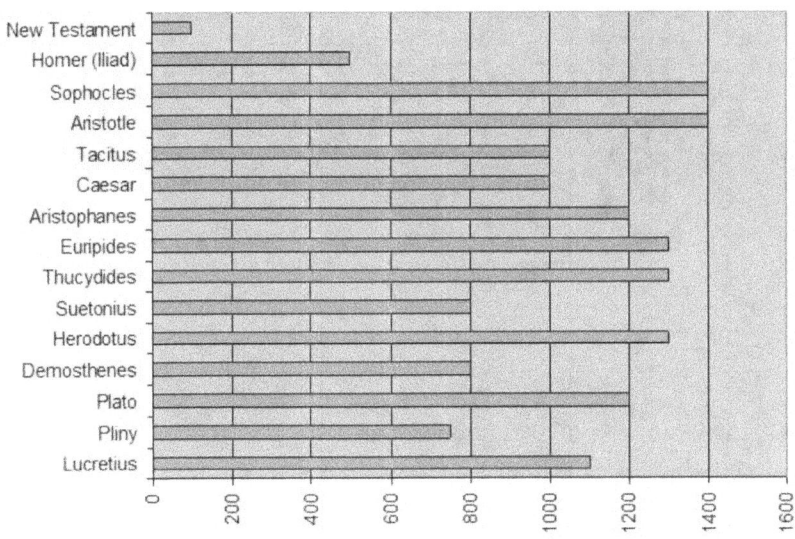

Approximate Time Span Between Original & Copy

- Regarding the New Testament documents, unlike other ancient works whether secular or religious, not enough time elapsed be-

313

tween when Jesus spoke and when His words were recorded to allow for misrepresentation or the development of legendary material.

Number of Available Witnesses

- There are more extant manuscripts of the New Testament than there are for any ten works of ancient history combined. Consider the following chart comparing the number of copies of the New Testament compared with Homer's *Iliad*.

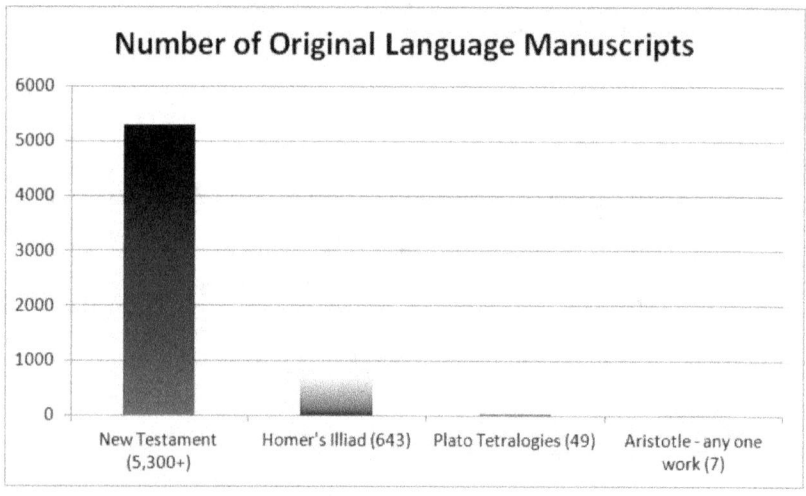

- There are over 86,000 known quotations of Scripture made by the church fathers. Even if we did not have any copies of the New Testament, we could still reconstruct all but eleven verses of the entire New Testament from material written by the church fathers within 150 to 200 years of the life of Christ.

Author	Book	Date Written	Earliest Copies	Time Gap	No. Of Copies
Homer	Iliad	800 B.C.	c. 400 B.C.	c. 400 yrs.	643
Herodotus	History	480-425 B.C.	c. A.D. 900	c. 1,350 yrs.	8
Thucydides	History	460-400 B.C.	c. A.D. 900	c. 1,350 yrs.	8
Plato		400 B.C.	c. A.D. 900	c. 1,300 yrs.	7
Demosthenes		300 B.C.	c. A.D. 1100	1,400 yrs.	200
Caesar	Gallic Wars	100-44 B.C.	c. A.D. 900	c. 1,000 yrs.	10
Livy	History of Rome	59 B.C.-A.D. 17	4th cent. (partial) mostly 10th cent.	c. 400 yrs. c. 1,000 yrs.	1 partial 19 copies
Tacitus	Annals	A.D. 100	c. A.D. 1100	c. 1,000 yrs.	20
Pliny Secundus	Natural History	A.D. 61-113	c. A.D. 850	c. 750 yrs.	7
New Testament		A.D. 50-100	c. 114 (fragment) c. 200 (books) c. 250 (most of the N.T.) c. 325 (complete N.T.)	+ 50 yrs. 100 yrs. 150 yrs. 225 yrs.	5366

EARLY CHURCH FATHER'S REFERENCES TO THE NEW TESTAMENT

WRITER	GOSPELS	ACTS	PAULINE EPISTLES	GENERAL EPISTLES	REVELATION	TOTALS
JUSTIN MARTYR	268	10	43	6	3 (266 allusions)	330
IRENAEUS	1,038	194	499	23	65	1,819
CLEMENT OF ALEXANDRIA	1,017	44	1,127	207	11	2,406
ORIGEN	9,231	349	7,778	399	165	17,922
TERTULLIAN	3,822	502	2,609	120	205	7,258
HIPPOLYTUS	734	42	387	27	188	1,378
EUSEBIUS	3,258	211	1,592	88	27	5,176
GRAND TOTALS	19,368	1,352	14,035	870	664	36,289

- There is more evidence for the reliability of the New Testament text than for any ten pieces of classical literature combined.
- The Bible is in better textual shape than the 37 plays of William Shakespeare written in the 17th century after the invention of the printing press.
- People do not question whether they have accurately understood Plato, Aristotle, or Socrates, yet they will doubt the veracity of the Biblical text when there is exponentially more historical/textual evidence supporting the New Testament. All of this demonstrates the huge bias that people have against the Bible in their thinking.

THE CHARGE OF CIRCULAR REASONING

- Unbelievers accuse Christians of using circular reasoning and unsupported assumptions to justify their beliefs. Christians allegedly take unsupported assumptions and use them, to justify other unsupported assumptions, in effect, using "fiction to support fiction." Here is a sample conversation that is illustrative of the Christian use of circular reasoning with respect to the Bible being the word of God, according to unbelievers:

    o   Unbelievers Question: "How do you know the Bible is true? How do you know it is the word of God?"

    Christian Answer: "Because the Bible says it is God's word. The Bible is internally consistent and harmonious. Its writers, who lived thousands of years apart, agree on the same message. It also contains many fulfilled prophecies from the Old Testament that were fulfilled in the New Testament. The odds of that happening by chance, according to Christian theologians, are astronomical. The Bible also agrees with history, archaeology and science. It is the only book that is complete with a chronicle of humanity's history, salvation, and future predicament."

- Definition — a use of reason in which the premises depends on or is equivalent to the conclusion, a method of false logic by which "this is used to prove that, and that is used to prove this"; also called circular logic. (Dictionary.com)

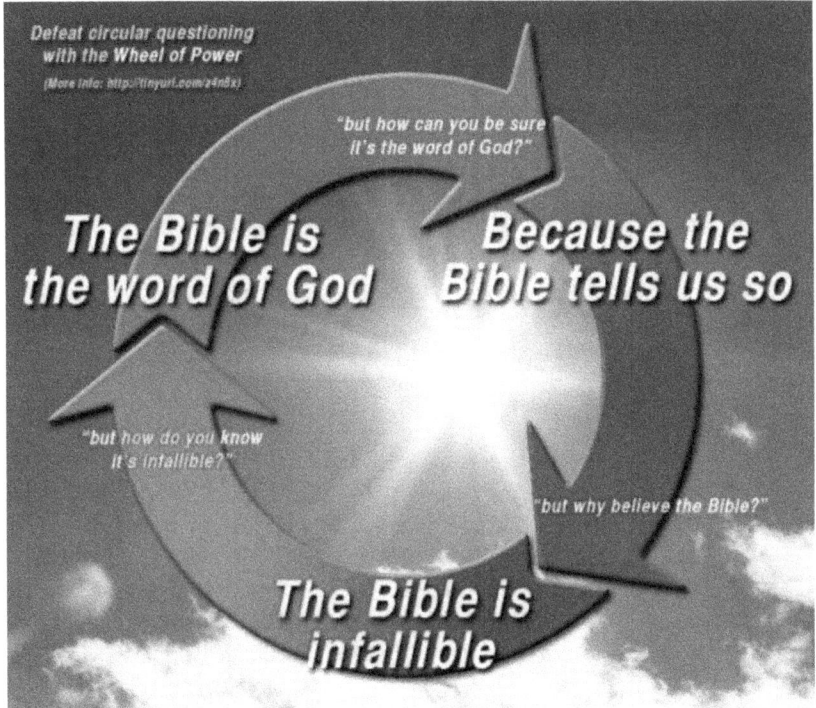

- Definition — a formal logical fallacy in which the proposition to be proved is assumed implicitly or explicitly in one of the premises. For example: "Only an untrustworthy person would run for office. The fact that politicians are untrustworthy is proof of this." (Wikipedia.org)
- The common accusation that Christians use circular reasoning is actually true. In fact, everyone uses some degree of circular reasoning when defending his ultimate standard (though not everyone realizes this fact). (Viet, *Circular Reasoning*)

- *All* philosophical systems start with *axioms* (presuppositions), or non-provable propositions accepted as true, and deduce *theorems* from them. Therefore, Christians should not be faulted for having axioms as well, which are the propositions of Scripture (a proposition is a fact about a thing, e.g. God is love). So the question for any axiomatic system is whether it is *self-consistent* and is *consistent with the real world*. (Sarfati, *Using the Bible to Prove the Bible*)

- *Self-consistency* — means that the axioms do not contradict each other. Indeed, allegedly circular reasoning at least demonstrates the *internal* consistency of the Bible's claims it makes about itself. If the Bible had actually disclaimed divine inspiration, it would indeed be illogical to defend it. (Sarfati, *Using the Bible to Prove the Bible*)

- *Consistent with the real world* — Christian axioms provide the basis for a coherent *worldview*, i.e. a thought map that can guide us throughout all aspects of life. Non-Christian axioms fail these tests, as do the axioms of other 'holy books'.

    o Biblical axioms logically and historically provided the basis for modern science. A major one is that the universe is orderly, because it was made by a God of order, not the author of confusion (I Corinthians 14:33). But why should the universe be orderly if there were no God, or if Zeus and his gang were in charge, or if the universe were one big Thought, as Eastern religions teach? It could change Its mind!

    Also very importantly, the Christian axioms provide a basis for *objective right and wrong*. Note, it is important to understand the point here — *not* that atheists cannot be moral but that they have *no objective basis for this morality from within their own system*.

    Christian axioms also provide a basis for voluntary choice, since we are made in the image of God (Genesis 1:26–27). But evolutionists believe that we are just machines and that our thoughts are really motions of atoms in our brains, which are just 'computers made of meat'. But then they realize that we cannot function in the everyday world like this. Science is supposed to be about predictability, yet an evolutionist can far more easily predict behaviour if he treats his wife as a free agent with desires and dislikes. For example, if he brings her flowers, then he will make her happy, i.e. for all practical purposes, his wife is a free agent who likes flowers. Nothing is gained in the practical world by treating her as an automaton with certain olfactory responses programmed by genes that in turn produce certain brain chemistry. So evolutionists claim that free will is a 'useful illusion'. (Sarfati, *Using the Bible to Prove the Bible*)

- The truth is that everyone uses some degree of circular reasoning when defending their ultimate standard (though not everyone realizes this fact). Yet, if used properly, the use of circular reasoning is not arbitrary and, therefore, not fallacious. Contrary to popular belief, circular reasoning is surprisingly a valid argument. Circular reasoning is a logical fallacy only when it is arbitrary, proving nothing beyond what it assumes. (Viet, *Circular Reasoning*)

- However, not all circular reasoning is fallacious. Certain standards must be assumed. Dr. Jason Lisle gave this example of a non-arbitrary use of circular reasoning:

    o   Without laws of logic, we could not make an argument.
    o   We can make an argument.
    o   Therefore, there must be laws of logic. (Viet, *Circular Reasoning*)

- While this argument is circular, it is a non-fallacious use of circular reasoning. Since we could not prove anything apart from the laws of logic, we must presuppose the laws of logic even to prove they exist. In fact, if someone were trying to *disprove* that laws of logic exist, he'd have to use the laws of logic in his attempt, thereby refuting himself. Your non-Christian friend must agree there are certain standards that can be proven with circular reasoning. (Viet, *Circular Reasoning*)

- The independent and extra Biblical evidence afforded by history and archaeology serves to break the cycle. If the Bible can be proven to be correct in all areas in which it can be checked extra Biblically, then we have the most compelling evidence for accepting its spiritual truth claims–including its own teaching regarding its own inspiration.

WORKS CITED

McDowell, Josh. *The New Evidence That Demands a Verdict*. Nashville: Thomas Nelson, 1999.

Sarfati, Jonathan. *Using the Bible to prove the Bible?* http://creation.com/not-circular-reasoning.

Viet, Darius & Karin. *Circular Reasoning*. https://answersingenesis.org/apologetics/circular-reasoning/.

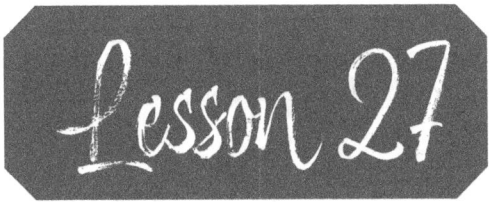

DISCLAIMERS REGARDING THE LIMITATIONS OF INSPIRATION

INTRODUCTION

- After studying the doctrine of inspiration for the better part of 26 weeks, I would like to conclude this section of the class by looking at some disclaimers regarding the limitations of inspiration.
- Just as it was vitally important to clearly identify and defend what inspiration is from the Bible; it is of equal importance to be aware of the doctrine's limitations.
- In order to accomplish this task, we will consider the following major points:

- o   Disclaimers Regarding Inspiration
- o   Four Summary Statements

- Please note that unless otherwise stated, these notes have been amended from the Sixth Lesson of Manuscript Evidence 101 taught by Pastor Richard Jordan in Grace School of the Bible.

DISCLAIMERS REGARDING INSPIRATION

Disclaimer Number One

- Inspiration does not mean that all parts of the Bible are dispensationally applicable to the members of the body of Christ during the dispensation of grace. It only means that all parts of the canon (Genesis through Revelation) are equally inspired.

    - o   This should be self-evident. Ephesians is more important to us as members of the body of Christ than the book of Revelation. That being said, it is all God's word, and, because of that, it is important and profitable; but you must remember to rightly divide the scripture to get the profit that God intended for you in the Bible. So, it is all equally inspired, but it is just not all of equal importance. When you talk about the inspired word of God, it is every bit inspired; but you are not describing the importance of it as far as its practical application to you.

Disclaimer Number Two

- Inspiration does not guarantee the inspiration of any particular modern or ancient translation.

o   Now, why would that be true? It is not the function of the doctrine of inspiration to deal with the issue of the transmission of the text. The doctrine of preservation is the doctrine that does that. We have been dealing with inspiration — the scriptures came out of the mouth of God, God breathed them, He speaks them out, and the scriptures come right out of His mouth. The idea of the transmission of the text and where the Bible is today is covered by the doctrine of preservation.

The reason I point that out to you is this. People will say, "Are you trying to say that the King James Bible is the inspired word of God?" They will try to make fun of you if you believe that the Authorized Version, or Luther's German Receptus, etc., are copies of the inspired word of God. They say, "Do you mean that the translators were inspired like the original writers were?" And the answer is "NO". We are not describing that.

I have learned this. You must be very careful in your statement of what you are trying to say because people have all kinds of false concepts. People jump to all kinds of conclusions about what they think they heard you say. You want to say it in the most proper and clear and persuasive fashion. You want to distinguish between inspiration and preservation. What you hold in your hand is the preserved word of God. Inspiration deals with the written text of the scripture. Inspiration deals with what God wrote down, not the process but the result. It deals with what He wrote down on the page. The words are inspired.

Now, what happened to those inspired words is determined by the doctrine of preservation. If you have a consistent doctrine of preservation (what God wrote down He has preserved through history and therefore you can hold it in your hands today), then you can say that you hold the preserved word. You have a copy of the original.

Therefore, if you have the preserved word of God, you have an inspired Bible. But, inspiration means that the original copies came out of the mouth of God. Preservation is what gets it to you.

So, the doctrine of inspiration does not guarantee the inspiration of any particular modern or ancient translation. Preservation does what inspiration ceased when the canon of scripture was completed. There is no inspiration today, but there is providential preservation.

Disclaimer Number Three

- Inspiration does not allow for any false information, but it does on occasion record the lie of someone. Just because something is recorded in the Bible that does not mean it is always the truth. It is always an accurate record of what went on; but if somebody lies to somebody else, the record of the lie is accurate, but the lie is still a lie.

    o Genesis 3:4 — "And the serpent said unto the woman, Ye shall not surely die:"
    - If I tell you that verse four is a lie, am I saying the text is wrong, or that the man who said it is wrong? I am saying that the man who said it is wrong. If I tell you that verse four is true, what am I saying? Am I saying that the devil did not tell a lie? No, I am saying that it is an accurate record of what Satan said. You must be really careful to distinguish between those things.

    o Job 42:7 — "And it was so, that after the LORD had spoken these words unto Job, the LORD said to Eliphaz the Temanite, My wrath is kindled against thee, and against thy two friends: for ye have not spoken of me the thing that is right, as my servant Job hath."
    - Well wait a minute! All of that stuff is recorded in the book of Job, and God says that it is not right. It is false information; it is bad information. It is off from center, meaning it is not accurate. But, God is not impugning the inspiration of the book of Job. He is not saying that the book of Job is not an accurate record. God is saying that it was accurately recorded, but what they said is not accurate.

    o You want to remember this. Inspiration does not allow for any false information. Everything that is recorded is true and accurate in its record, but that does not mean that God did not record someone's lie or some misinformation that someone put out.

Disclaimer Number Four

- Inspiration does not mean that all Bible writers had personal illumination. Every Bible writer did not have personal illumination about all that he was writing down.

    - This is one of the ways you know that the Bible had to come out of God's mouth. The dynamic inspiration idea is that it goes into the mind of man, and he comprehends it, and he spits it out. Consequently, that would mean there is no way to transfer the thought if it was incomprehensible to the man.
    - I Peter 1:10-11 — "Of which salvation the prophets have enquired and searched diligently, who prophesied of the grace that should come unto you: Searching what, or what manner of time the Spirit of Christ which was in them did signify, when it testified beforehand the sufferings of Christ, and the glory that should follow."
        - The Old Testament prophets searched their own writings diligently. They were trying to figure out what the Spirit meant when he wrote through them about the sufferings of Christ and the glory to follow. Therefore, it is pretty obvious that the OT prophets did not all have personal illumination at all times with respect to everything that they wrote.
    - Daniel 7:1, 15, 28 — "In the first year of Belshazzar king of Babylon Daniel had a dream and visions of his head upon his bed: then he wrote the dream, and told the sum of the matters. . . I Daniel was grieved in my spirit in the midst of my body, and the visions of my head troubled me. . . Hitherto is the end of the matter. As for me Daniel, my cogitations much troubled me, and my countenance changed in me: but I kept the matter in my heart."
        - Daniel did not grasp what was going on. He writes the dream down in verses 1-28, but he does not fully understand what is happening. He had the facts but he did not have the illumination to understand the facts, and that is not unusual. He writes 27 verses there, and in half of them he is just writing the dream down, and in the other half of them, you have the explanation that was given him. Yet, he still does not understand it.

- One needs to understand that just because a Biblical writer wrote something that does not necessarily mean that he understood everything that he wrote down. This is why it is very important for one to understand the issue of progressive revelation. Something can be written down in time past and not understood by the men that wrote it down. Yet, it is inspired, and it is right.

Disclaimer Number Five

- Inspiration does not prohibit personal research by a writer.

  - That is very important because a lot of people will try to get after you about the issues of inspiration. They will claim that you are saying that the man who wrote it had to sit on a stump somewhere knowing nothing, and God just bore a hole in his head and poured the information in. That is not what is implied by inspiration. Inspiration does not imply that God does not take into account the activities, and the knowledge, and the frame of reference of the man who wrote it. Nor does it imply that when you read about someone in the scripture who has personally investigated things, that therefore God could not have inspired him because the man was not in a trance and all that kind of stuff.

    I have never read about anybody or heard about anybody that teaches plenary verbal inspiration and believes that the men were put into a trance, or a vision, or whatever in order to write the text of the scripture. If you ever hear anybody say that, please know that they are wrong. God did not just blank-out their mind and pick up their pen in a magical kind of operation and cause them to write. He reached into the library of their vocabulary; and out of that He chose words and moved upon them in such a way that the words they wrote down were the very words that He wanted them to write down. The words came out of His mouth through them onto the paper.

  - Luke 1:1-4 — Luke is saying [paraphrase], "Listen Theophilus, I am writing this to you, and I want you to know at the outset that I have been a good historian. I checked the references; I talked to the eyewitness accounts; I talked to the people that were there – the people that know. When I got this piece of information, I checked it out." It is amazing how many historical references there are in the book of Luke. As you read Luke sometime, mark down the dates, and the references, and that kind of thing, and you will be impressed with the job that Luke did. My point to you is that Luke personally researched the data, and he said, "I've checked all the facts that you are going to read in this book." Yet, the book of Luke is inspired by God.

- Thus, inspiration does not mean that the writer is prohibited from doing personal research.

Disclaimer Number Six

- Inspiration does not deny the use of extra-biblical sources.

  - I say it that way because I cannot come up with any better way to communicate what I have in my mind.
  - Acts 17:28 — "For in him we live, and move, and have our being; as certain also of your own poets have said, For we are also his offspring."
    - When Luke wrote Acts 17:28, he wrote it down under the inspiration of the Holy Spirit, and that is an inspired passage. That does not mean that God Almighty put those words in the poet's mouth, but it does mean that God Almighty accurately recorded them here. If you look back in history books, you can find the source.
  - Titus 1:12 — "One of themselves, even a prophet of their own, said, The Cretians are alway liars, evil beasts, slow bellies."
  - I Chronicles 29:29 — "Now the acts of David the king, first and last, behold, they are written in the book of Samuel the seer, and in the book of Nathan the prophet, and in the book of Gad the seer,"
    - When he says, "the book of Samuel the seer (see I Samuel 9:9 for a definition of "seer"), and the book of Nathan the prophet, and in the book of Gad the seer" that demon-

strates that the nation Israel had extensive archives of public records. What is written in Chronicles is easily checkable; it is easy to verify the information. It is taken from well-known public records that only prove the legitimate nature of the work that you are reading in Chronicles as having been done by a well-informed author.

- o There are at least fourteen different source references recorded in I Chronicles and II Chronicles.
  - II Chronicles 9:29, 12:15, 13:22, 20:34, 24:27, 26:22, 27:7, 32:32 — Do you see the historic references when you read these things? They show you that Israel had extensive archives and that the guys that compiled this information back there had it readily available to them. The public also had it readily available to them, and they are referring people to the records.
- o Inspiration does not allow for any false information. It does not necessarily mean that God, on occasion, does not record something that was not originally inspired. He takes it and puts it in the Bible; and the part that is in the Bible is inspired, because it is what is written down in this book. If God can record Satan's lie, he can record public records.

Disclaimer Number Seven

- Inspiration does not overwhelm the personality of the human author. Inspiration does not mean that a guy just goes into a catatonic state while the Lord gives him the words.

  - o See our discussion of Divine Dictation in Lessons 14 through 18.

Disclaimer Number Eight

- Inspiration does not mean uniformity in all the details given in describing the same event.

- An example of that are the books of Matthew, Mark, Luke, and John. You have four inspired accounts of the earthly ministry of Christ each given from a different perspective. So, inspiration does not mean that all of the details are the same, rather, it shows the design and purpose in giving a particular viewpoint, which might necessitate different details.
- See our discussion of Undesigned Coincidences in Lessons 21 and 22.

FOUR SUMMARY STATEMENTS

Summary Statement Number One

- Plenary Verbal Inspiration assures us that God included all of the necessary things that He wanted us to know and excluded everything else.

  - In other words, everything that you need is in the Bible and what is not in the Bible, you do not need. That is pretty simple. If God wrote the very words down, then you can be sure and confident that everything that He wanted written down is there and that everything that is excluded is unnecessary.

Summary Statement Number Two

- Inspiration has been completed.

  - Colossians 1:25 — the word of God has been completed in its contents, in its subjects, and in its canon. There is no more revelation being given today. Revelation has been completed. Revelation produces inspiration. Illumination produces preservation. Revelation is completed; inspiration is completed. They do not function today.

The Charismatic movement teaches that God is still revealing himself today. According to Pentecostalism, Jesus shows up and speaks to people when they are speaking in tongues. They profess to believe in a continuing revelation, which means that there is a continuing inspiration, meaning that the word of God is not completed. It is being added to every time they speak and every time they preach. That is a dangerous doctrine! The reason it is so dangerous is because that would mean that your Bible is not complete, therefore, it is not the last word, and it is not completely and absolutely authoritative. (That is Satan's design – to cause you not to believe that it is complete and absolutely authoritative.)

When you believe as do the Charismatics, (that revelation and inspiration are not finished), you get into Joseph Smith, Mary Baker Eddy, Charles Russell, and Herbert Armstrong type stuff. They believe that the Bible is not complete, and that they are getting further revelation. They believed that what they wrote was of equal inspiration and authority as the canonical scriptures.

Summary Statement Number Three

- The Bible is complete.

    o Revelation and inspiration are completed. God has completed it, and it is finished. The writing of the scripture is complete, which means if verbal inspiration assures you that God included everything that is necessary, all that He wanted you to have is in the Bible, then the Bible is complete. If you add those two things together, you come up with the fact that the canon is complete without any *Apocrypha* or any extra books.

    Paul says in Colossians 1:25 that the scripture is completed as to its content – its subject matter. In Colossians 1:25, Paul is saying that the dispensation of the grace of God is given to me to fulfil the word of God — to bring the word of God to its completion. Without Paul's revelation, the word of God would never be complete in its subject matter.

    Therefore, the scripture is infallible; it is authoritative; it is sufficient; it is effective.

Summary Statement Number Four

- The Bible should not be treated like any other book.

    o   Many encounter problems studying manuscript evidence because they approach the subject from the vantage point of human viewpoint. In other words, the subject is broached with a lack of thorough understanding of the fundamental underlying doctrines.

    o   "The Christian Church has long confessed that the books of the New Testament, as well as those of the Old, are divine Scriptures, written under the inspiration of the Holy Spirit. . . Since the doctrine of divine inspiration of the New Testament has, in all ages, stimulated the copying of these sacred books, it is evident that this doctrine is important for the history of the New Testament text, no matter whether it be a true doctrine or only a belief of the Christian Church." But what if it be true? What if the original New Testament manuscripts actually were inspired of God? If the doctrine of divine inspiration of the New Testament is a true doctrine, then New Testament textual criticism is different from the textual criticism of ordinary books." (Hills, 1-2)

    o   "Thus there are two methods of New Testament textual criticism; the consistently Christian method and the naturalistic method. These two methods deal with the same materials, the same Greek manuscripts, and the same translations and biblical quotations, but they interpret the materials very differently. The consistently Christian method interprets the materials of New Testament textual criticism in accordance with the doctrines of the divine inspiration and providential preservation of the Scriptures. The naturalistic method interprets these same materials in accordance with its own doctrine that the New Testament is nothing more than a human book." (Hills, 3)

    o   Grounding ourselves in these basic concepts will help us wade through the manuscript and textual issues later on. Possessing the ability to judge the textual and historical information from the vantage point of what the Bible teaches about itself is the only source of clarity on these difficult issues. In short, if our doctrine is correct it ought to commend itself to us in both history and our experience.

WORKS CITED

Hills, Edward F. *The King James Version Defende*d. Christian Research Press, 1956.

Jordan, Richard. *Manuscript Evidence 101, Lesson 6*. Chicago, IL: Grace School of the Bible.

Trust Publishers House,
the trusted name in quality Christian books.

Trust House Publishers
PO Box 3181
Taos, NM 87571

TrustHousePublishers.com

www.ingramcontent.com/pod-product-compliance
Lightning Source LLC
Chambersburg PA
CBHW071954110526
44592CB00012B/1088